LE CORBUSIER
Early Works by Charles-Edouard Jeanneret-Gris

ARCHITECTURAL Monographs 12

LE CORBUSIER

Early Works by Charles-Edouard Jeanneret-Gris

**With contributions by
Geoffrey Baker and Jacques Gubler**

ACADEMY EDITIONS · LONDON / ST. MARTIN'S PRESS · NEW YORK

ARCHITECTURAL
Monographs 12

Subscriptions and Editorial Offices
7/8 Holland Street, London W8

Publisher
Dr Andreas C Papadakis

Editor
Frank Russell

Published in Great Britain in 1987 by
Academy Editions, 7/8 Holland Street, London W8

ISBN 0 85670 804 6 (paper)
ISBN 0 85670 892 5 (cased)

© 1987 Academy Group Ltd

All rights reserved
No parts of this publication, including the text, drawings and photographs, may be reproduced in any manner whatsoever without permission in writing from the copyright holders.

The opinions expressed by writers of signed articles appearing in this publication are those of their respective authors for which the publisher and editors do not hold themselves responsible.

Publisher's Note
All original drawings in this publication are copyright © Academy Group Ltd and may not be reproduced without permission in writing from The Secretary, Architectural Monographs, 7/8 Holland Street, London W8.

Published in the United States of America in 1987 by
St Martin's Press, 175 Fifth Avenue, New York, NY 10010

Library of Congress Catalog Card Number 8613010
ISBN 0 312 47583 7 (paper)
ISBN 0 312 47582 9 (cased)

Printed and bound in Hong Kong

Cover: Villa Favre-Jacot, axonometric from the east (Geoffrey Baker)
Title verso: Charles-Edouard Jeanneret (centre) working with two other Art school students on the sgraffito wall of the Villa Fallet, c 1907. (La Chaux-de-Fonds Library) *Title page*: Villa Stotzer, front elevation. (La Chaux-de-Fonds Library)

Acknowledgements
We would like to express our thanks to the Fondation Le Corbusier in Paris and the Municipal Archive, Library and Historical Museum in La Chaux-de-Fonds for permission to reproduce drawings in their collections. Individual credits are as follows. Original drawings, including analytical and didactic diagrams, specially drawn by Geoffrey Baker for Architectural Monographs 10(2-3), 11(5-6), 15(16-18), 16(20-21), 17(22-24), 18(28-29), 19(30-32), 23(39). Perspectives and axonometrics created by Geoffrey Baker based on drawings, photographs and other information researched by Geoffrey Baker 14(14-15), 50, 56-58, 64-66, 72-74, 80-82, 90-92. Plans, sections and elevations drawn by Geoffrey Baker to represent the as-built projects based largely on on-site measurements and drawings by René Chapallaz, Charles-Edouard Jeanneret and other unnamed draughtsmen deposited with the Municipal Archive at La Chaux-de-Fonds and reproduced here with their permission 52-55, 60-63, 68-71, 76-79, 84-89, 94-99: the drawings on 104-109 were shared with Geoffrey Bowles. Geoffrey Baker also supplied the following drawings and photographs 6, 8, 10(4), 12(7-8), 13(9-12), 14(13), 16(19), 18(26-27), 20(33-35), 21(36), 22(37-38), 24(40), 25, 27(5-8), 28(10-12), 29(13), and those on pages 30-48 which are not otherwise credited. Photographs 26(2), 28(9) and 30(14) are by Guy Collomb. Jacques Gubler provided the photographs on 112(2)(Swissair Photo by Walter Mittelholzer), 114(3), 115(4) (own photo), 116(5) (private collection), 117(6) (Bauhausbuch), 118(7), 119(8), 120(1-2), 122(3, 5), 123(4, 6), 124(7-8, 10), 125(9), 126(11), 127(12) (La Chaux-de-Fonds Historical Museum), 128-29.

The authors and publisher are grateful to the owners of the buildings for allowing them to be photographed.

This issue of Architectural Monographs is published to coincide with the centenary of Le Corbusier's birth in 1887, and an exhibition of his work at the Hayward Gallery, London.

Contents

- 7 Foreword
- 9 *The Early Villas of Le Corbusier in La Chaux-de-Fonds*
  Geoffrey Baker

Colour Illustrations
- 18 Art School Drawings
- 26 Villa Fallet
- 30 Villa Stotzer
- 34 Villa Jaquemet
- 36 Villa Jeanneret-Perret
- 40 Villa Favre-Jacot
- 44 Villa Schwob
- 48 La Scala Cinema

Projects
- 50 Villa Fallet
- 58 Villa Stotzer
- 66 Villa Jaquemet
- 74 Villa Jeanneret-Perret
- 82 Villa Favre-Jacot
- 92 Villa Schwob
- 102 La Scala Cinema

- 110 *From Feeling to Reason: Jeanneret and Regionalism*
  Jacques Gubler

- 120 *In Time with the Swiss Watchmakers*
  Jacques Gubler

- 128 List of Early Projects in La Chaux-de-Fonds and Le Locle

- 130 Selected Bibliography

- 131 Résumés in French, German, Spanish and Italian

Foreword

The centenary of Le Corbusier's birth in 1887 provides an opportunity for a major reassessment of his œuvre. As the most influential architect of the first half of the twentieth century he is best known for his leadership of the Modern Movement during the 1920s and for that powerful and sculptural series of buildings during the 1950s which include the Unité at Marseilles, the chapel at Ronchamp, the monastery at La Tourette, the Jaoul houses and Chandigarh. Inevitably, three decades on, the pendulum of architectural fashion has swung away from an uncritical deification of the masters of Modern architecture and their icons towards a pluralistic cacophony of images and styles. After such a short time it seems also inevitable that the masters, including Le Corbusier, should come under attack, even if the criticisms are at best uninformed and at worst malevolent.

Clearly more time must elapse before a dispassionately objective position can be taken regarding Le Corbusier's position in the twentieth century. However, the present view is impaired by substantial gaps in many people's knowledge which prevent a proper understanding of his aims and objectives. Seldom is account taken of the way Le Corbusier's creative output was affected by the formative influences on him and by the prevailing spirit of an age in which significant changes were happening almost decade by decade. It is not, for example, generally understood how far the circumstances of his training in La Chaux-de-Fonds set him on course for all his later achievements.

In this sense it is unfortunate that the least-known period of his life should in retrospect now seem probably the most important. The early years in La Chaux-de-Fonds have until recently been so neglected that even now many are unfamiliar with those writings, sketchbooks and buildings created in his own name of Charles-Edouard Jeanneret, between 1904 and 1916. This Monograph sets out to remedy this deficiency by documenting the early houses in and near La Chaux-de-Fonds. As built works, these houses crystallise Jeanneret's philosophical position and show how his design technique was beginning to develop. The built work expresses the architect's intentions more clearly than his other forms of expression and these early houses explain the changes in Jeanneret's perception of architecture induced first by study and then by travel.

Because so little is known of these works, this Monograph addresses itself to the task of a full documentation of the early houses in terms of drawings and illustrations. Geoffrey Baker has been commissioned to redraw the existing plans, sections and elevations of these buildings, and to provide axonometrics. In addition to furnishing most of the illustrations of the houses, he has contributed an article in which each house is analysed in relation to its context and is considered in relation to Jeanneret's evolving design technique. Baker also discusses the way Jeanneret's education in La Chaux-de-Fonds and on various study tours affected his development as a designer and details those changes in technique which took place as he moved away from a local vernacular imagery towards a more classical approach. This development is shown to have taken place as a result of an awareness of the potential of geometry, which was organised in the later villas so that movement towards and into the building became part of the geometrical concept.

Baker's study is complemented by two essays written by Jacques Gubler. The first of these, 'From Feeling to Reason: Jeanneret and Regionalism', gives the background to the early projects in La Chaux-de-Fonds, placing them in the context of Jeanneret's education. His discussion embraces the twin topics of nature and the machine which preoccupied Le Corbusier throughout his life. The second essay, 'In Time with the Swiss Watchmakers', reveals how Jeanneret's early career was influenced by the predominance of the watchmaking industry in his native town, and traces his evolution from apprentice watchcase engraver to architect via commissions from watch manufacturers in La Chaux-de-Fonds.

Pencil sketch showing (below) a mountain peak drawn in different formats, the second lower drawing making geometric patterns of the first. Above this two pine trees are shown in detail alongside a group of pine trees to the right with a small sketch (top left) showing mist sliding down between the mountain with a stream in the foreground.

THE EARLY VILLAS

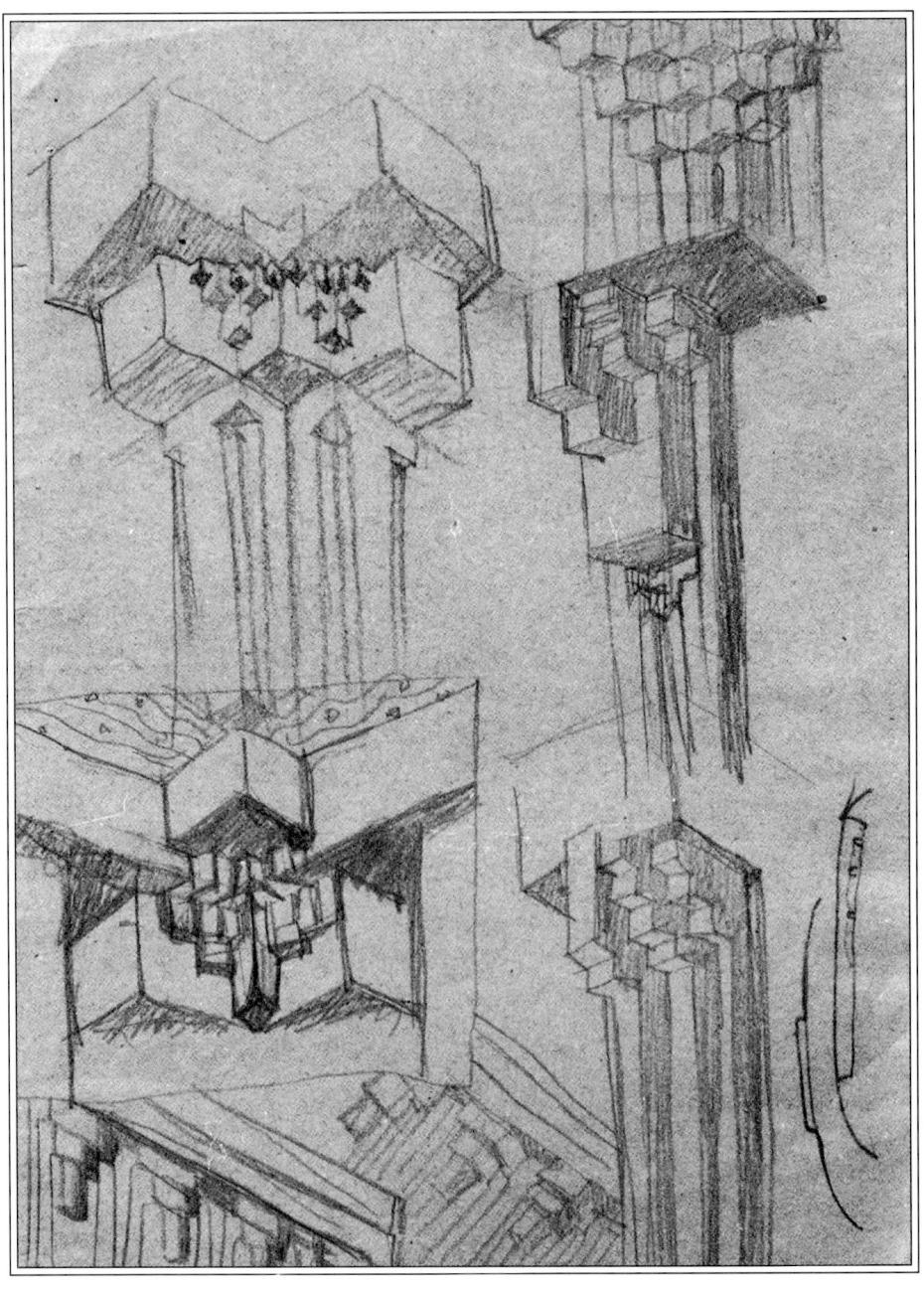

The Early Villas in La Chaux-de-Fonds by Charles-Edouard Jeanneret-Gris[1]

Geoffrey Baker

Le Corbusier's work is generally thought of in two distinct phases: works of the post-Purist period after 1918, characterised by his abstract planar language of the 1920s and culminating in such didactically heroic monuments as the Villa Savoye and the Pavillon Suisse; this being followed by the post-war reassessment which led to Jaoul, Ronchamp, La Tourette and Chandigarh. Although these two periods seem disconnected, in fact they form part of a continuous thread of development which began with another phase that is much less well known or understood. Of all the periods of Jeanneret's life, the formative years which he spent at the Art School in La Chaux-de-Fonds are arguably the most rewarding to the historian or design analyst, if only because they reveal aspects of his character that were later sublimated when, as Le Corbusier, he took his place on the world stage and became involved in the struggle to establish a new architectural language. Le Corbusier was fond of the paradox, so it is not entirely inappropriate that he, the architect perhaps most associated with the reversal of stylistic eclecticism, should himself have relied on nineteenth-century theory and techniques when, as a student, he laid the foundations for his own architectural philosophy. In fact, the range and depth of his enquiry into architectural history was only possible because of the emphasis placed on such study around 1900, and it is the knowledge gained as a result which gives his work that informed sense of historic continuity which effectively separates him from the Post-Modernists and their successors.

During his period at the Art School in La Chaux-de-Fonds, Jeanneret was profoundly influenced by his teacher and mentor L'Eplattenier, who ran an intensive and enlightened course of training in the visual arts. Having met Clement Heaton, an English artist in stained glass who had settled in Neuchâtel, L'Eplattenier became familiar with the English Arts and Crafts movement and the writings of William Morris, Walter Crane, John Ruskin and Owen Jones. Two key works used by L'Eplattenier and later referred to by Le Corbusier were Owen Jones's *Grammar of Ornament*[2] and Eugène Grasset's *Méthode de composition ornementale*.[3] The *Grammar* was kept in L'Eplattenier's classroom and Jeanneret copied out several of the beautifully illustrated pages which dealt so comprehensively with the history of ornament. Jones insisted that nature's laws reveal the principles which underlie all good design and believed that the relationship between structure and growth had an architectural correlation in the way the decoration of structure proclaimed the characteristics of an architectural style.

The main ideas and principles advocated by Eugène Grasset and Owen Jones had been anticipated by John Ruskin, who always believed that nature was a direct revelation of God's truth. *Modern Painters*, which he published in five volumes between 1843 and 1860, demonstrates in particular the way in which he could use natural phenomena such as clouds, rocks or trees to make pronouncements on moral laws. Ruskin's style may be alien to us now, but his ideas were based on meticulous and searching analysis. *The Stones of Venice*, *The Seven Lamps of Architecture*, *The Elements of Drawing* and *Modern Painters* were all listed in the Art School catalogue and became key source material for Jeanneret.[4]

When L'Eplattenier established the 'Cours supérieur d'art et de décoration' in 1905, (to which Jeanneret, then aged eighteen, transferred), an important element of the course was the study of nature through the medium of drawing. This technique, encouraging

1 Pencil sketches of corners based on geological formations

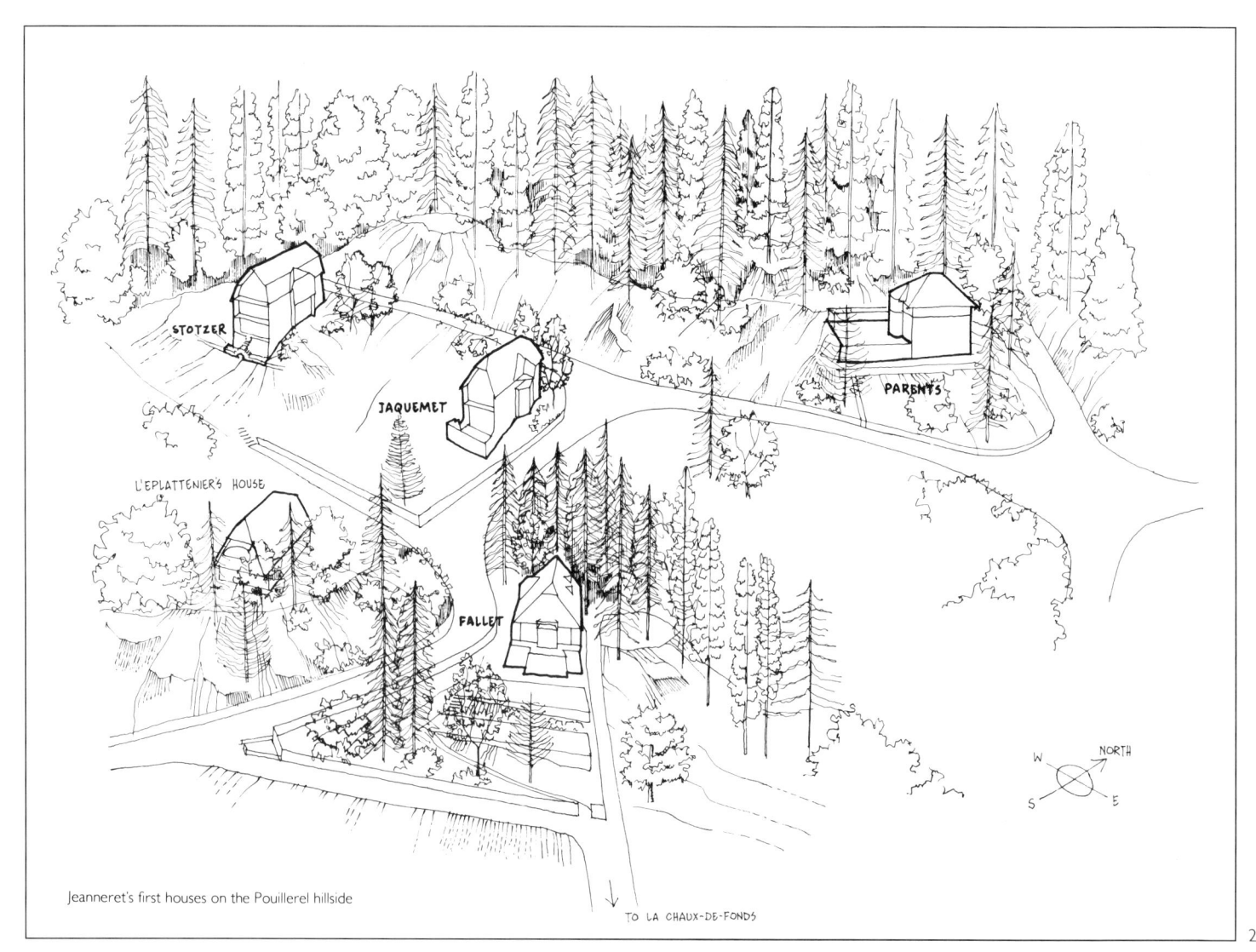

THE EARLY VILLAS

Jeanneret's first houses on the Pouillerel hillside

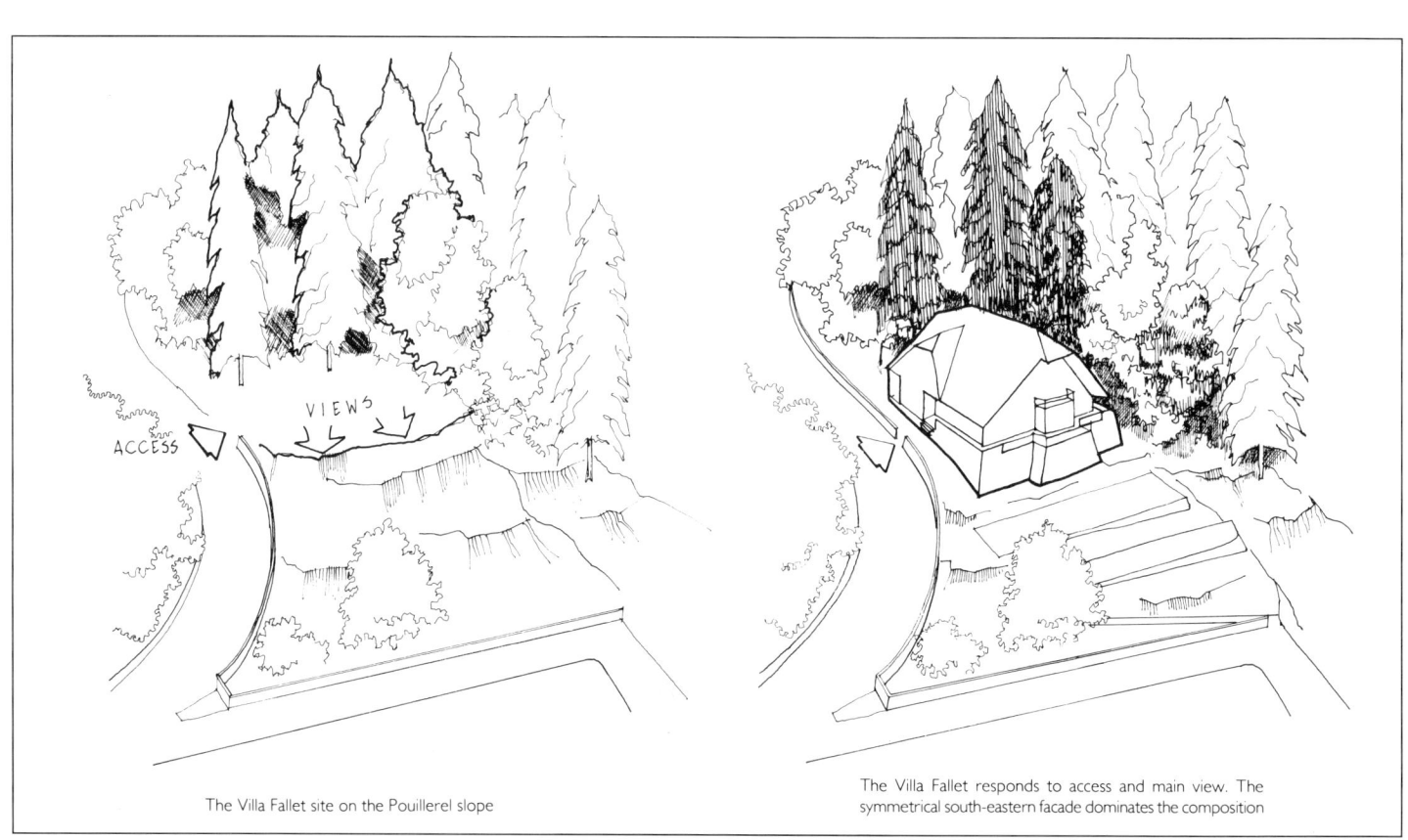

The Villa Fallet site on the Pouillerel slope

The Villa Fallet responds to access and main view. The symmetrical south-eastern facade dominates the composition

THE EARLY VILLAS

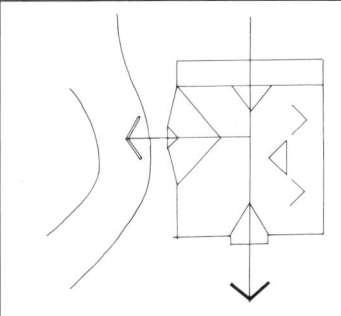

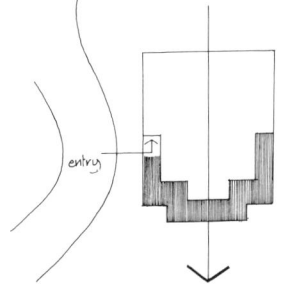

2 Hillside locations of houses
3 Villa Fallet site
4 Villa Fallet, south elevation
5 Villa Fallet, axis diagrams
6 Villa Fallet, gable treatment

Villa Fallet, the centroidal form becomes directional as the ridge produces a linear axis. The secondary axis relates to the entry point

The linear theme is preserved by a low-key entry point and by twin covered loggias

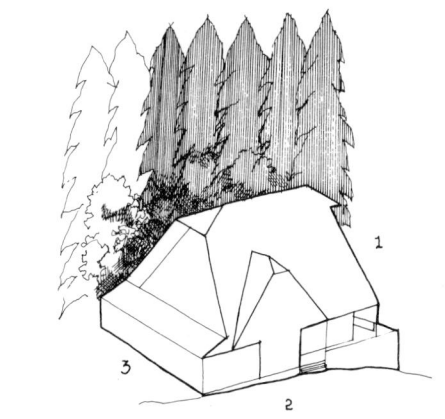

Villa Fallet, elevational hierarchy by gable treatment: the lean-to roof reduces the power of the rear elevation

powers of concentration and the ability to record detail, lay at the very heart of Ruskin's teaching and is manifest in his own drawings and writings. Jeanneret studied these drawings closely and, in retrospect, Ruskin's nineteenth-century 'labour-intensive' approach seems to have left a deep mark, inspiring him to see and record the world in a similar way.

As Kenneth Clark has pointed out, Ruskin loved 'not merely detail … but inner construction, the rhythms and tensions that are revealed to a steady penetrating gaze'.[5] Similarly, Jeanneret's sketches constantly probed behind the surface towards the hidden structure and its rhythmic consequences. He would approach each task in the way he thought appropriate, drawing the essentials swiftly and reducing the main points to a kind of shorthand about the size of a postage stamp. Often he selected a series of different perspectives or drew the same subject under changing conditions, and his style altered according to whether a scene was being documented or the structure of a plant was being analysed. Sometimes the rendering is precise and descriptive whilst at other times it is bold and atmospheric. Usually the drawings are vigorous; and they are always informative, never pictorial in an artistic sense, even when they describe the mood of a landscape. Direct links with Ruskinian subject matter occur too frequently to record in detail here, but they include mist on the mountains, many impressions of the pine tree, and studies based on geological formations. From the first it seems that Jeanneret preferred to rationalise our emotional reactions to visual phenomena, and there seems little doubt that the kind of rules and theoretical principles underlying the writings of authors such as Ruskin, Jones and Grasset helped to form his own ideas.

Jeanneret started at the Art School intending to be a watch engraver; it was his teacher, L'Eplattenier, who persuaded him to become an architect, and who also secured his first commission. When Louis Fallet, a well-known local jeweller, asked L'Eplattenier to design a villa next to his own recently completed house on the Pouillerel hillside overlooking La Chaux-de-Fonds, L'Eplattenier gave the job to his precocious student, then only seventeen and a half, displaying a confidence in his ability which took account of his lack of experience.[6] Like so many of Jeanneret's works, the villa consolidates a whole area of exploratory research.[7] It consummates his adolescent forays into the mysteries of nature, being essentially an essay in form and surface treatment which takes its inspiration from the pine trees surrounding it.[8] In his design synthesis, Jeanneret followed the processes of abstraction from nature which he had been using in L'Eplattenier's classes, acknowledging such major forces as symmetry and orientation in geometrically regularising nature's randomness.

The Villa Fallet is located at a bend in the road ascending Pouillerel from La Chaux-de-Fonds, where a shallow slope begins to fall sharply away to the south-east. A bank of trees screen the north-eastern side and access is from the west (Figure 3). The main view is south-east towards La Chaux-de-Fonds and, although the plan is almost a square, Jeanneret gave this centroidal form a linear axis with the ridge line of the roof. The south-eastern facade with its terrace and balcony dominates the composition with the linear axis governing the bilateral symmetry of this elevation (Figure 3).

The elevated terrace to the south-east extends along each side to form covered loggias. Movement is turned into the house at right angles at the end of the south-western loggia, thus giving entry a low-key role. This ensures the dominance of the south-east facade and preserves the symmetrical linear theme (Figure 5). If the south-west elevation is second in the elevational hierarchy, the north-western (rear) elevation is third by virtue of its lean-to roof, the north-east elevation being relegated to fourth as it is hardly seen (Figure 6).

Ruskinian references proliferate in a design in which every element seems to be a literal transcription of nature. Railings, strapwork to doors, elevations, timber brackets and stucco patterns are all abstractions of the pine tree[9] while the railings on the porch balcony resemble clouds. Ruskin was fond of heavily rusticated stonework[10]: the Villa Fallet is built of large blocks of masonry which contrast with the dressed stone lintels

THE EARLY VILLAS

7 Abstractions of the pine, charcoal and pencil
8 Tree root sketches, charcoal and pencil
9 Villa Fallet, wrought iron balcony railings designed as an abstraction of the pine
10 Villa Fallet, strapwork to the doors as an abstraction of the pine
11 Villa Stotzer, west facade
12 Villa Jaquemet from the south-west

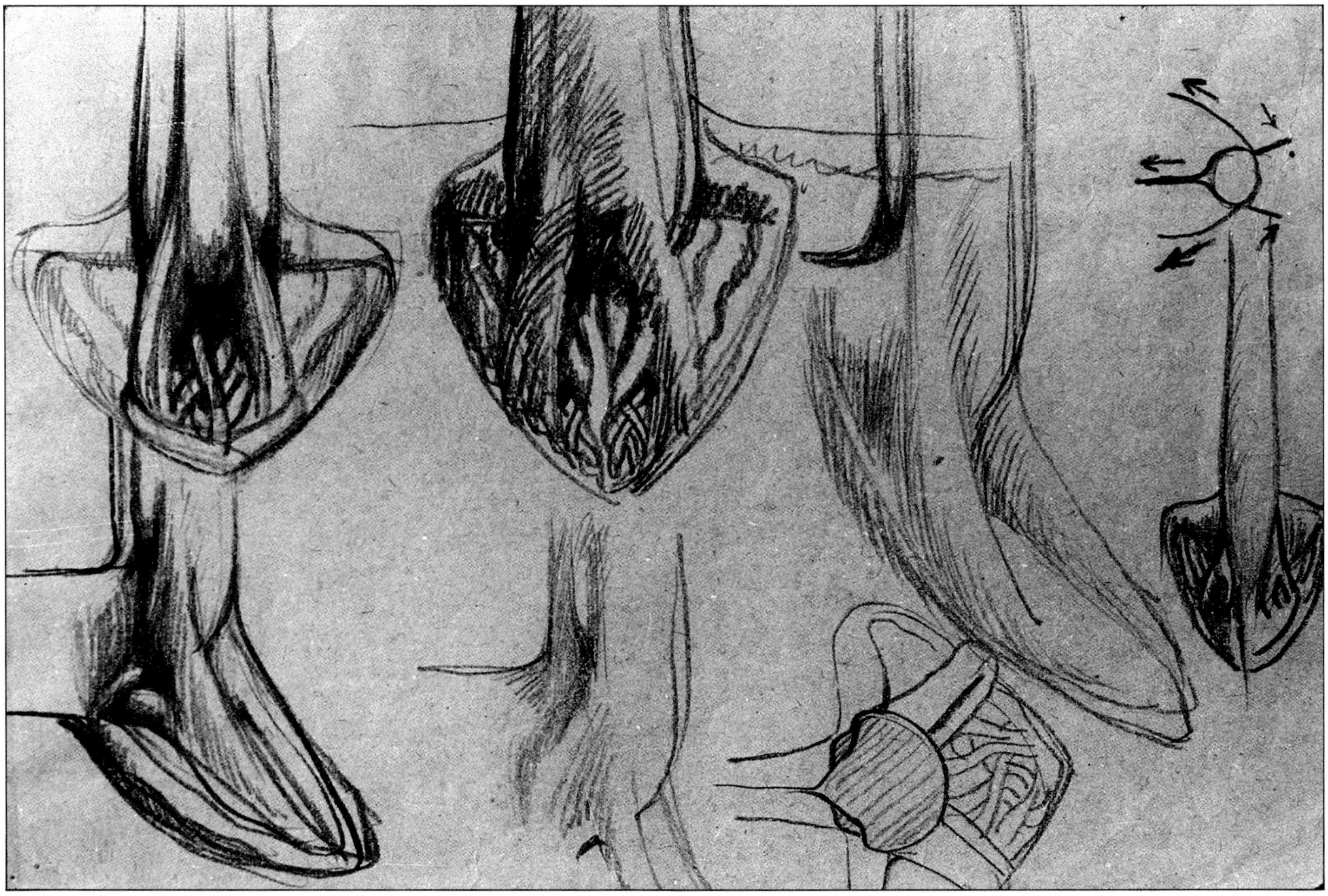

THE EARLY VILLAS

and frames on the windows and doors. The corbelling effect used for both timber and stone construction was inspired by Jeanneret's studies of geological formations while the lizard door latches epitomise his obsession with nature. The villa – in effect, the distillation of all that he had been taught at the Art School – resonates with the richness of its content and surface treatment.

In 1907, when he was twenty, Jeanneret embarked on one of his most important study tours and saw for the first time some of the greatest masterpieces of European art and architecture. With Léon Perrin he visited Italy, equipped with Ruskin's *Mornings in Florence*[11] and Hippolyte Taine's *Voyage en Italie*.[12] As part of their tour, the students decided to see for themselves the two buildings which Ruskin praised most, the cathedral at Pisa and the Doge's Palace at Venice. They also visited Florence where Jeanneret produced some of his finest sketches and watercolours, their quality reflecting his own feelings towards the works he saw. In *Mornings in Florence* Ruskin advises his reader at the end of the first day to drive the charterhouse at Ema to see a tomb by Donatello: this Jeanneret did on September 15th, so beginning an association with the monastic lifestyle which helped condition his view of the relationship between the individual and the community.[13]

During the tour Jeanneret sometimes sketched buildings, but he spent as much time sketching frescos and works of sculpture, relying largely on *Mornings in Florence* for his selection of subject matter. He limited his architectural studies mainly to pre-Renaissance buildings, concentrating on such examples as the Palazzo Vecchio and the Bargello, each of which was favoured by Ruskin. While Jeanneret was already conversant with the grandeur of nature, this tour gave him his first real insight into the majesty of art. Although on one level he was still gathering information about the massing and surface treatment of buildings, he found the broader vision of art as the supreme vehicle for emotional expression to be the great challenge, even if he had not yet found the means to realise this in his architecture.

This tour led Jeanneret to Vienna, where he designed the Villas Stotzer and Jaquemet, relying once more on René Chapallaz to produce the working drawings. The houses are situated close to the Villa Fallet but a little higher up on the hillside, with access from a road running across the slope and the best views to the south-east, towards La Chaux-de-Fonds (Figure 16). They are almost identical in plan, being built to virtually the same brief, and follow a strategy similar to the one used in the Fallet design.

These first three houses aptly demonstrate Jeanneret's technique at this time and have several points of similarity. First, each house is composed on the basis of a rusticated stone podium with an elaborate and expressive roof (Figure 17). Second, each design is controlled by a dominant linear axis with a lateral axis providing contrasting secondary gables (Figure 18). Third, each house has an impressive symmetrical main facade which responds to the view and to its own particular character. Their respective characters are largely determined by the sites they occupy. Thus Fallet is an individual and elaborate 'jewel' placed at a bend in the road so that it is seen side on, whereas Stotzer commands its situation, being higher on the hill than the neighbouring Villa Jaquemet. Consequently, Jeanneret made Stotzer a very powerful statement, extending its cranked roof beyond the facade and thereby increasing both its linearity and dramatic content. Jaquemet, by comparison, is more passive, and the indents and pronounced side gables of its roof formation increase its centroidality (Figure 16).

In each house subsidiary themes complement the main design idea. Having extended the roof and side walls beyond the south-east facade in the Villa Stotzer, Jeanneret reinforced this framing of the facade by stretching the balcony and roof overhang across it. This tautness, with a suggestion of muscular tension, increases the drama and is accentuated by the insistent window rhythm at balcony level, which is in turn echoed by the rhythm of the balustrade itself (Figure 14). The balcony is supported by cantilevered reinforced concrete beams which extend from the concrete floor. The podium on which the villa rests is of heavily rusticated stone with large copings and, as with the Villa Fallet, the dressed stone lintels and jambs of the windows are contrasted with the rough texture of the masonry. The door to the terrace is framed by

THE EARLY VILLAS

particularly heavy members proclaiming the idea of support with an almost Egyptian sense of permanence. Placed centrally, the door forms part of a deliberate stressing of the central axis to which the heart-shaped upper window and arched void under the steps leading to the terrace also contribute. In all these early buildings, Jeanneret composed by using the framing principle: each facade is framed by stone piers with areas of stucco in between, and the upper window of the main facade is elaborately framed in timber. The minimal side projection preserves the linear theme and the gable is cranked up and given a deep fascia. Sturdy timbers are used and the main support member projects out obliquely against its neighbouring support, enriched by a corbelled profile and by the framing of the windows on either side (Figure 14). As in the Villa Fallet the glazing box pattern is an abstraction of the pine tree.

Although their plans are almost identical, the Villa Jaquemet is the opposite of the Villa Stotzer in several respects. Jaquemet is centroidal, only part linear, giving an image of passivity rather than strength, and settles into the landscape with soft curved edges to its south-eastern flanks. Its ground floor treatment has the same powerful expression as the Villa Stotzer, but the central axis of the main facade is not emphasised; there is no balcony, and the paired window rhythm is innocuous and placid compared with the vigour of its neighbouring equivalent (Figure 15). The side projections are not dramatic, but are more elaborate and pronounced than Stotzer's in support of the centroidal theme. It has V-shaped balconies covered by a roof composed of elegant curved timber supports, a diamond and triangles.

13 Villa Stotzer, south facade
14 Villa Stotzer, side gable
15 Villas Stotzer and Jaquemet, facade treatment
16 Villa Stotzer, roof treatment
17 Roof and podium concepts
18 Axis diagrams

This early phase of intensive observation and drawing, dominated by L'Eplattenier and the writings of nineteenth-century theorists, gave Jeanneret certain design maxims that he was to retain. The almost musical sense of rhythm and structure which pervaded his sketching and design at this time may have been instinctive; but it was certainly reinforced by what he learnt. The strong sense of thematic development in the three villas may also have been intuitive, but it was carried through with a rigour and attention to detail that may have been influenced by Ruskin. Jeanneret's letters from this period reveal an engagingly youthful mixture of determination and confidence tempered by uncertainty and humility. His prose style is poetic and romantic yet meticulous in recording detail, as when he wrote to L'Eplattenier of the cathedral at Pisa:[14] 'I will never recapture that peace of six o'clock in the evening lying in the grass when everyone is far away and the fireworks display is at its height; I have taken notes at some such moments: they will remain unforgettable: "The Duomo at six in the evening is a fairyland of colour, the quintessence of yellows of every quality and value, of ivory white, black patinas, all this on an ultramarine of extraordinary intensity; if you keep on looking at it you begin to see it as black. The part upon which the Baptistery projects its shadow is a gentle vibration of rich yellows, of inlaid red marbles coming to life, and of black marbles turning to blue; it is in counterpoint to the smooth surfaces which vibrate and speak quietly – seven o'clock, and this dome is even lovelier than ever, what tones! Behind me the sky is orange and purple; the green of the door is dead, yellow marbles begin to stand out, they are natural sienna while the columns are a white pink, like the petal of a wild rose." '

Villa Stotzer, side gable

In 1910 Jeanneret visited Germany, having been commissioned by the Art School to report back on the latest developments in design and production there. Whilst in Germany he had read a book by Cingria-Vaneyre entitled *Entretiens de la ville de Rouet* (Geneva 1908) in which it was argued that, as the Swiss countryside is similar to the Greek, the most suitable architectural language for the Swiss Romande would be 'a calm, simplified Classicism'. Jeanneret wrote in the book: 'For me it [the book] unlocks the Germanic vice. In one year in Rome I will re-read it and through sketches I will found my discipline of the Jura, my discipline of Neuchâtel'.

Just before this visit, he had met William Ritter,[15] who gradually took over L'Eplattenier's role as confidant and mentor, and it was partly at Ritter's instigation that he embarked in 1911 on his celebrated *Voyage d'Orient*. He wrote to Ritter: 'To finish my student life, I am preparing a very great journey ... My spring will soon be shining. Summer arrives too soon ... Gone is the period of voluntary concentration! Let everything rush out! Let everything in me live.'[16]

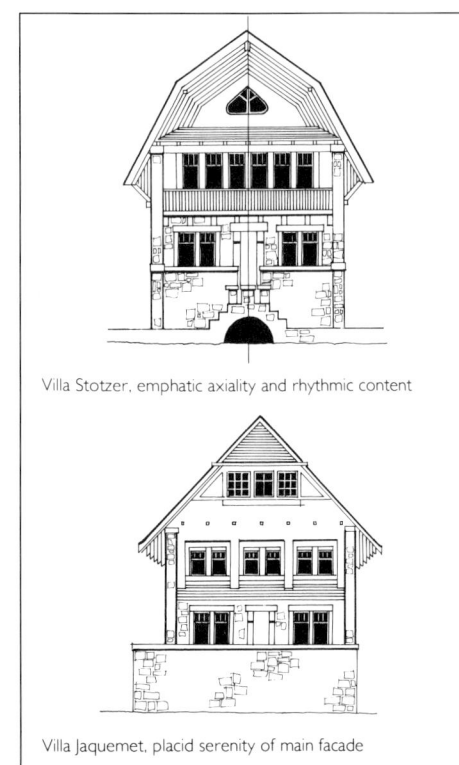

Villa Stotzer, emphatic axiality and rhythmic content

Villa Jaquemet, placid serenity of main facade

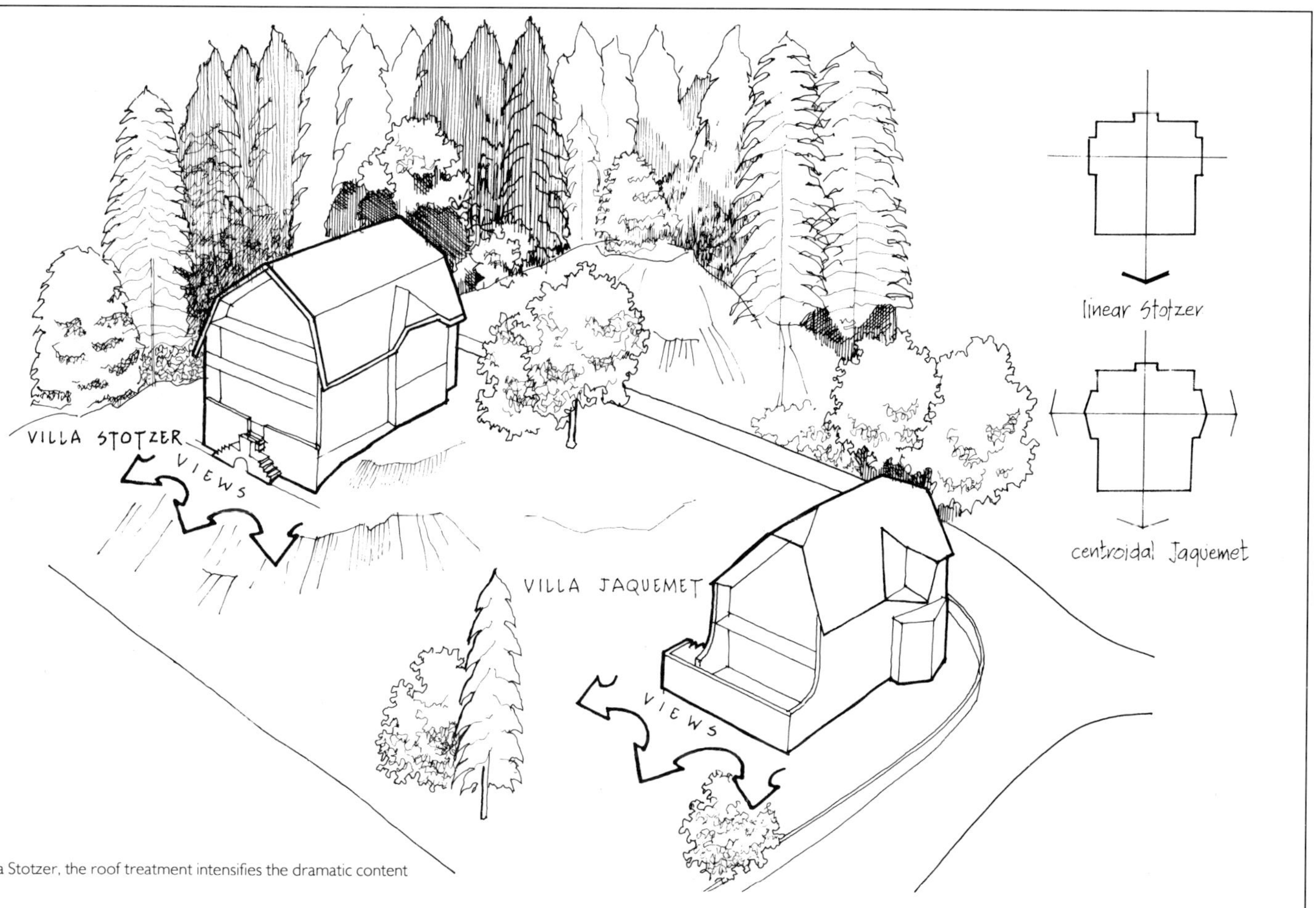

THE EARLY VILLAS

Villa Stotzer, the roof treatment intensifies the dramatic content

Each villa has a rusticated stone podium and an elaborate roof

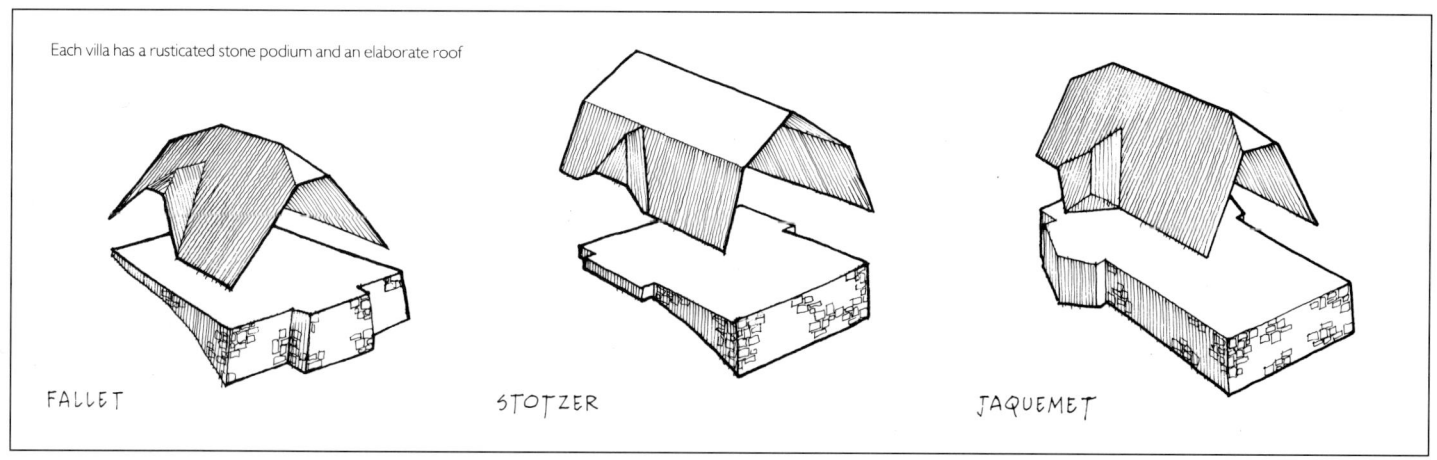

Each design is controlled by a dominant directional axis

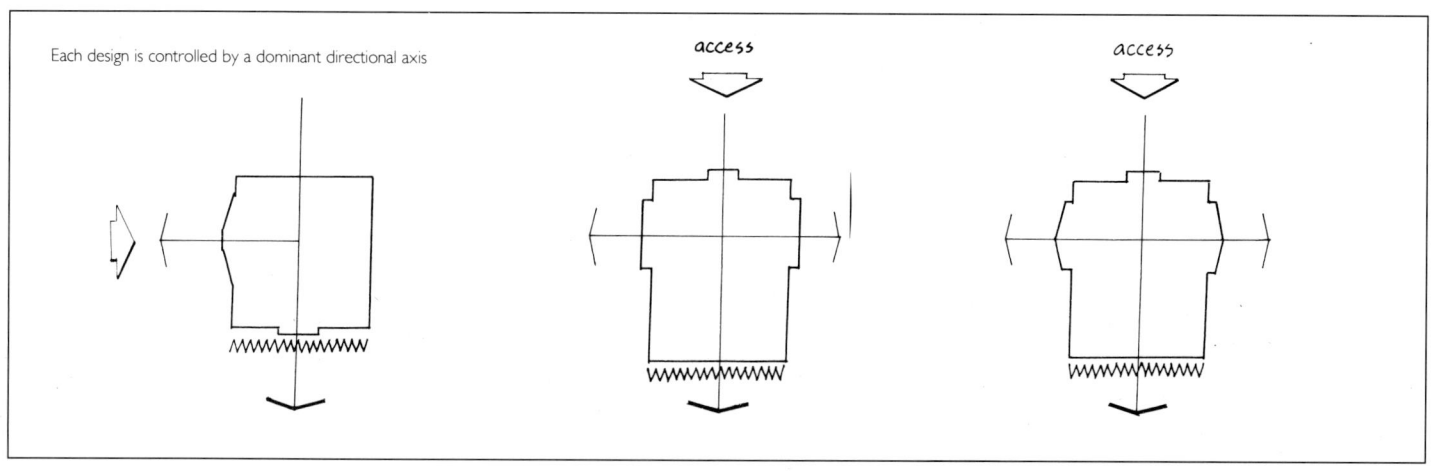

THE EARLY VILLAS

Although the trip was undoubtedly the supreme artistic and intellectual experience of Jeanneret's formative years, it was in many ways confirmatory, as he had already convinced himself that certain theoretical principles underscored great works of architecture. The mosques of Constantinople, for instance, only clarified his ideas about architectural geometry and confirmed his view that major works of architecture resulted from the application of structural logic and the deployment of primary forms. Over and above this, the mosques gave him a better understanding of space and light. The Parthenon verified his view that Classicism held the key to his future progress but had a humbling effect in the unexpected power and emotional impact of its forms.[17] As far as his design technique was concerned, the main lesson lay in the way movement towards and through buildings can be a design generator. He put this knowledge to the test in 1912 when he designed a villa for his parents in La Chaux-de-Fonds and the Favre-Jacot residence for the owner of a large watchmaking factory in nearby Le Locle.

Although the houses show signs of the influence of Behrens, Hoffmann and Wright,[18] they also contain ideas peculiar to Jeanneret, which as Le Corbusier he was later to use to far greater effect. The main difference from the earlier houses lies in the abandonment of the complex massing and expressive structure and materials in favour of the cool statements in which accepted classical tenets are transformed. Jeanneret also shows a greater awareness of spatial potential both inside and out and for the first time controls the movement sequence towards the houses in a positive way.

His parents' house, the Villa Jeanneret-Perret, is sited a short distance from the Villa Jaquemet on a plateau carved out of the Pouillerel hillside. It has a south-east aspect similar to the Jaquemet, and it relates to a terrace, its rectilinear volume being delineated in stucco. On the main axis, an apsidal projection faces the elevated terrace and the axis is terminated by a rectilinear bay projection poised at the edge of a steep part of the slope. The controlled ascent towards the villa through a series of space zones provides several references to the Acropolis. A path through the garden reaches the terrace (temenos enclosure) by an enclosed stair (Propylaea) which gives access to a pergola whose axis takes the route through an arch into a small transitional space prior to entry (Figure 20). As with the processional route around the Parthenon, the two main facades are seen before entering at the rear. Once inside, a hall and cloakroom lit by a circular 'porthole' precede an interior space whose grand dimensions are made possible by the use of four reinforced concrete columns supporting concrete floor slabs (Figure 21).

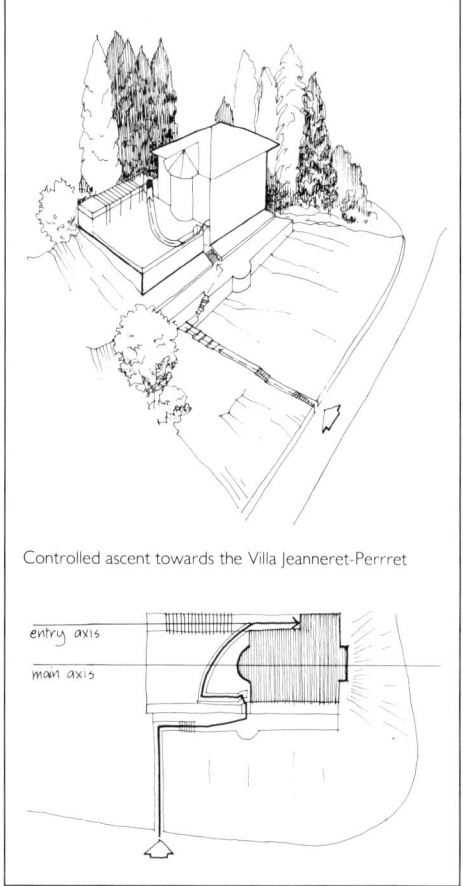

Controlled ascent towards the Villa Jeanneret-Perrret

The main impact, as with the earlier villas, is concentrated on the bilaterally symmetrical south-east facade which has a base, piano nobile and 'frieze' immediately below the overhanging roof. A row of columns with cubic bases and capitals rhythmically punctuate the frieze and each elevation is framed by a stucco projection. With its classical inference, almost open plan at main floor level, and controlled movement through a series of space zones, the villa anticipates Le Corbusier's design strategy in the 1920s, although it lacks the compositional virtuosity which Purism and the orthogonal grid were later to provide.

The Villa Favre-Jacot is poised on a long, narrow plateau looking towards Le Locle. Here again Jeanneret controlled movement towards the building. Curved walls wrap around a turning circle in front of the villa to provide an enclosed entry zone which opens out to maintain visual contact with the valley. The rectilinear villa is placed behind

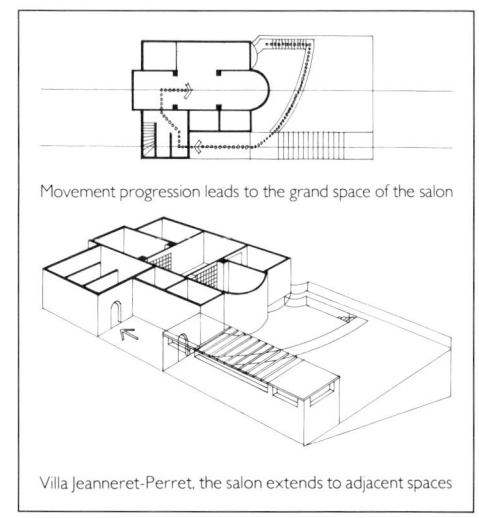

Movement progression leads to the grand space of the salon

Villa Jeanneret-Perret, the salon extends to adjacent spaces

THE EARLY VILLAS

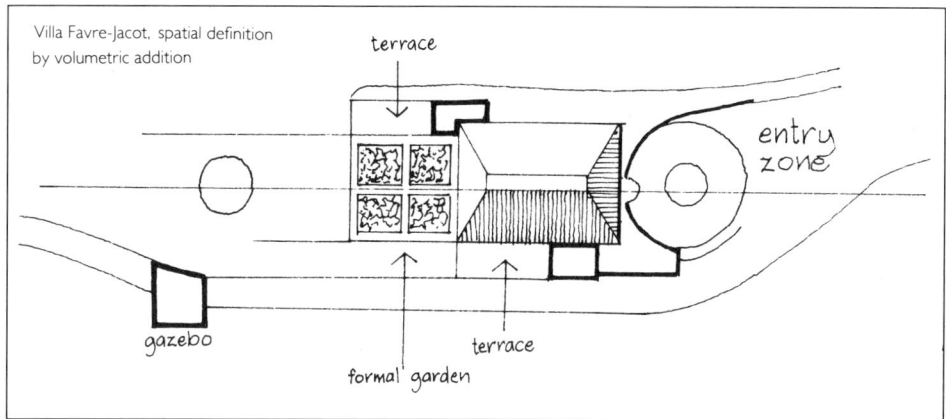

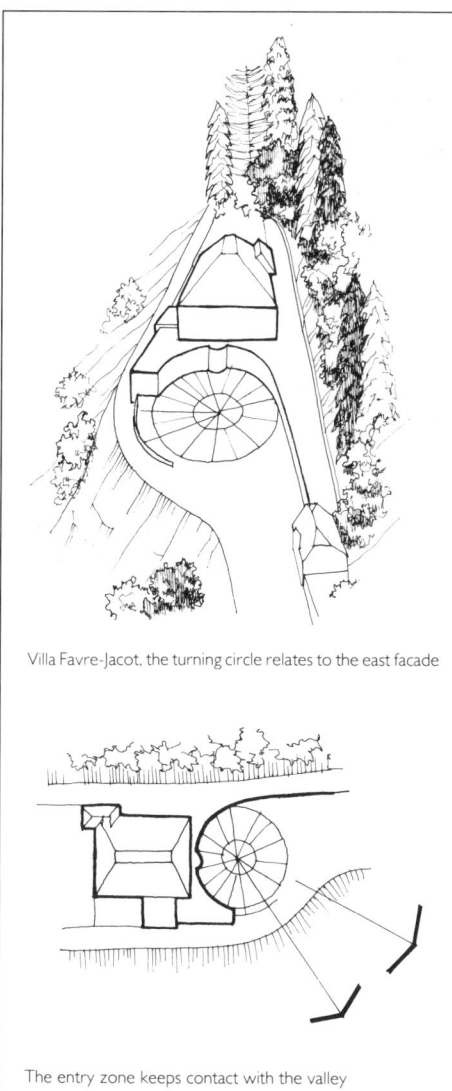

Villa Favre-Jacot, the turning circle relates to the east facade

The entry zone keeps contact with the valley

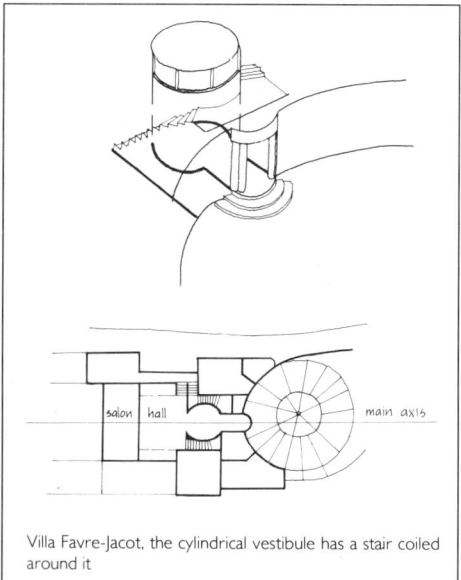

Villa Favre-Jacot, the cylindrical vestibule has a stair coiled around it

19 Sketches by Jeanneret of the Villa Favre-Jacot
20 Villa Jeanneret-Perret, south-west corner
21-22 Villa Jeanneret Perret, movement sequence
23 Villa Favre-Jacot, turning circle
24 Villa Favre-Jacot, cylindrical vestibule
25 Villa Favre-Jacot, spatial definition

this screen, and the plane of its eastern facade stabilises the turning effect of the circle (Figure 22). Inside, the main staircase is coiled around a cylindrical staircase. This cylinder is locked into the outer system by a projecting half-cylindrical porch, so that the route provides a series of different spatial and volumetric constructs (Figure 23). The idea is only partially successful because the cylinder is underlit, and what follows in the hall and salon, each placed on the axis, is ordinary enough. However, with this house Jeanneret was already experimenting with the kind of shock treatment offered by a carefully programmed series of visual experiences that was to characterise his work of the 1920s and be dramatically exploited at La Tourette some forty years later.

The villa locks into its landscape by additive massing which defines terraces and a formal garden (Figure 25). It was intended that the ensemble be completed by a gazebo spanning the road immediately below the site, with a curved pergola leading to a dome, and a circular pool on the axis. This solution has a Florentine flavour, with its crisp corner pilasters[19] and pedimented balcony, but the columns projecting out from the study resemble those used by Frank Lloyd Wright in his Unity Church of 1906. The pigeon and leaf capitals were carved by Léon Perrin and the elevations are precisely framed, with a sub-frame for the upper windows.

The fresh attitude to volume, space, zonal arrangement and movement which Jeanneret acquired on his journey to the East and which he first explored in the villas of 1912 was taken a stage further in the Villa Schwob, built in 1916 on his first urban site in La Chaux-de-Fonds. Known locally as the 'Villa Turque', with its flat roof, apsidal wings and bold massing, the house can be related in a general sense to the mosques of Constantinople. References to Hagia Sophia can be seen in the sophisticated relationship of the central volume to adjacent spaces and in the positive use of curves. However, it also develops ideas suggested in the parents' house, and seems more directly inspired by the Thomas P Hardy house built by Frank Lloyd Wright in 1905. Both houses are sited at the edge of a slope (although the Hardy slope is much steeper), and both have paired entrances, an almost blank wall to the street, and a central living space with rooms on either side. However, where Schwob differs is in its geometrical complexity and sense of continuous space (the Hardy house is by comparison cellular).

Both Hagia Sophia and the Villa Schwob are based on the generic idea of a cube with a half-cube. In Hagia Sophia the central volume is raised above the surrounding space, and apsidal projections extend along the main linear axis. In the Villa Schwob Jeanneret added half-cylindrical projections along the linear axis parallel with the rue du Doubs but overlaid this with a lateral axis which becomes primary by being expressed as a double-height volume (Figure 28). Absolute bilateral symmetry had not been possible in either Favre-Jacot or Jeanneret-Perret, but Jeanneret came closer to this kind of geometrical purity in the Villa Schwob.

Although the outer walls of the villa are clad in brickwork, Jeanneret used reinforced concrete construction for the first time throughout.[20] Four slender columns at the core of the plan allow an extension of the ground floor volume vertically and horizontally, unimpeded by support walls. As with the Stotzer, Jaquemet and his parents' villas,

17

THE EARLY VILLAS

26

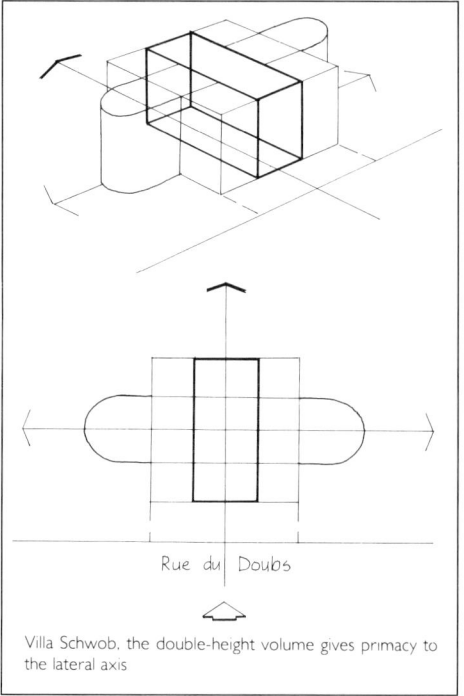

Villa Schwob, the double-height volume gives primacy to the lateral axis

Jeanneret played off the two main axes against each other, but this time extended the constrast by exploiting the vertical dimension. As with the previous designs, the main axis becomes directional towards the view overlooking the town; here, the linearity of this space is most pronounced at the upper level where it is reinforced by the squeezing effect of projections to a boudoir and bedroom (Figure 29). Curved balconies to the rear support this directional overlay with a large window defining the volume and confirming the axis.

At ground level the apsidal projections, with their curved ends thrusting outwards, extend the space laterally and horizontally, but this volumetric dynamism is countered by the cubic format in which the axial forces are contained. This format gave Jeanneret the flexibility to organise the corners, which are left open at the ground floor southern edge so that a continuous space exists towards the view, but closed at the opposite side to define the central volume's vertical directionality (Figure 30).

Jeanneret expressed the various space zones with clarity: taking the street as a baseline, he established a flat plane which anchors the villa to its setting (Figure 31). This symbolic barrier does not invite penetration but is punctuated by two entrances defined by a projecting canopy. Behind this plane, the volume expands with, first, the entry zone and staircase and, beyond, the living space with apsidal projections. The sleeping level above is capped by an overhanging concrete cornice[21] which separates it from the upper level with the roof terrace. The form fans outwards from the base plane and the upper level is set back to allow a radial vista from the roof terrace. Fenestration is deployed in accordance with the geometrical format, and the brick veneer is expressed literally, forming a precise ochre frame for the grey plaster panels. For the first time, Jeanneret used a proportional system to organise the elevations. A panelled wall along the rue du Doubs extends the barrier theme, and low relief sculptures by Léon Perrin embellish the flanks of the apsidal projections. Jeanneret preserved the essential solidity of the massing by incising vertical slit windows at either side of a cruciform mullion arrangement at the first floor level. The theme of curves against orthogonals is maintained where the villa meets the ground, with curved grills allowing light to the basement and acting as containers for plants and flowers (35). An extension of the kitchen wing forms a garden pavilion which is in plan a small-scale replica of the main form;[22] on the opposite side is a terrace with a pergola. The garden, although small in dimensions, is grand in concept like that of Favre-Jacot, with steps down the main axis and corner pavilions at each end of the southern boundary.

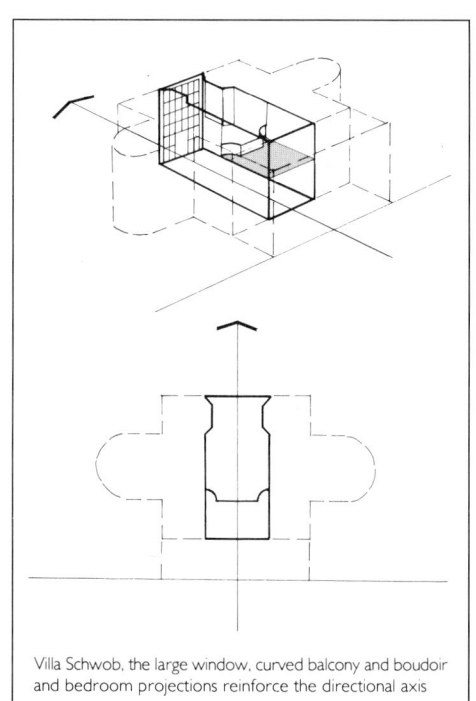

Villa Schwob, the large window, curved balcony and boudoir and bedroom projections reinforce the directional axis

THE EARLY VILLAS

The Villa Schwob summarises Jeanneret's theoretical position in 1916, when he was twenty-nine years old. Previous design experiments, reading and travel, had weaned him away from a Ruskinian decorative approach that concentrated mainly on the exterior surface treatment towards an idea of internal space as one of the generators of external form. He had now achieved a three-dimensional geometric approach which could accommodate sophisticated spatial interaction, while the dialogue between form and function begins to resemble that of his next phase of development. The symmetrical format and proportional relationships give the design a serenity, sense of order and grandeur which Jeanneret had not previously achieved.[23]

Jeanneret's understanding of nature was founded on techniques devised by L'Eplattenier to enable ornament to be 'extracted' from a close study of natural phenomena. His early training in sketching techniques at the Art School provided him with a means to understand the structure of organisms and to rapidly analyse both paintings and buildings. It was this ability to examine natural phenomena from several viewpoints simultaneously which led Jeanneret towards the comprehensive analytical appraisal of architecture using a method whereby he could examine those aspects of any building which he believed to be important.

If the Villa Fallet represents Jeanneret's early preoccupation with ornament, structure, and above all surface decoration, he was awakened to other possibilities at this time by reading Provensal, who emphasised the importance of unity, number and harmony, and Schuré,[24] who insisted upon the primacy of spiritual values. These two authors inspired an idealism linked to the notion of an artistic elite acting as responsible 'guardians' for society that was to remain with Jeanneret, materially affecting the course of his development.

Although nature had always inspired Jeanneret, his artistic awakening in Italy prompted a close study of the arts during his later formative years. He became a connoisseur of the arts, and the great works of Italy established standards to which he could relate and aspire. His dedication was reaffirmed in sketches and letters to his mentor L'Eplattenier. However, this somewhat academic aesthetic development did not improve his grasp of constructional technology, which had been poorly taught at the Art School. With this in mind, Jeanneret set out for Vienna, hoping to learn more about construction by working with a good architect. In the event, this did not materialise, but Vienna nonetheless provided a useful extension of his architectural education by giving

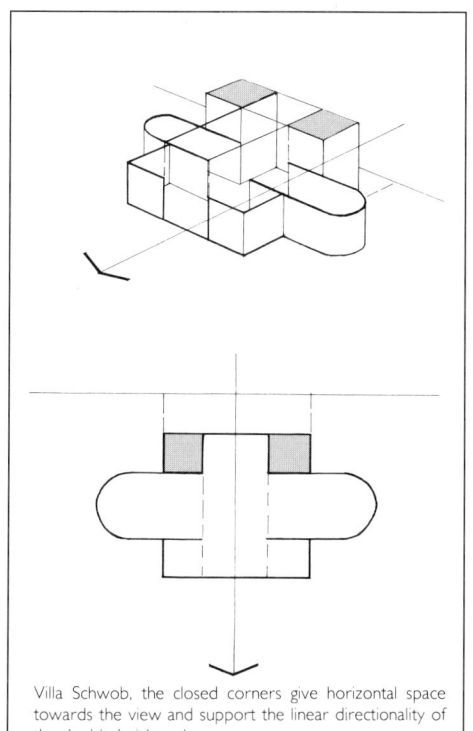

Villa Schwob, the closed corners give horizontal space towards the view and support the linear directionality of the double-height volume

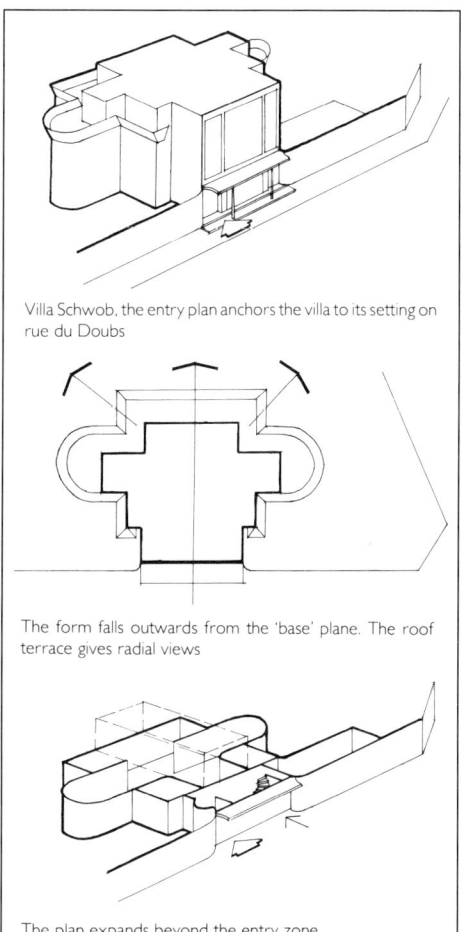

Villa Schwob, the entry plan anchors the villa to its setting on rue du Doubs

The form falls outwards from the 'base' plane. The roof terrace gives radial views

The plan expands beyond the entry zone

26 Study of Hagia Sophia copied from a drawing by Auguste Klipstein, 1911
27 Villa Schwob, view from rue du Doubs
28-29 Vila Schwob, axis diagrams
31 Villa Schwob, entry
32 Villa Schwob, basement lights

THE EARLY VILLAS

access to the works of avant-garde contemporaries such as Wagner, Hoffmann and Olbrich. However, his next two buildings, the Villas Stotzer and Jaquemet, show that he was not yet able to demonstrate a coherent architectural philosophy that could reflect current developments in technology and the arts.

Although imaginative in their detailed surface treatment and in the way the form is handled, these houses are conventional and rather pedestrian in comparison to, say, the advances being made by Wright in the USA: Jeanneret's particular skills in composition and ornament were insufficient to enable him to evolve an architectural language which reflected emerging cultural change. He seems to have realised that the very provinciality of his native town prevented a full exposure to those events which were to give a separate identity to the twentieth century. And just as a visit to Italy had awakened a commitment to the values which are inherent in great periods of artistic evolution, so a visit to Paris in 1908 opened up an awareness of the possibilities of the emerging technology and the attitudes which this encouraged.

During Jeanneret's stay in Paris he worked for Auguste Perret, who became a mentor during these years, establishing the importance of the programme, structural technology, and materials appropriate to the age in his emerging architectural philosophy. This new understanding of the importance of structure led Jeanneret towards a detailed study of Romanesque architecture, and also convinced him that Perret's faith in reinforced concrete was fully justified.

The exposure to new ideas and the opportunity for quiet contemplation afforded by the Paris sojourn caused the first break in Jeanneret's close relationship with L'Eplattenier. The arguments advanced in an important critical letter to L'Eplattenier written in November 1908 show how much he now believed that a new architectural language was necessary – one which reflected twentieth-century life as former styles had reflected each successive age. He was particularly critical of the way L'Eplattenier encouraged his students to believe that they emerged from their studies equipped to tackle current problems, and implied that his teaching lacked a certain substance and depth – that it was impossible to sing when you haven't got lungs'.

The letter confirms the seriousness of Jeanneret's search, and its mystical overtones suggest an obsessive missionary idealism that was leading him towards distant goals. The realisation that L'Eplattenier no longer held the key to a full understanding of the arts served to bring Jeanneret close to William Ritter, who encouraged him to travel to Germany. There he learnt a great deal about the Deutscher Werkbund and current attitudes towards design and industry, but the experience persuaded him that Teutonic rationalism was not enough – its results lacking the emotional content that he had encountered in Italy – and he became more than ever convinced that a new architectural language should be founded on an understanding of the great buildings which emerged in the ancient civilisation of the eastern Mediterranean. Once again, it was Ritter in whom he confided about the forthcoming journey, and it was Ritter who advised him not to return immediately to La Chaux-de-Fonds.

Jeanneret's journey to the East consolidated his conviction that the Parthenon held the key to certain basic architectural principles, namely the way the forms respond to the site and the impact which certain arrangements of shapes can have upon the senses. Overwhelmed by the sheer power of the Parthenon, his own subsequent work often strove to command a similar impression by the handling of the mass. The mosques of Constantinople also helped to give Jeanneret a better understanding of the potential of mass arrangements, enabling him to come to terms with the three-dimensional manipulation of space more fully than before. The effects of lighting and of the combination of vertical and horizontal space he saw there may have sparked the exploration of these possibilities in the Villa Schwob, which itself observes so many principles directly traceable to the mosques. That the Parthenon and the mosques were based on primary forms disciplined by axes was fully appreciated by Jeanneret before he visited them; what he seems not to have grasped prior to the journey was the way in which light can animate both form and space and how movement towards a building and through it becomes a key factor in architectural composition.

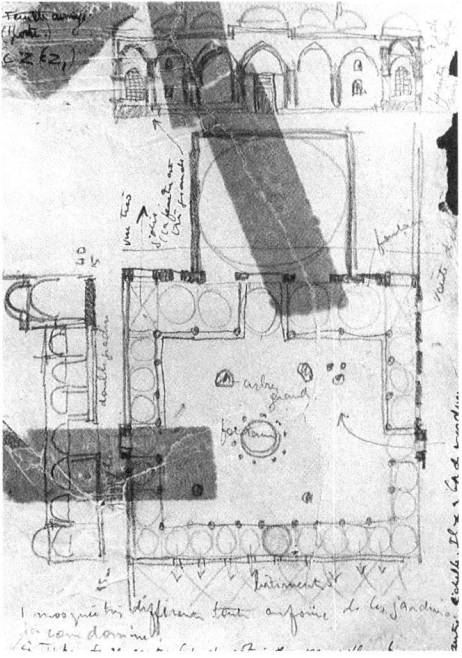

THE EARLY VILLAS

Approaching the Parthenon by the steep ascent towards the Propylaea and arriving at the mosques through a controlled spatial sequence brought home the message that buildings have to take account of each successive movement of the observer. Jeanneret's parents' house is composed so that a visitor ascends towards the building and moves around it as one does when approaching the Parthenon. The Villa Favre-Jacot embraces both the valley and the visitor by the curved projections in front of the facade. Thus, the movement route, or *promenade architecturale*, was already a feature of Jeanneret's strategy ten years before it was celebrated in the La Roche-Jeanneret houses in Paris, and it seems likely that his perception of the importance of successive experience towards and through a building was enhanced by his method of looking at landscapes and architecture from a multiple viewpoint. Similarly, his ability to comprehend a complex by means of sketching techniques developed at the Art School enabled him to come to terms with the sophisticated three-dimensionality of the great buildings of Greece and Byzantium.

Jeanneret's contemplative nature and interest in spirituality gave his visit to Mount Athos special importance, and observations he made on the journey reaffirmed the high respect for the monastic vocation he had felt previously on his visit to the charterhouse at Ema. He studied the churches on Athos with great care, perceiving, in one example, how the stones were arranged so that 'a spirit emanates from it' and referring to 'a mysterious link between shapes and colours, opening in a rhythm of withheld light only to the upward prayer and the lips of song'. Although he was not to design a church for another forty years, the messages learnt at Athos re-emerge in the pilgrimage chapel at Ronchamp and in the monastery at La Tourette. Throughout the journey, Jeanneret seems to have been as interested in landscapes, people and peasant houses as he was in the monumental buildings, and his writings contain numerous anecdotes relating to mood and to impressions of all kinds. His perception of the relationship between architecture, site and the people who use it relates to his concept of growth in nature as being dependent upon needs and conditions. He contrasts the healthy and correct growth of certain towns with the malignant determining circumstances discernible in certain others. This argument recurs with moralistic overtones, and seems focused on a considerable distrust of what Jeanneret felt to be artificial; thus, for example, his enjoyment of a musical instrument played spontaneously one evening is contrasted with his dislike of the forced conditions imposed by a concert hall.

Jeanneret's view of integrity, whether in a work of art, a building or whatever, seems based on what he considered to be appropriate for the particular conditions in operation: this led him to prefer simplicity when this seemed necessary, and his rapturous admiration for peasant art and architecture arose partly from his feeling that this reflected the kind of growth patterns he had observed in nature. Although he read widely, he relied a good deal on personal conclusions drawn from his observations during his various study tours, and he believed that man's artefacts could achieve a kind of perfection when they reflected the harmony which he thought possible between man, nature and the cosmos. The journey to the East was a watershed in Jeanneret's development because it consolidated some already established views about what might constitute an ideal lifestyle and identified key factors impinging on design technique. The next five years, 1912 to 1917, when he was between twenty-five and thirty, were transitional in that he was building the bridge that would take him from the localised teaching of L'Eplattenier to the larger world beyond.

William Ritter was instrumental in cultivating higher ambitions and broader aims, and Jeanneret's work during these years seems always to show an awareness of a future that would take him away from La Chaux-de-Fonds to emerge eventually in Paris as a leading member of the avant-garde. To an extent, this work was experimental, as Jeanneret was gaining vital professional experience, making mistakes and discovering that being an architect demands much more than being able to design. The period must have been a very difficult one for him as for long stretches he was engaged as an interior decorator and frustrated in his main intention. Yet with the Villa Jeanneret-Perret and the Villa Favre-Jacot he was able to advance his design technique by establishing a more considered relationship between the building and site, and by

33 Sketch showing disposition of internal space
34 Composite plan, section and elevation study of Hagia Sophia, 1911
35 Sketch of Tirnova, Bulgaria 1911
36 Studies of street life in Constantinople

THE EARLY VILLAS

37 Study of a street in Constantinople, 1911
38 Sketch of a balcony with pergola
39 Villa Savoye, Poissy, 12929-31

designing in a way that took account of a movement progression. He became aware of the need to regard architectural arrangement as zonal, volumetric and spatial, where formerly he had given too much weight to surface decoration.

The basic discipline of these houses was Classicism, but the primary volumes of his parents' house point towards his Purist architecture of the 1920s. While the Villa Favre-Jacot is the most literally classical design, it employs the curve imaginatively in the embracing gesture around the turning circle in front of the main facade. Each house anticipates strategems to be used in Jeanneret's later language, leading him immediately towards the Villa Schwob, the culminating work of the early phase.

The Villa Schwob is more advanced than the earlier buildings partly because it is more abstract, achieving a happier homogeneity, but mainly because of its clarification of certain elements within the general organisation. The circulation is clearly defined and separated from the rest of the configuration, and is used as a positive element in the plan. The plane of the street facade responds to the requirements of its context; the roof accommodation is separated by the cornice overhang from the main configuration and the roof terrace appears for the first time in a completed project. This classification of functional components expressed as separate elements within the building is the beginning of the next phase of Jeanneret's development; for in his Purist buildings he exploits inherent differences between the dynamics of circulation and volumetric arrangements disposed in accordance with functional needs. One of the most important links between the pre-Purist Classicism of Jeanneret's early villas and the language he was about to evolve lies in the use of curved elements. These were to play a vital role in his Purist paintings and in his later architecture, with the tensioning of curves within an orthogonal grid emerging as basic to his technique. As a continuous undercurrent to Jeanneret's evolving design strategy, the Domino system is no less significant. It was the Domino system which determined Le Corbusier's attitude not simply towards concrete as an ideal material but – fuelled by his interest in the ieas of Tony Garnier, the Futurists and the English Garden City movement – towards standardisation[25] and town planning as well. If the Domino structure helped to persuade Jeanneret of the virtues of concrete, it was the planar organisation which this made possible that provided him with a more potent means of organising primary geometry.

Jeanneret decided to leave La Chaux-de-Fonds after an embarrassing law suit over the Villa Schwob. He went to Paris in 1918, thus embarking on the final period of his education in which his relationship with Amédée Ozenfant was to provide the decisive direction for his work during the next decade.

THE EARLY VILLAS

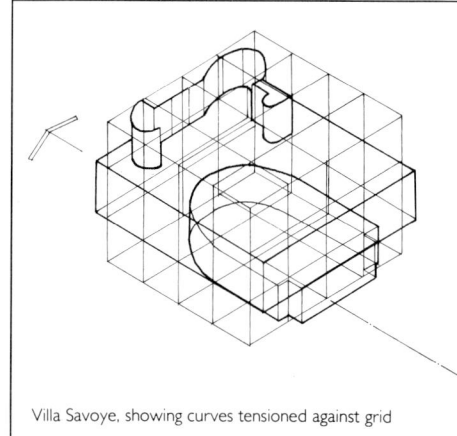

Villa Savoye, showing curves tensioned against grid

NOTES

1. Charles-Edouard Jeanneret-Gris (1887-1965) adopted the pseudonym Le Corbusier in 1920, although he continued to sign his paintings 'Jeanneret' until 1928.
2. Le Corbusier later acknowledged the importance of Jones's *Grammar*: 'We had been told: "Go to the quiet of the library and look at Owen Jones's great book, the GRAMMAR OF ORNAMENT". That was a more serious study. There we saw a succession of purely decorative motifs that man had created completely out of his own head. But wait, what we found there was rather the man of Nature, and if Nature was omnipresent, man was there completely, with his capacity for crystallisation, and his geometric shape-making. We went from Nature to man. From imitation to creation. That book was beautiful and true because everything in it was a distillation of what had been made, and *made* (or created) from the depths: the ornamentation of the Savage, of Renaissance man, of Gothic, Romanesque and Roman man, the Chinaman, the Indian, the Greek, the Assyrian, the Egyptian, etc. This book made us feel that the problem facing us was this: man *creates works of art that are capable of moving him.*' Le Corbusier, *L'Art décoratif d'aujourd'hui* (Paris 1925), p 135.
3. In 1897 Eugène Grasset published *La Plante et ses applications ornementales* in a folio-sized volume comparable with Jones's *Grammar* in the richness of its illustrative material. Decorative themes were extracted from a selection of plants, and the resultant patterns were widely copied. Jeanneret certainly read his *Méthode de composition ornementale* which was published in 1905 in two volumes, the first dealing with *Eléments rectilignes* and the second with *Eléments courbes* (right-angled and curved elements). Grasset used line drawings and sketches to show how patterns could be formed and then used in the design of ceramics, wallpapers, metalwork and stained glass.
4. Later Corbusier wrote of Ruskin: 'In our childhood we listened to the admonitions of Ruskin: an intricate, complex, contradictory and paradoxical apostle. His message was that those days could not be endured; things could not continue as they were; everything revealed a stupid, crushing Philistinism, bathed in materialism, garlanded with meaningless, completely mechanical decorations: decorations manufactured by machines that went on beyond the power of anyone to control, producing papier-mâché objects and cast iron scrolls ... Ruskin spoke about spiritual concerns. In his SEVEN LAMPS OF ARCHITECTURE it was the Lamp of Sacrifice, the Lamp of Truth and the Lamp of Humility that shone ...' Le Corbusier, *L'Art décoratif d'aujourd'hui*, op cit, p 134.
5. Kenneth Clark, *Ruskin Today* (London 1964), p 351. In this excellent study, Kenneth Clark gives a balanced critical appraisal of Ruskin's strengths and weaknesses and includes a wide-ranging selection of his writings.
6. In fact, L'Eplattenier insisted that the working drawings should be prepared and the work supervised by Rene Chapallaz, a local architect who had helped him design his own house. Chapallaz had begun his career in La Chaux-de-Fonds in 1902 in the offices of Architects Pignet and Ritter who had an excellent reputation. From 1905 to 1908, Chapallaz had an office in Tavannes and it was from there that he produced working drawings for all three of Jeanneret's first houses. For a detailed survey of the role of Chapallaz and L'Eplattenier see the article by Jacques Gubler, 'Jeanneret and Regionalism: From Feeling to Reason', pp 110-20.
7. This is a recurrent feature in Le Corbusier's œuvre as, for example, in the way the Villa Schwob culminates his early work and the Villa Savoye his heroic period, with Jaoul and the Unités summarising areas of research extending back over three decades.
8. Mary Patricia May Sekler has dealt with the symbolic importance of the tree in Jeanneret's early work in La Chaux-de-Fonds in a discussion entitled 'Ruskin, the Tree and the Open Hand', in *The Open Hand*, edited by Russell Walden (Cambridge, Mass 1977), pp 43-95. This subject is also dealt with by Dr Sekler in *The Early Drawings of Le Corbusier* (New York 1977), ch IV, pp 130-64.
9. Of the pine, Ruskin wrote: 'The pine, placed nearly always amongst scenes disordered and desolate, brings into them all possible elements of order and precision ... these two great characteristics of the pine, its straightness and rounded perfectness ... the pine rises in resistance, self contained.' (J Ruskin, *Modern Painters*, vol V, pp 78-80.
10. Ruskin argued that the contrast between large stones and 'divided masonry' should be properly organised 'like that of the continuous bones of the skeleton as opposed to the vertebrae'. The logical result of this was that not only must masonry be shown, but 'the smaller the building the more necessary its masonry should be bold' and 'if we build in granite or lava ... it is wiser to make the design granitic itself'. J Ruskin, *The Seven Lamps of Architecture* (London 1897).
11. This was translated by E Bypels under the title *Les Matins à Florence*, Paris 1906.
12. Paul Turner has discussed the significance of this book, explaining how Taine distinguished 'between art objects whose beauty can be conceptualised and understood, and nature, whose beauty is so grand and noble as to be beyond analysis'. He preferred the simplicity of classical buildings to the complexities of the Baroque or Gothic, believing the classical to have a sublime quality normally only found in nature. See Paul Turner, *The Education of Le Corbusier* (New York 1977), pp 37-42. Significantly, Jeaneret's sketches on this trip form two groups: impressionistic sketches of buildings, and drawings which are copiously annotated with detailed analytical information.
13. For a discussion of the significance of the monastery in Le Corbusier's development, see Peter Serenyi, 'Le Corbusier, Fourier and the Monastery of Ema', in *The Art Bulletin*, XLIX (1967).
14. Translated by Sekler, *The Early Drawings of Le Corbusier*, op cit, p 430.
15. William Ritter was a painter and art critic living in Neuchâtel whom Jeanneret had met during the winter of 1909. He wrote reviews for the Paris-based magazines, *La Gazette des Beaux-Arts*, *L'Art et L'Artiste* and *Mercure de France*, as well as the *Feuille d'Avis de La Chaux-de-Fonds*.
16. For this quotation I am indebted to Joyce Lowman's research into correspondence between Jeanneret and Ritter. Joyce Lowman, 'Le Corbusier 1900-1925: The Years of Transition', unpublished doctoral dissertation submitted to the University of London in 1979, p 33.

THE EARLY VILLAS

17 Of the Acropolis Jeanneret wrote: 'Seeing the Acropolis is a dream which one caresses without even thinking that one will be able to realise it. I don't really know why this hill should contain within itself the essence of artistic thought. I can measure the perfection of its temples and recognise that there are no others elsewhere which are so extraordinary.' Of the Parthenon he said: 'But why after seeing so much else must I designate as the incontestable master this Parthenon, when it rises from its plate of stone, and bend even angrily in front of its supremacy?' Both of these quotations are taken from one of the articles which Jeanneret wrote for the local newspaper, *Feuille d'Avis de la Chaux-de-Fonds*. These had been prompted by Ritter, who suggested that Jeanneret should correspond with him with a view to publication. Ritter's connections with the local newspaper ensured that several articles appeared, and these were eventually published in book form as *Voyage d'Orient*, (Paris 1966).

18 Stanislaus von Moos compares the parents' residence with Behrens's Villa Schröder at Eppenhausen, near Hagen (1908-09), and the Villa Favre-Jacot with Behrens's Villa Goedecke, also at Eppenhausen (1911-12). See S von Moos, *Le Corbusier: Elements of a Synthesis* (Cambridge, Mass 1979), pp 17 and 18. The south elevation of the parents' villa is similar to Wright's Winslow House (1893), whilst the framing of facades in each house resembles Hoffmann's treatment of the Palais Stoclet (1905).

19 This corner treatment resembles Schinkel's Altes Museum which Jeanneret would have seen in Berlin.

20 Jeanneret had been interested in reinforced concrete since he worked for Perret in Paris in 1907 but this interest was furthered by contact with an engineer friend, Max du Bois. In 1914 du Bois and Jeanneret worked out a concrete construction system based on principles advocated by Professor E Mörsche, who taught du Bois at the Zurich Polytechnic. This was later called the 'Domino' system because of the way houses constructed using this method could be placed next to each other like dominoes, with the columns relating to the slab. Jeanneret's sketchbooks for 1915 show various housing layouts using the system but he was only able to build in concrete in the Villa Schwob.

21 This resembles the cornice to the Cuno residence by Peter Behrens's (1909-10) on which, according to von Moos, Jeanneret worked whilst in Behrens's office. Von Moos, *op cit*, p 34.

22 This sort of 'repetition in a minor key' is referred to by Le Corbusier in *Towards a New Architecture* in connection with the Green Mosque at Broussa, on that occasion referring to spaces of a similar size but in half-light. See Le Corbusier, *Towards a New Architecture* (London 1946), p 168.

23 For a detailed analysis of these buildings see G H Baker, *Le Corbusier: An Analysis of Form* (Wokingham 1984).

24 For a full discussion of Jeanneret's reading see Paul Turner, *op cit*. Three books which exerted considerable influence were Henri Provensal's *L'Art de demain* (1904), Edouard Schuré's *Les grands initiés* (1907) and Nietzsche's *Thus spake Zarathustra* (1883-85).

25 Jeanneret optimistically assumed that standardisation and technical advance generally would transform society for the better, as when he later described one of his 1915 designs for a middle-class house in reinforced concrete: 'The architectural resources . . . permit a large and rhythmical arrangement and make a real architectural treatment possible. It is here that the mass-production principle shows its true value: some sort of link between the rich man's house and the poor man's; and some sort of decency in the rich man's dwelling.' *Towards a New Architecture, op cit*, pp 216 and 217.

40 Framed sketch of mountain view with tree-covered slopes in the foreground

THE EARLY VILLAS

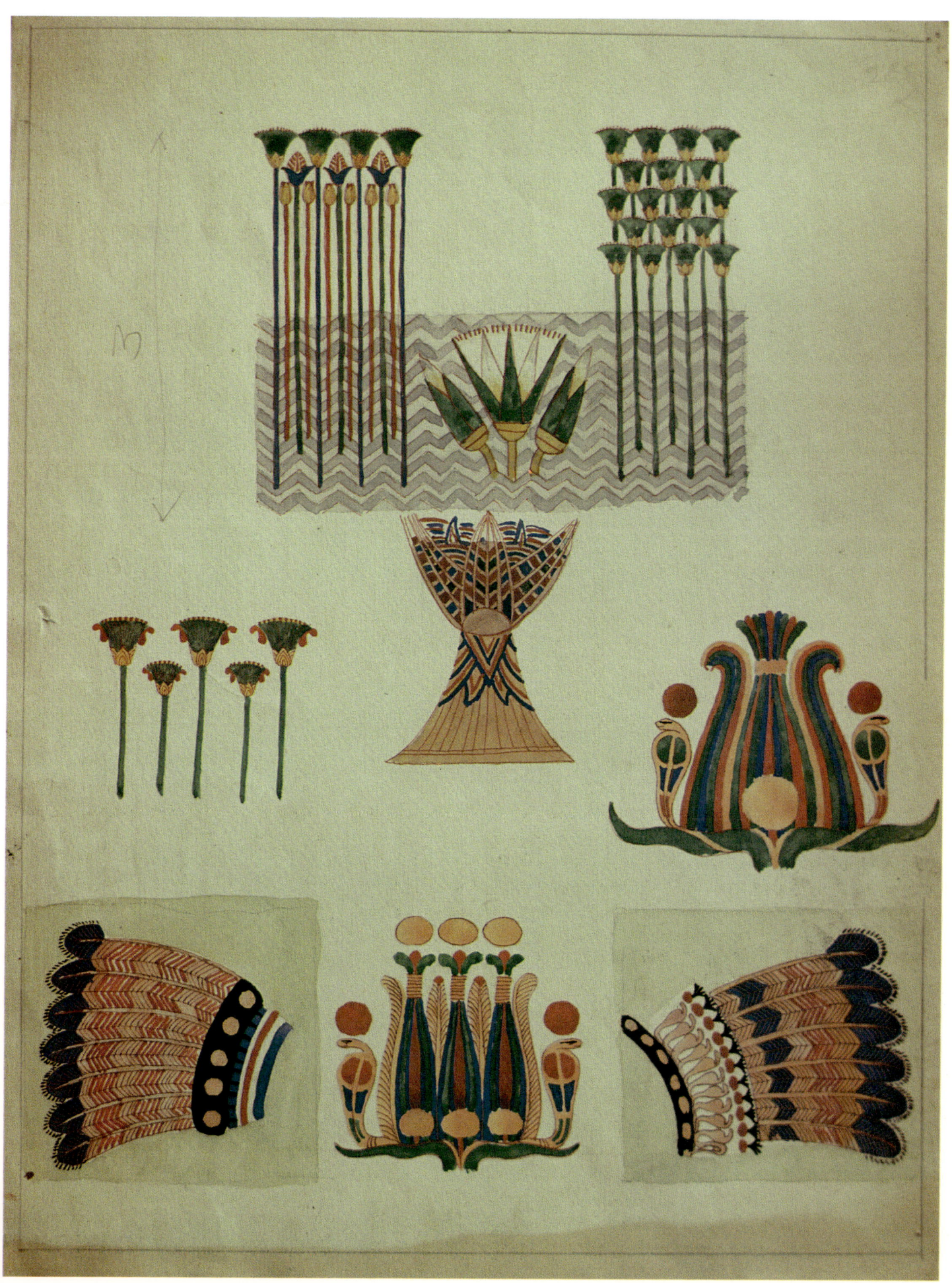

1 Sketches based on Owen Jones's *Grammar of Ornament*

VILLA FALLET

2 South elevation

3 Timber support column and white limestone corbel

4 View of salon

VILLA FALLET

5 Timber bracket support on sgraffito wall

6 Pine mullions and cloud-shaped railings

7 Wrought iron railings of pine abstraction

8 View from north-west

VILLA FALLET

9 Stucco decoration and corner junction of projecting porch, south elevation

10 White limestone corbel on west elevation

11 Door to salon

12 Lizard door handle

13 Upper landing to hall

VILLA STOTZER

14 View from south-east

15 Door to southern terrace

16 North facade

17 East gable

VILLA STOTZER

18 View from south-west

19 Rusticated masonry on southern terrace

VILLA STOTZER

20 View from south-east

22 Salon

VILLA STOTZER

23 View from south

24 East facade

VILLA JAQUEMET

25 View from south-east

26 View from south-west

VILLA JAQUEMET

27 South facade

28 West facade

VILLA JEANNERET-PERRET

29 Garden approach from south

30 South facade

VILLA JEANNERET-PERRET

31 View from south-west

32 Pergola leading to entrance

VILLA JEANNERET-PERRET

33 Bay on west facade

34 View from terrace towards entrance

35 View towards salon

VILLA JEANNERET-PERRET

36 Charles-Edouard Jeanneret's study

VILLA FAVRE-JACOT

37 Approach route to villa

38 East facade

VILLA FAVRE-JACOT

39 Column capital with acanthus leaves by Léon Perrin

40 Pilaster at south-west corner

41 West facade (roof addition not by Jeanneret)

VILLA FAVRE-JACOT

42 Detail of south facade showing typical framing of elements by Jeanneret

43 Detail of south facade above main entrance

VILLA FAVRE-JACOT

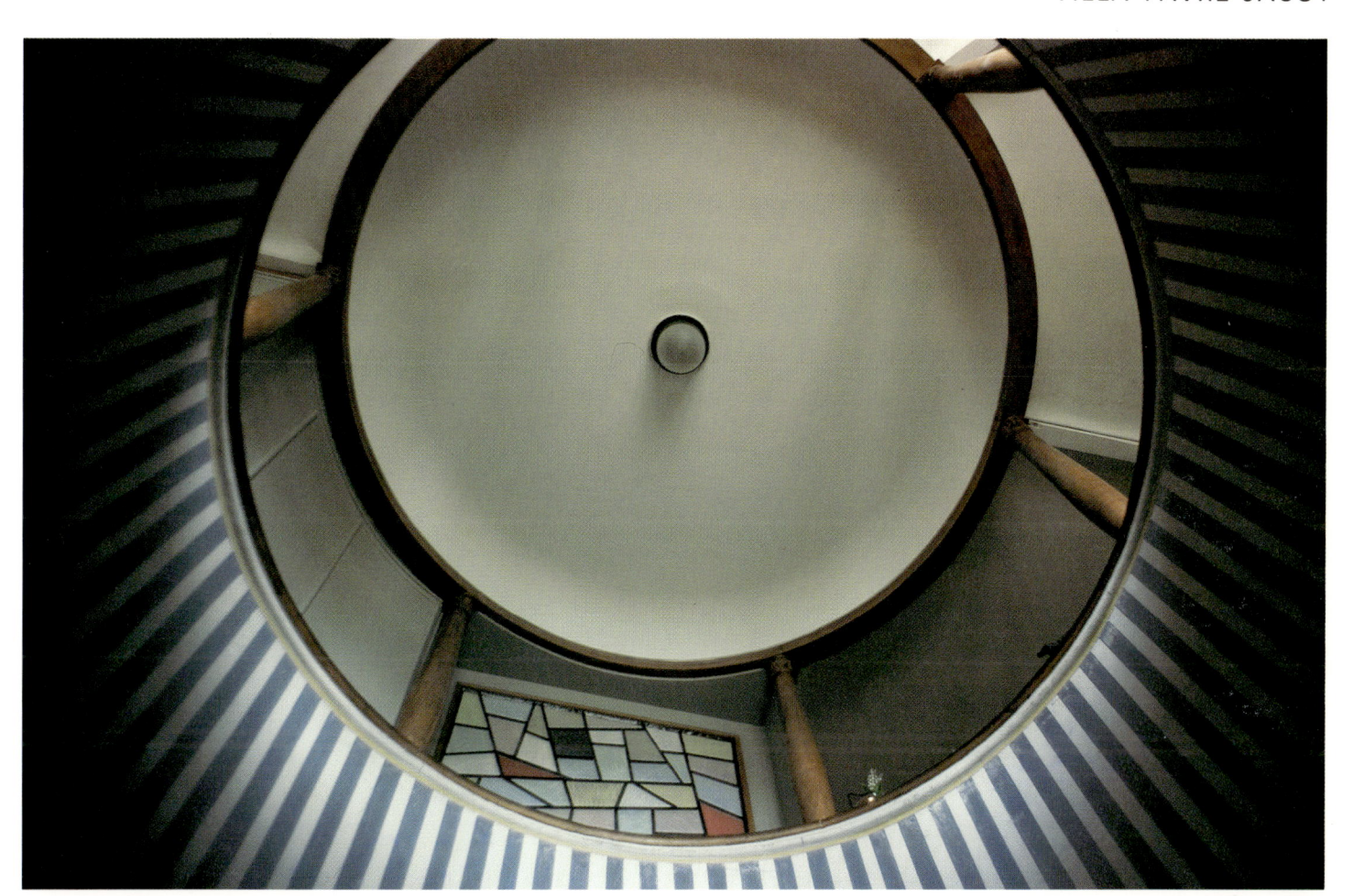

44 Upper gallery around vestibule

45 Cylindrical vestibule at first floor level

VILLA SCHWOB

46 North facade

47 Apsidal projection from east

VILLA SCHWOB

48 View from north-west

49 Window to salon on south facade

VILLA SCHWOB

50 Entrance portico from rue du Doubs

51 Apsidal wing with sculpted panel by Léon Perrin

52 Staircase behind north facade

VILLA SCHWOB

53 Balcony to salon

LA SCALA CINEMA

54 Rear of cinema from rue de la Parc

55 Projection booth and rear escape stair

56 Corner detail from rue de la Serre

The Early Projects
1905-1916

Villa Fallet
- 50 Perspective Drawing
- 51 Project Description and Notes
- 52 Plans and Sections
- 54 Elevations
- 56 Axonometric Projections

Villa Stotzer
- 58 Perspective Drawing
- 59 Project Description and Notes
- 60 Plans and Sections
- 62 Elevation
- 64 Axonometric Projections

Villa Jaquemet
- 66 Perspective Drawing
- 67 Project Description and Notes
- 68 Plans and Sections
- 70 Elevations
- 72 Axonometric Projections

Villa Jeanneret-Perret
- 74 Perspective Drawing
- 75 Project Description and Notes
- 76 Plans and Sections
- 78 Elevations
- 80 Axonometric Projections

Villa Favre-Jacot
- 82 Perspective Drawing
- 83 Project Description and Notes
- 84 Plans
- 86 Plans and Sections
- 88 Elevations
- 90 Axonometric Projections

Villa Schwob
- 92 Perspective Drawing
- 93 Project Description and Notes
- 94 Plans
- 96 Site Plan Section and Elevation
- 98 Elevations
- 100 Axonometric Projections

La Scala Cinema
- 102 Perspective Drawing
- 103 Project Description and Notes
- 104 Plans
- 106 Sections
- 108 Elevations
- 110 Axonometric Projection

VILLA FALLET

VILLA FALLET 1905

VILLA FALLET
La Chaux-de-Fonds 1905
Charles-Edouard Jeanneret and René Chapallaz

The Villa Fallet is located on the wooded Pouillerel hillside which overlooks La Chaux-de-Fonds. Built in the local vernacular 'chalet' style, the house is dominated by its roof which overhangs loggias to the east and west, with entry from the western loggia into a central hall.

The arrangement of the villa is typical of the region in having a cellar, a main floor elevated by a stone podium, bedrooms at first floor level and an attic storey in the roof. Externally, the southern facade becomes a major event, whilst internally, the main spatial feature is that of the hall which extends through two floors. The hall forms the circulation core of the plan, giving access to the south-facing ground floor rooms. A stair on its northern side gives access to the bedrooms via an L-shaped landing which helps to contain the space below. Further modelling of the space is provided by the extension of the staircase stringer to form an arch containing an area under the stair. The hall ceiling is angled along the ridge axis of the villa to echo the roof pitch, thus furthering the three-dimensional modelling of the space. The hall is well lit by a window to the north side which is angled to coincide with the internal roof arrangement.

Both internally and externally structural fact is exploited to provide decorative incident, this being maintained by the high level of timber craftsmanship in the region. The villa interacts with its context by its organisation and by its surface treatment, in which a series of allegorical references to the pine tree are abstracted to form various kinds of ornament. This surface decoration is furthered by an exploitation of the textural and rhythmic potential of stone and timber, deployed in an expression of structure inspired by Jeanneret's analysis of natural organisms.

In several ways this first building by Jeanneret demonstrates design characteristics that were to remain part of his repertoire as Le Corbusier. These include the positive handling of form, the elaborate orchestration of architectural elements, the sense of compositional balance with a hierarchical deployment of facades, the dramatic exploitation of one particular facade and the creation of an internal space of quality. Again as in Le Corbusier's work, the villa states a philosophical position as a crystallisation of the theoretical teachings of L'Eplattenier.

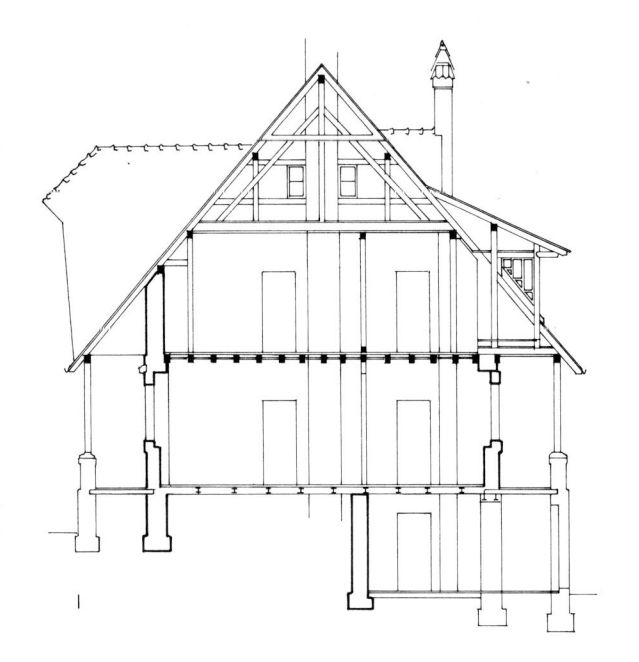

VILLA FALLET

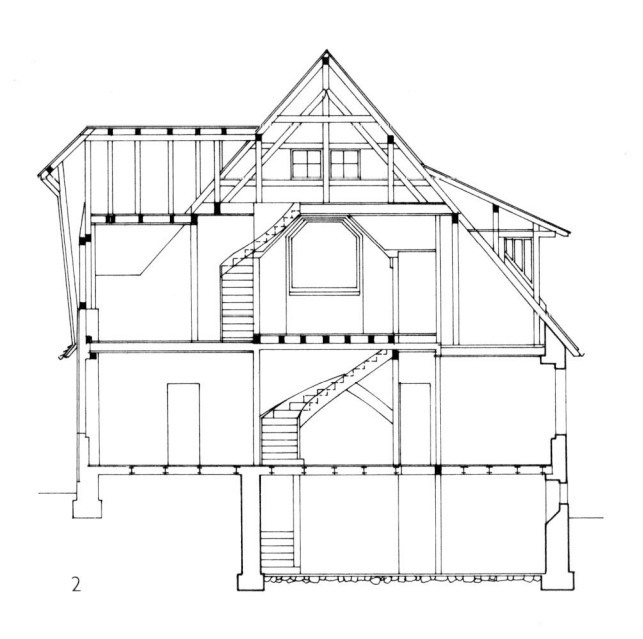

1 Cross section through front bedrooms
2 Cross section through hall
3 Longitudinal section
4 Roof detail
5 Basement plan
6 Ground floor plan
7 First floor plan
8 Layout of joists
9 Roof beam structure

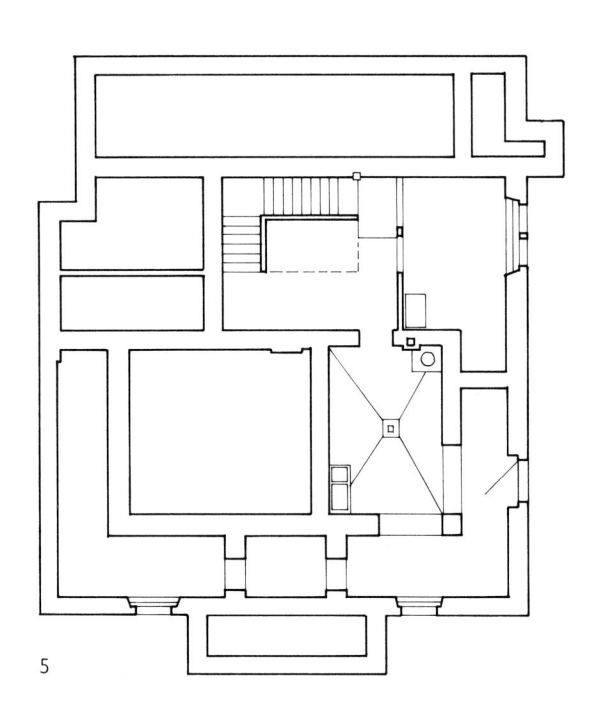

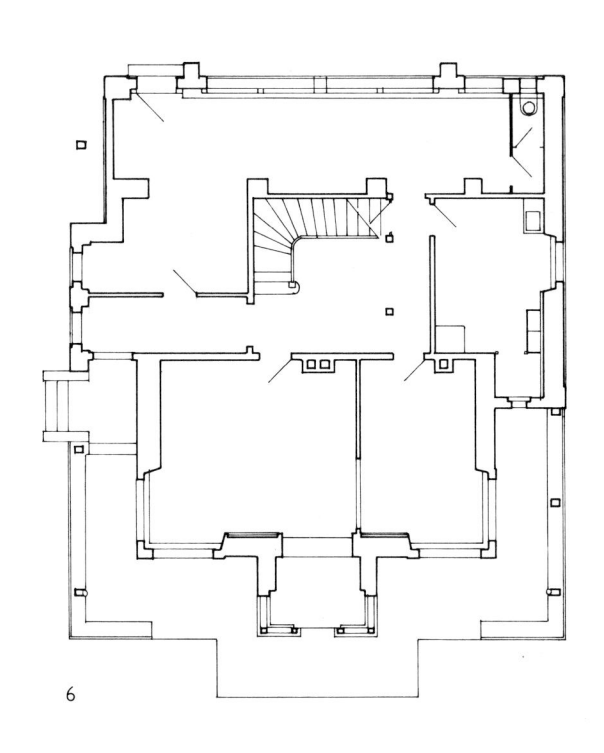

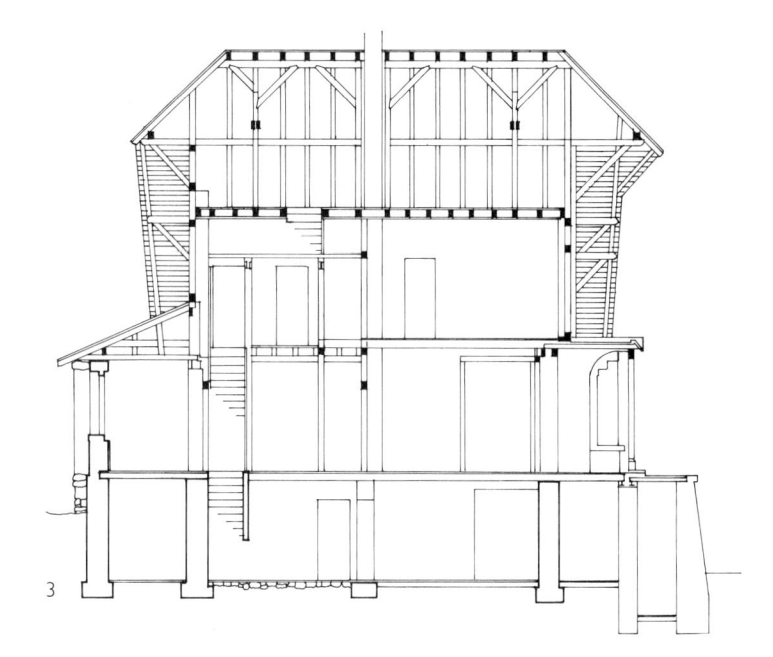

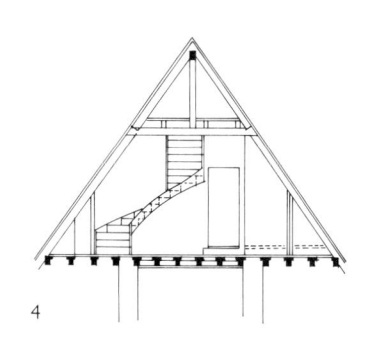

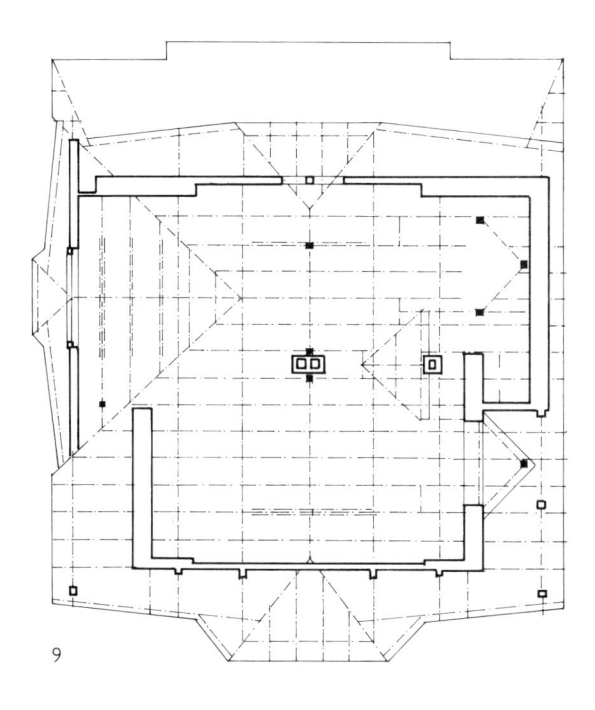

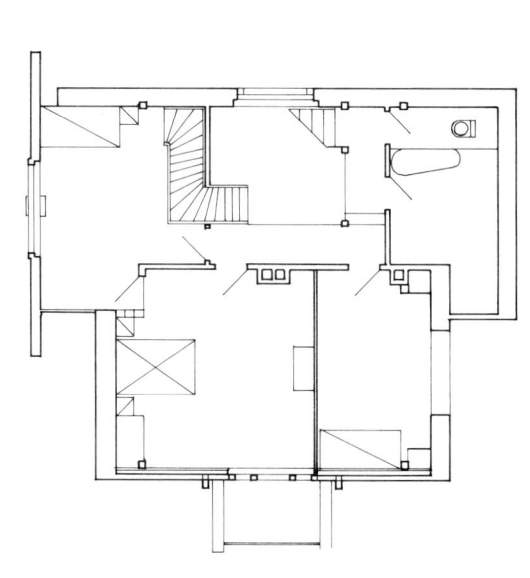

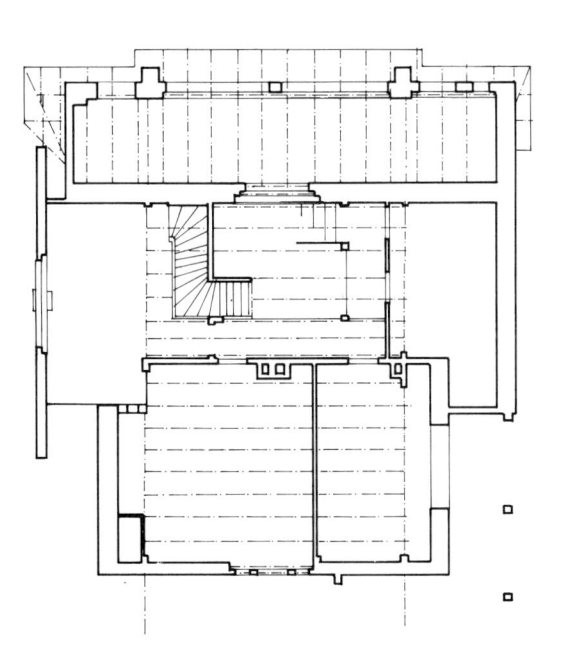

VILLA FALLET

VILLA FALLET

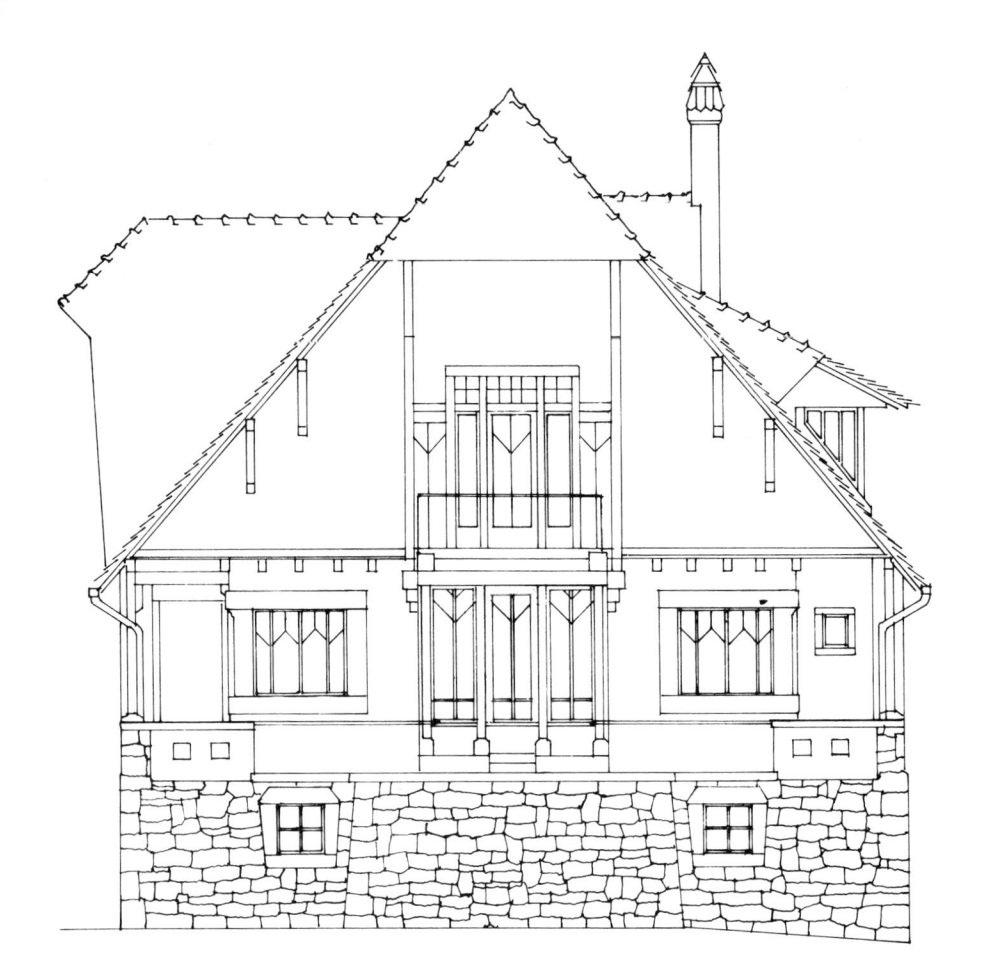

10 South elevation
11 North elevation
12 East elevation
13 West elevation

10

11

54

VILLA FALLET

12

13

VILLA FALLET

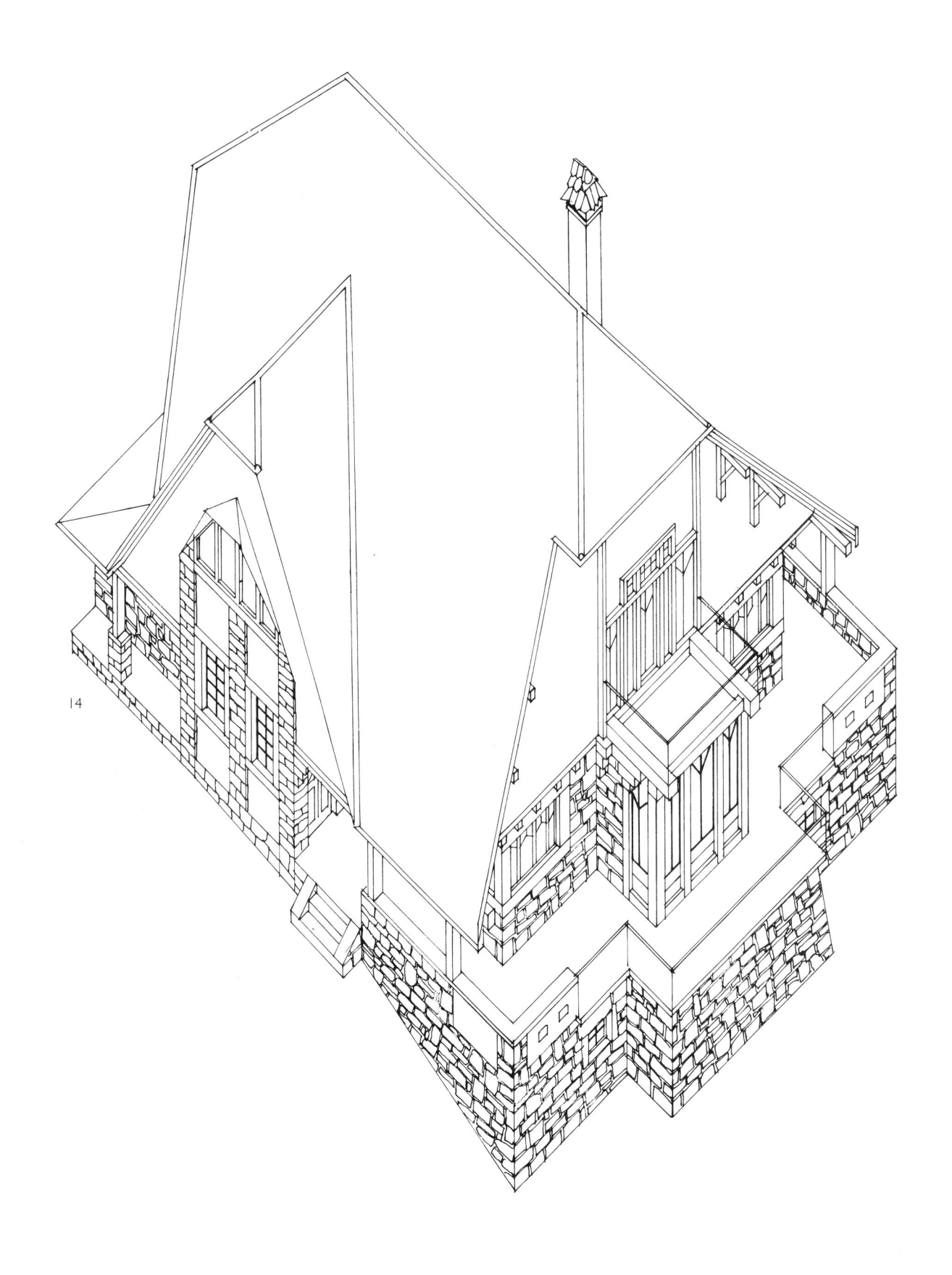

14

14 Axonometric from the south-west
15 Cut-away axonometric from the south-west

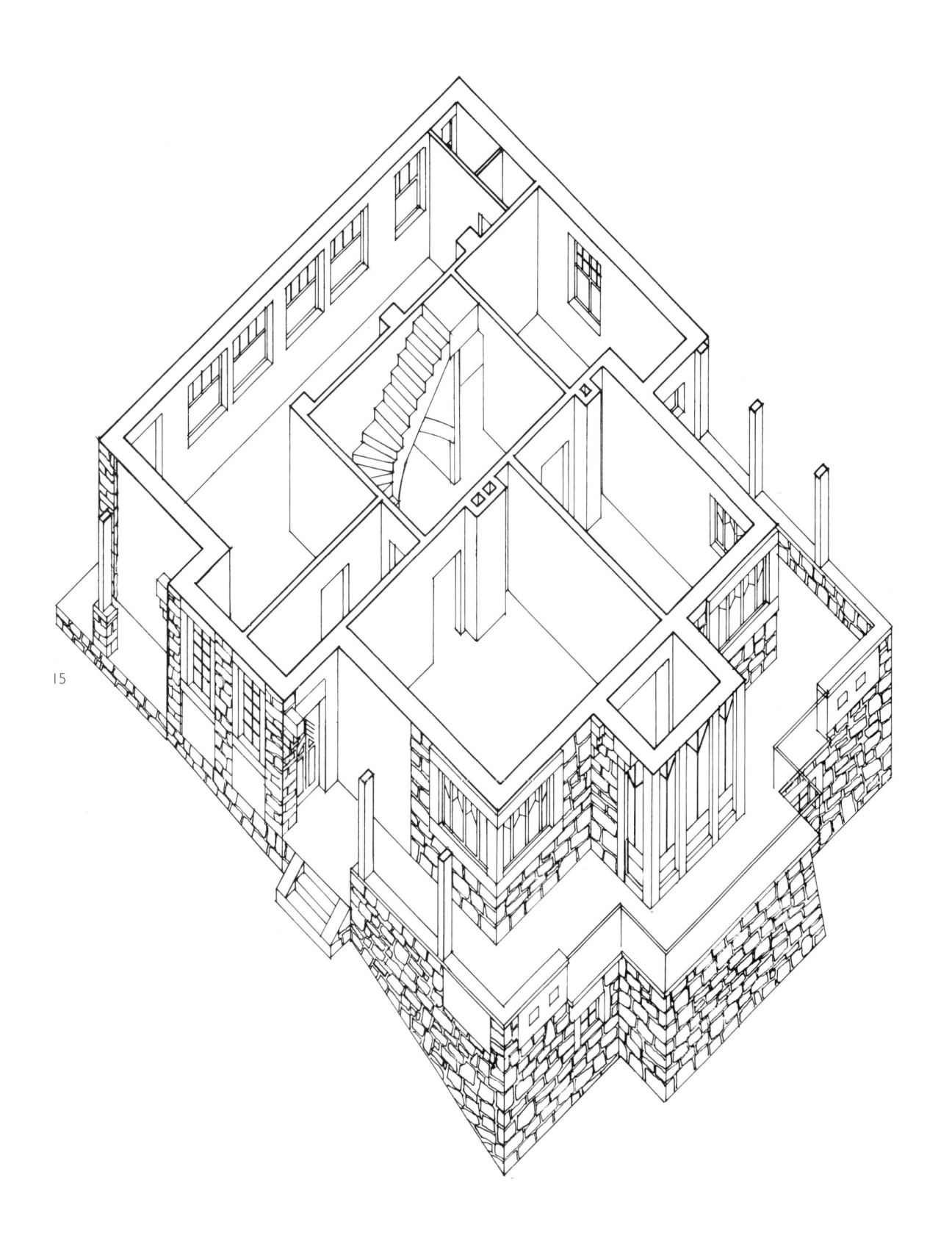

VILLA FALLET

15

VILLA STOTZER

VILLA STOTZER
1908

VILLA STOTZER
La Chaux-de-Fonds 1908
Charles-Edouard Jeanneret and René Chapallaz

The Villa Stotzer was built for Albert Stotzer-Fallet, a designer of jewellery in La Chaux-de-Fonds. Correspondence between Jeanneret and L'Eplattenier suggests that his teacher was in some way involved in his gaining the Stotzer and Jaquemet commissions. Both villas are built higher on the same sloping hillside as the Villa Fallet.

Jeanneret designed the Villa Stotzer in collaboration with René Chapallaz. He worked on the Villas Stotzer and Jaquemet whilst in Vienna, forwarding design suggestions to L'Eplattenier and Chapallaz for comment. The working drawings, dated January 1908, were almost certainly prepared in the Chapallaz office in Tavannes.

Access is from the north, with the best views towards the south-east. The planning strategy resembles that of the Villa Fallet inasmuch as the villa is organised around a main north-south axis with a dominant southern gable. The more open situation permits a bilaterally symmetrical organisation, and secondary gables express a transverse axis with a hall to the rear leading to the main south-facing rooms (as in the Villa Fallet).

The stairs are placed on the main longitudinal axis so that their slight projection on the north facade reinforces the symmetry of this elevation. The symmetry is also emphatically proclaimed on the south elevation, which has a distinctly linear general arrangement. As in the Villa Fallet, a podium helps to resolve the sloping terrain, giving a south-facing terrace to the villa.

The oblique planes of the southern gable are reinforced by a deep barge board; the extremities of the flank walls by rusticated masonry. The taut balcony contributes to a total effect in which a dynamic resolution of vertical and horizontal forms is surmounted by the contrasting oblique planes of the roof. This gable treatment is made more visually compelling by the centrally located leaf-shaped window which acts as a focus and is deeply incised into the stucco wall face and then framed by timbers which follow the gable profile. The glazing bars to this window are like the trunk and branches of a tree, and both its shape and position reinforce the symmetry of the south elevation.

The stucco external treatment of the villa is animated by randomly placed and slightly projecting stones – in the same way that the small holes in the east wall of the chapel at Ronchamp enliven its mass. Although the upper window on the main southern facade is a reminder of the importance of Art Nouveau to Jeanneret and L'Eplattenier, in other respects the villa demonstrates a clear rationale in the deployment of structure, materials and ornament which distances it from that movement.

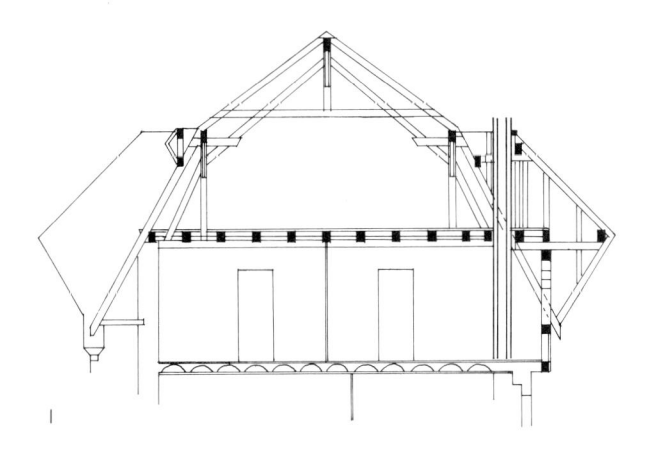

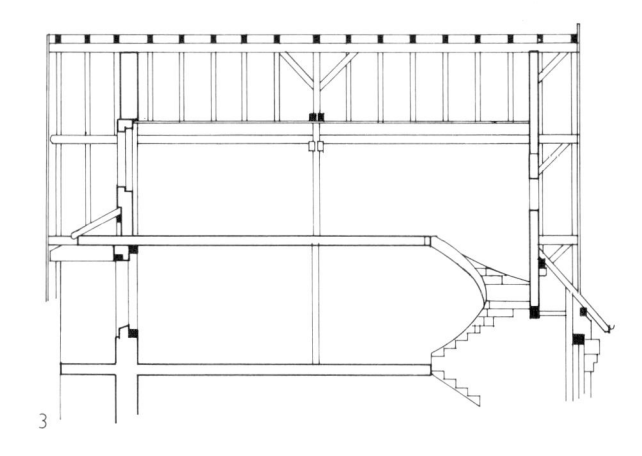

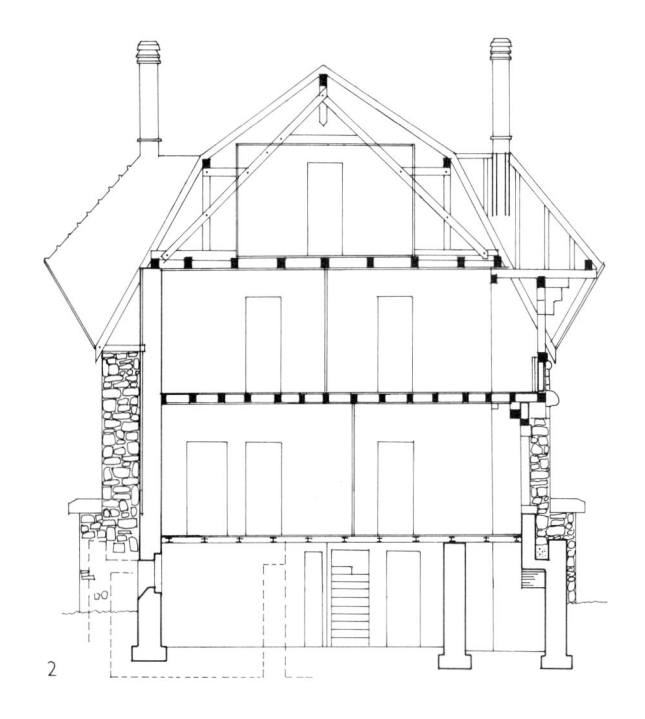

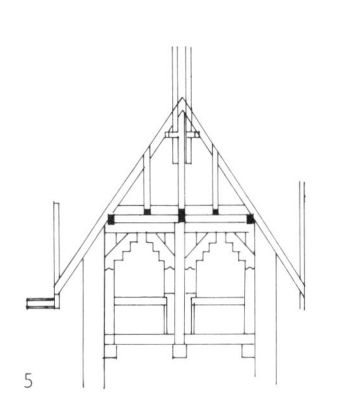

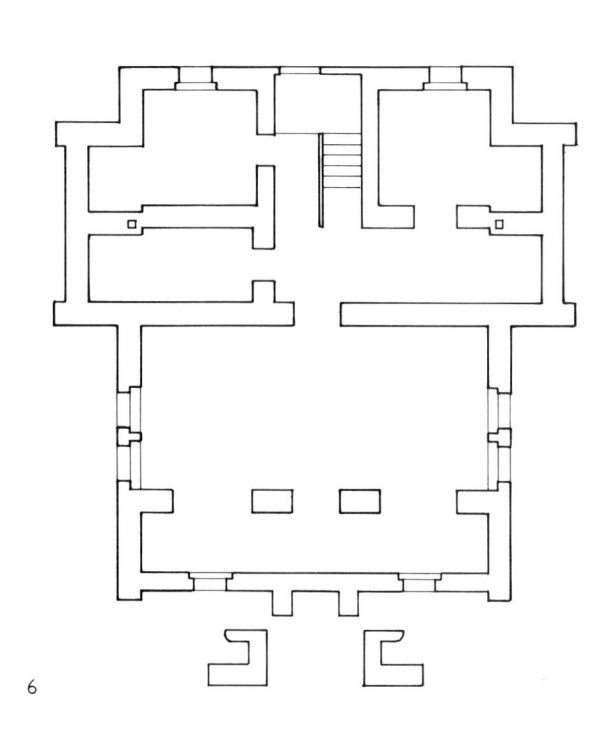

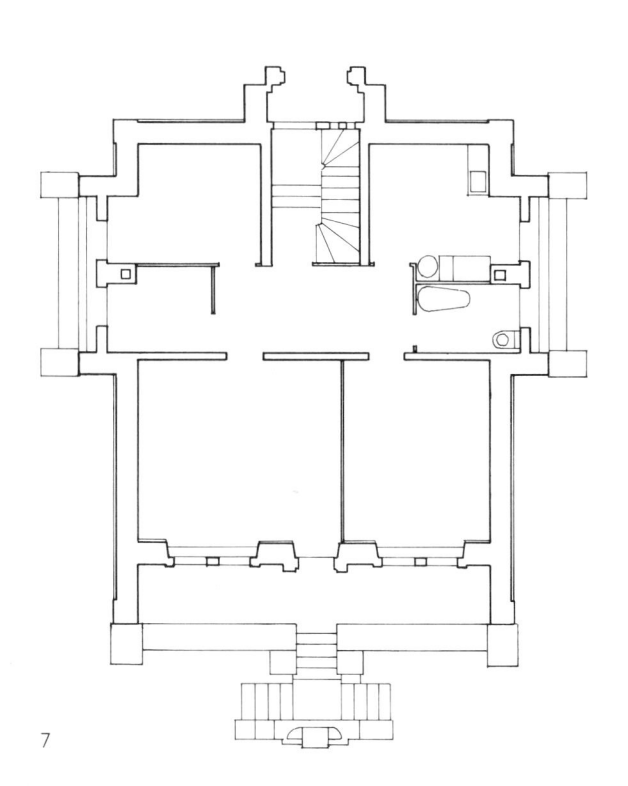

VILLA STOTZER

VILLA STOTZER

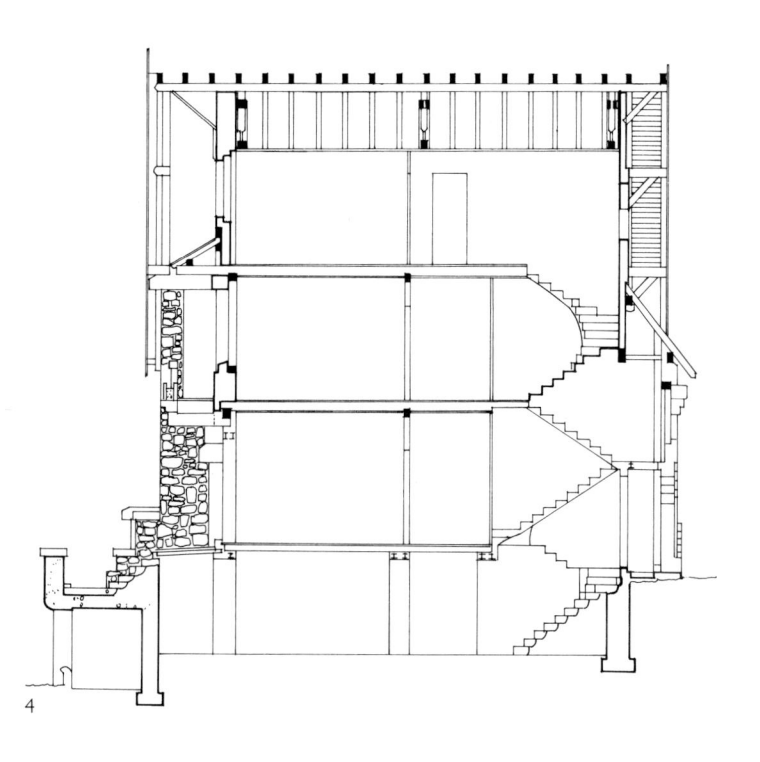

1-2 Cross sections
3-4 Longitudinal sections
5 Ridge detail
6 Basement plan
7 Ground floor plan
8 Layout of joists
9 First floor plan
10 Attic plan
11 Layout of roof beam structure

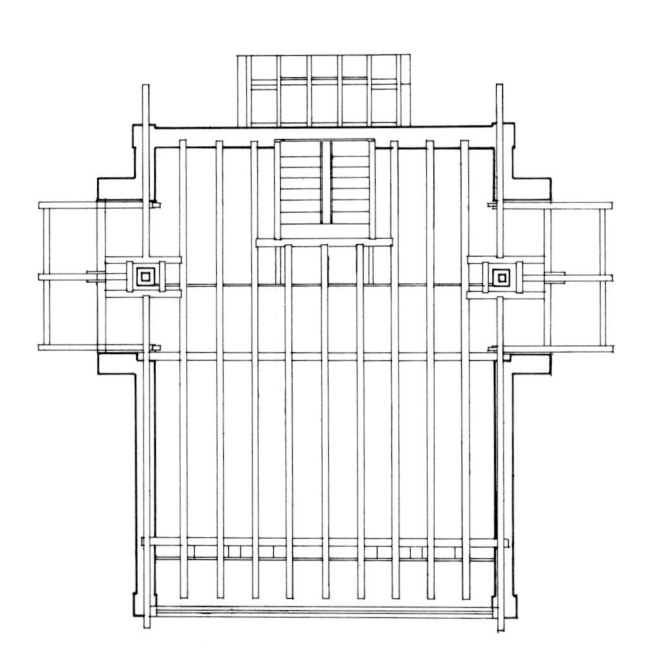

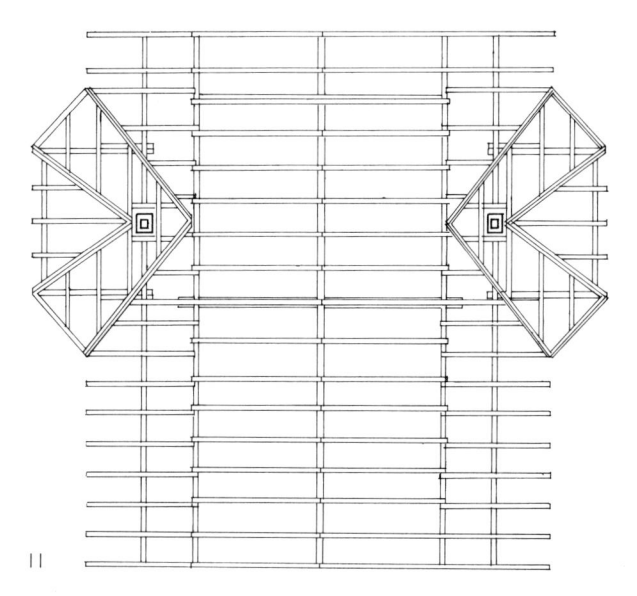

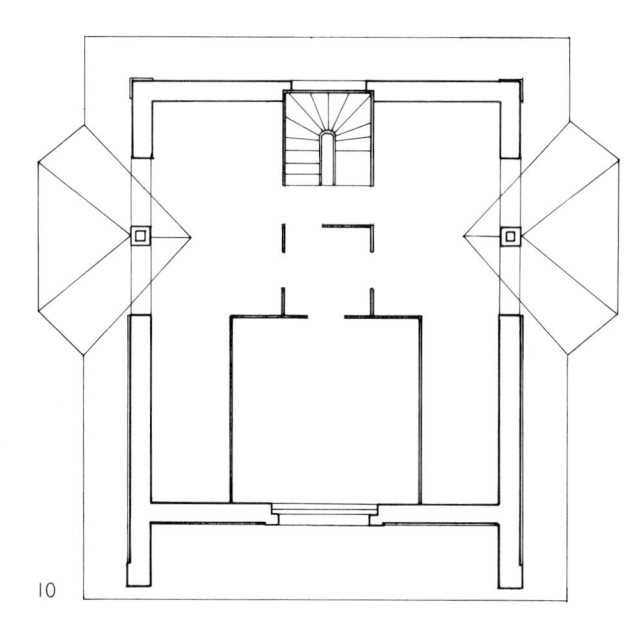

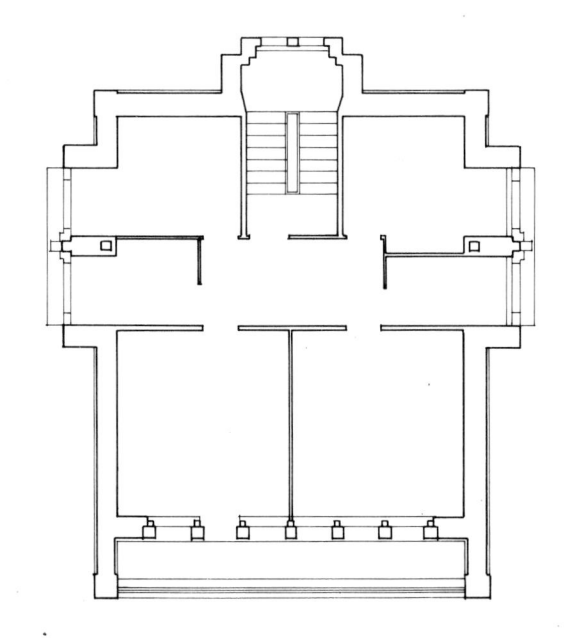

61

VILLA STOTZER

12

12 South elevation
13 East elevation
14 North elevation

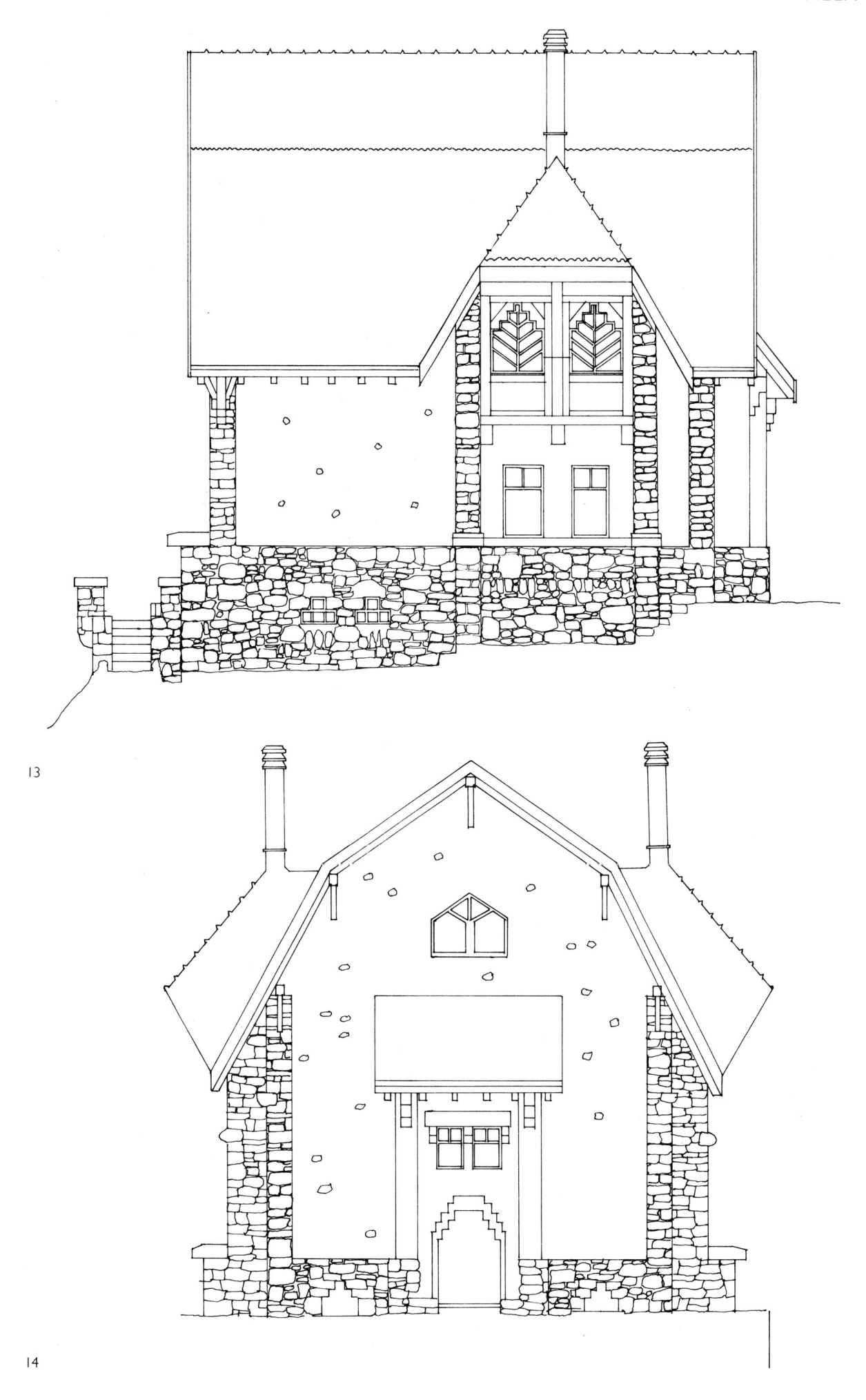

VILLA STOTZER

13

14

63

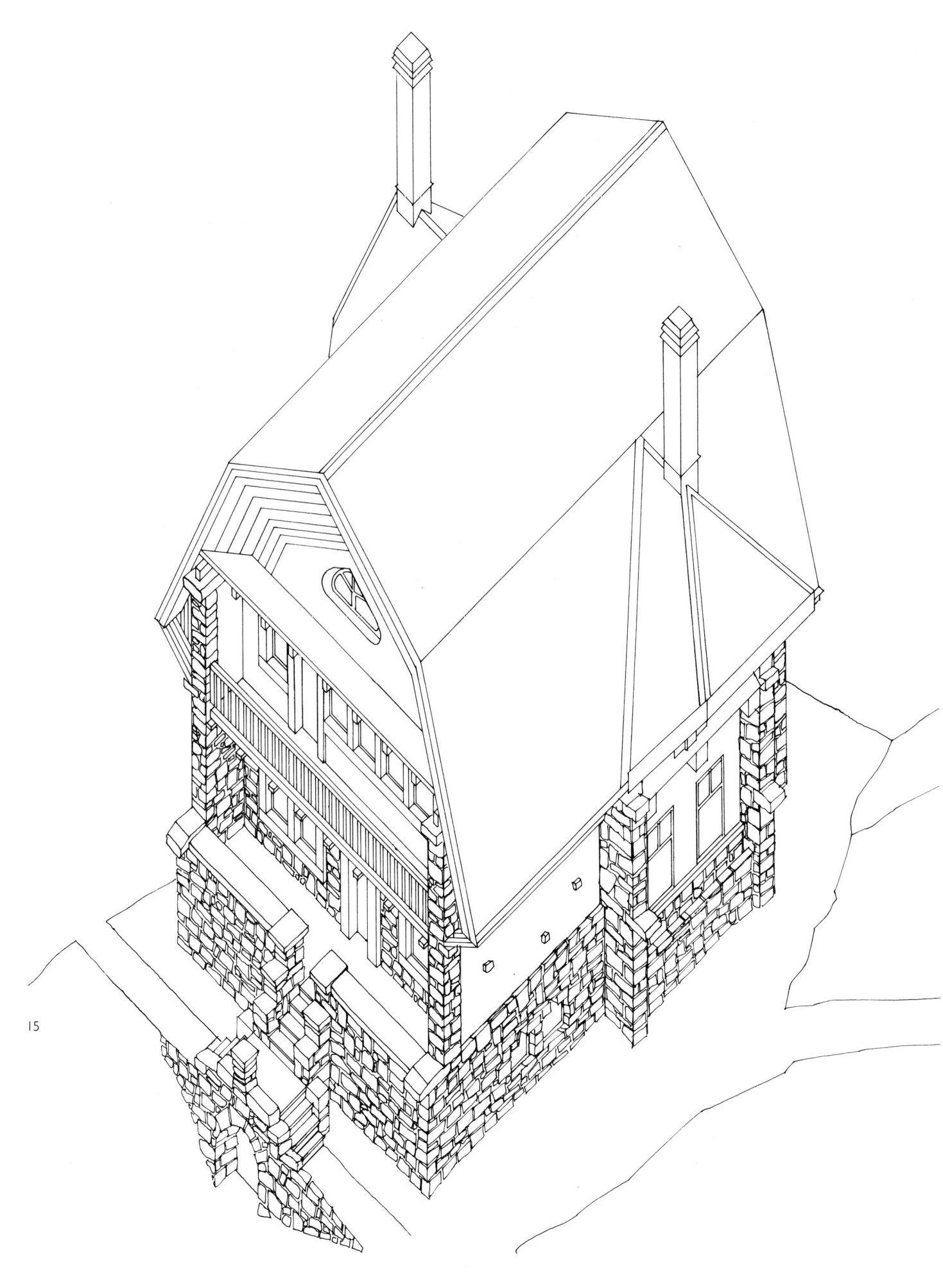

VILLA STOTZER

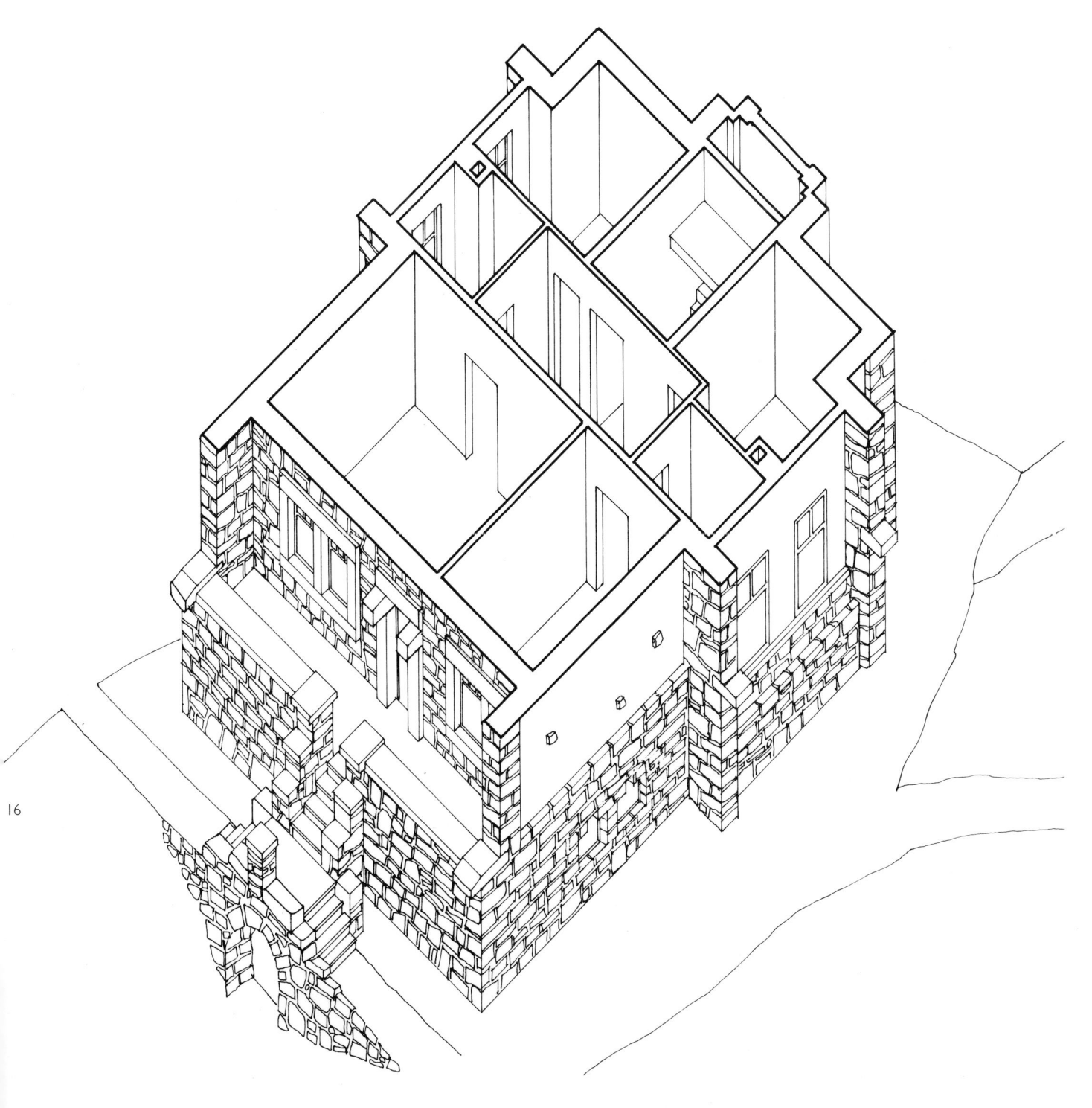

VILLA STOTZER

15 Axonometric from the south-east
16 Cut-away axonometric from the south-east

VILLA JAQUEMET

VILLA JAQUEMET
1908

VILLA JAQUEMET
La Chaux-de-Fonds 1908
Charles-Edouard Jeanneret and René Chapallaz

The Villa Jaquemet was built for Jules Jaquemet-Fallet close to the Villa Stotzer. The plans of the two houses are almost identical, but Jeanneret developed contextural differences to suggest contrasting themes in each.

As with the Villa Stotzer, access is from the north and the organisation is based on a north-south axis with an accentuation of the southern gable. The main south-facing rooms at ground level face onto an elevated terrace which forms part of a rusticated stone podium.

The Villa Jaquemet contains little of the nature-inspired decoration of the Villas Fallet and Stotzer, and its theme is one of low-key restraint. The geometrical complexity of the site projections shows Jeanneret using support timbers to elegantly express their structural role. The exploitation of the potential of materials is a feature of Jeanneret's first three houses in La Chaux-de-Fonds.

The Villas Stotzer and Jaquemet are less directly allegorical than the Villa Fallet in their surface treatment, so their overall richness is dependent partly on the massing, in which the roof and gable formation play a key role, and partly on the textural contrasts between stone and stucco, assisted by the rhythmic deployment of fenestration. Structural members support the decorative intention with an elaborate treatment of secondary gables and a clear demonstration of the trabeated potential of stone on the southern facades.

Although the houses appear to be individual family units they were in fact designed as apartments with the ground and first floors being identical and self-contained in their provision of living and sleeping spaces. Jeanneret was already experimenting with reinforced concrete floor slabs using the Hennebique system and these occur in both Jaquemet and Stotzer, with projections in the form of cantilevered concrete beams supporting the balcony of the latter house.

VILLA JAQUEMET

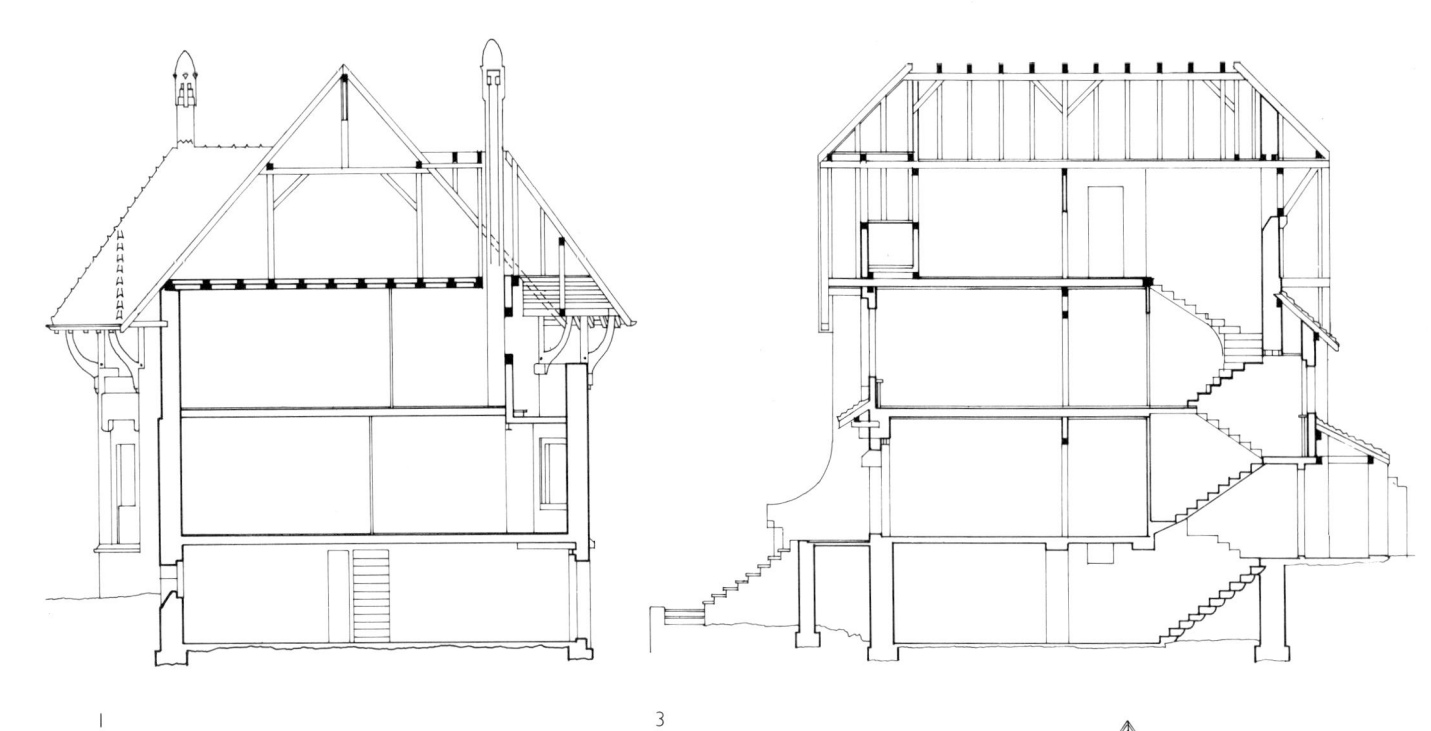

1 Cross section
2 Ridge detail
3 Longitudinal section
4 Basement plan
5 Ground floor plan
6 First floor plan
7 Attic plan
8 Layout of joists
9 Roof beam structure

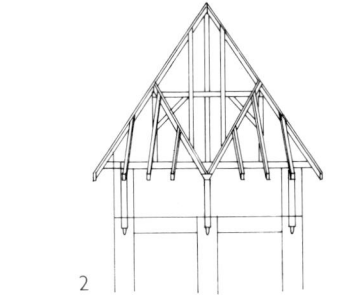

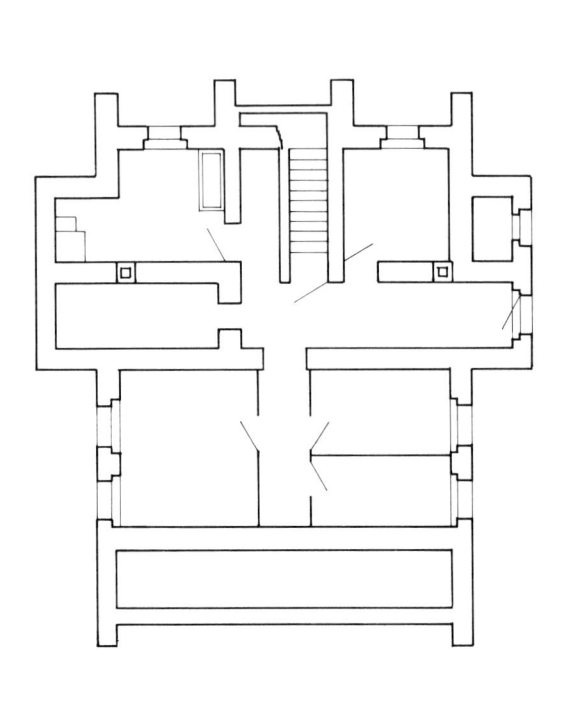

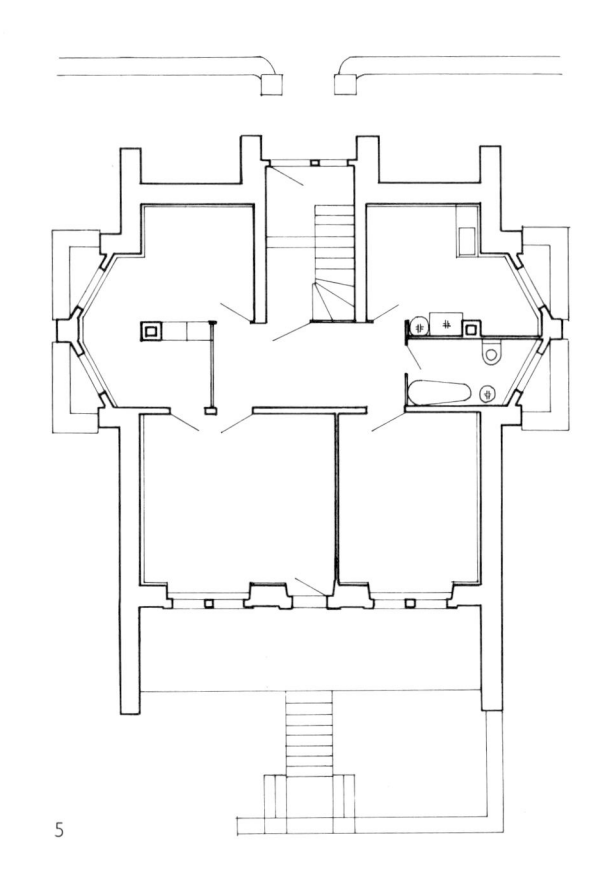

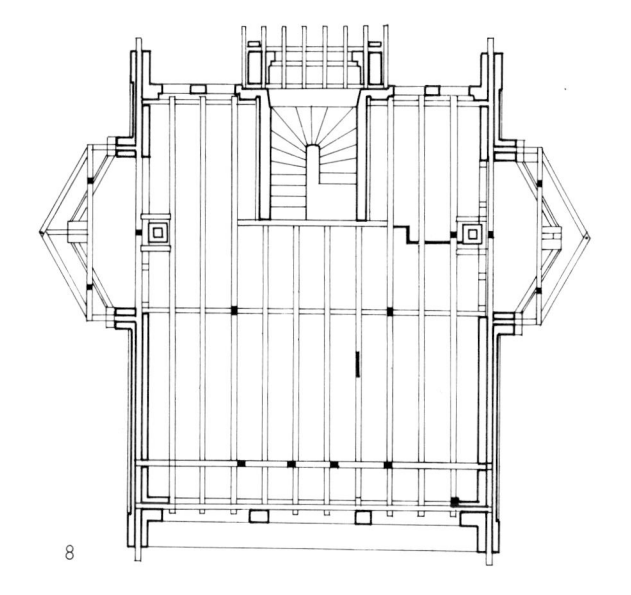

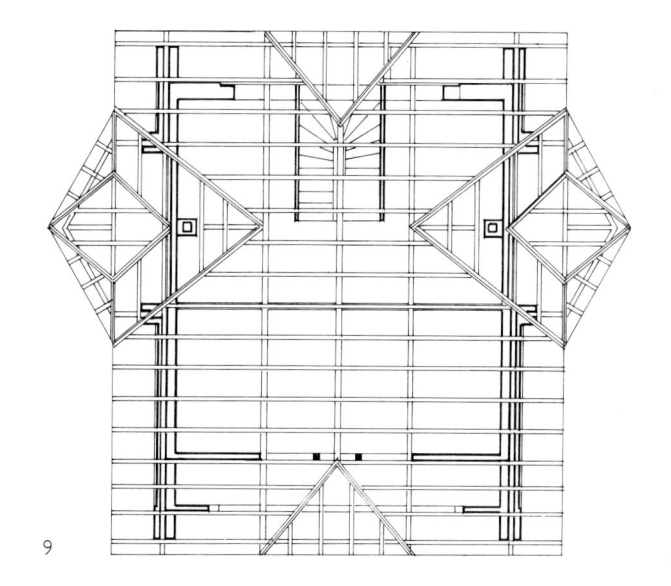

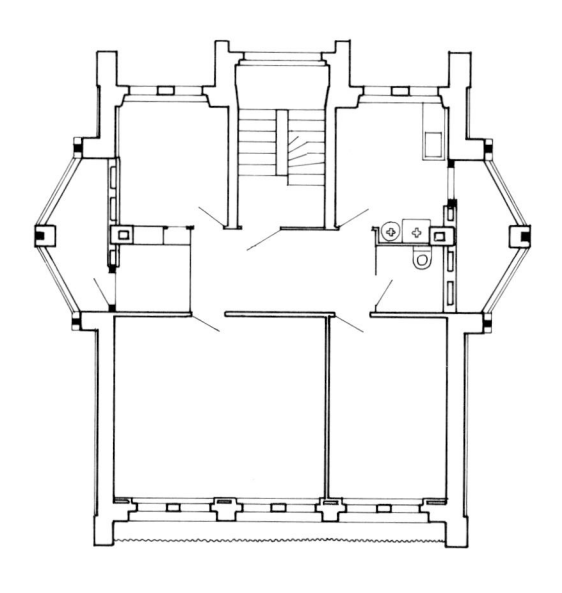

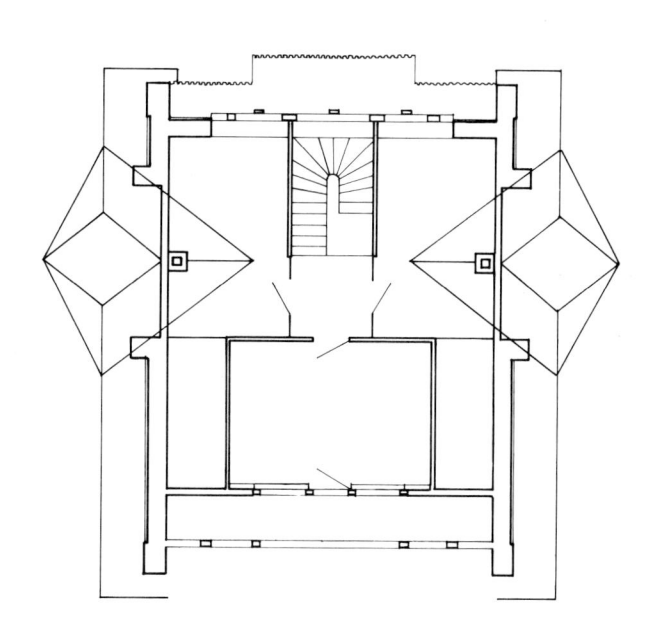

VILLA JAQUEMET

VILLA JAQUEMET

10 South elevation
11 East elevation
12 North elevation

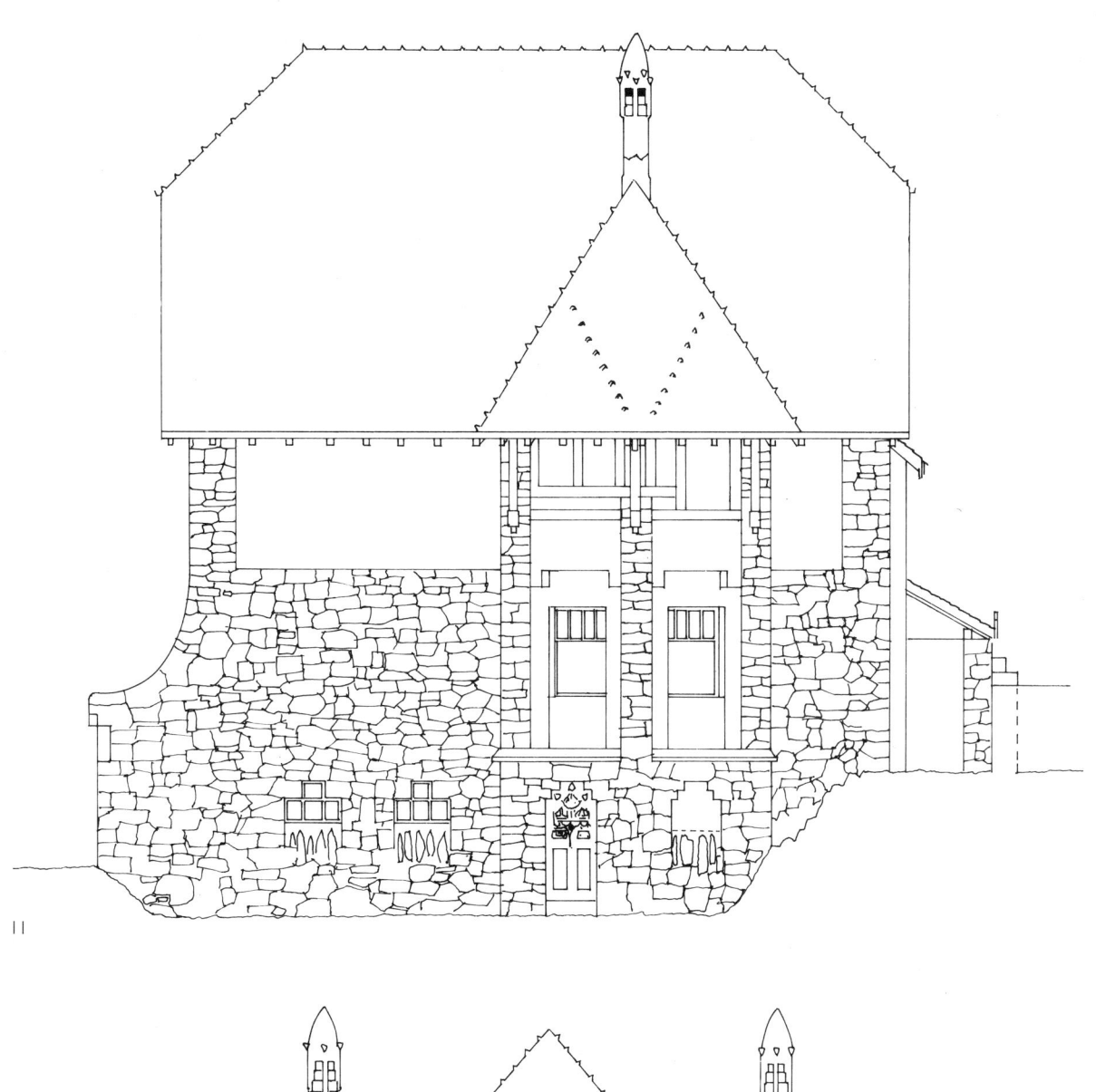

VILLA JAQUEMET

11

12

71

VILLA JAQUEMET

13 Axonometric from the south-east
14 Cut-away axonometric from the south-east

13

VILLA JAQUEMET

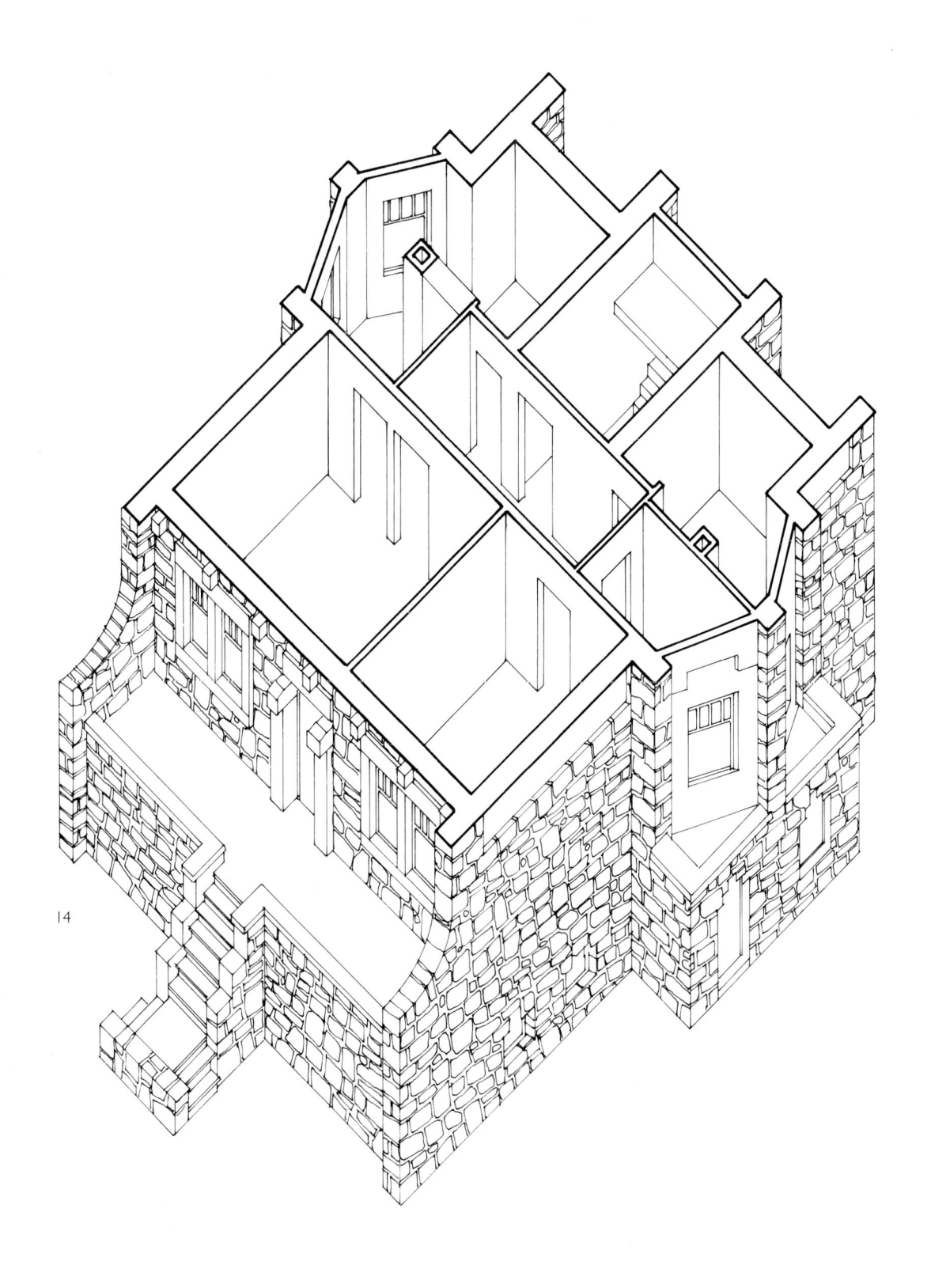

14

VILLA JEANNERET-PERRET

VILLA JEANNERET-PERRET 1912

VILLA JEANNERET-PERRET
La Chaux-de-Fonds 1912
Charles-Edouard Jeanneret

This medium-sized family house known locally as the 'Maison Blanche' was built on the Pouillerel hillside for Jeanneret's parents the year after he returned from his Voyage to the Orient. The house projects out from the hillside so that the main floor has an adjacent terrace to which access is gained by a staircase from a lower level. As in the earlier houses, the basement contains a cellar, and this lower level is set into the hillside. Again as in the earlier houses, entry and circulation are placed at the rear so that the main rooms enjoy an uninterrupted view to the south. A sketch by Jeanneret dating from this period bears such a close similarity to the villa that it may have been an early design proposal. Drawn boldly and economically, it contains the essentials of the final composition of the villa and is shown on a tree-lined hillside similar to the actual site.

Externally, the white cubic form relies on contrasts within the modelling, with the projecting bay defining the east-west linear axis. In the surface subdivision, decoration based on pattern and texture is abandoned in favour of a studied deployment of elements in accordance with classical design principles. Houses by Behrens, Hoffmann and Tessenow have been suggested as influences on the design but there is also a resemblance in general handling to Frank Lloyd Wright's Winslow House, which has a similar overhanging roof with windows in a band below it. Wright's work was known in Europe as a result of the *Wasmuth* publication of 1910.

Internally, the central salon is linked to adjacent rooms through glazed doors to form one grand space, the first example of this in Jeanneret's work. On the first floor, the staircase leads to an ample linen room lit by a pair of glazed double doors which give access to a small curved balcony with a simple wrought-iron balustrade. A corridor on the central axis of the plan leads to a bedroom facing the terrace, with the master bedroom centrally placed on the south side. To the north of the central corridor, Jeanneret designed himself a study with a west-facing window and a rooflight giving illumination to the centre of the room. In the roofspace, behind the frosted glass which admits light, he placed electric light bulbs to give indirect lighting. A further innovation was the provision of central heating radiators in wooden casings under the large windows of the main salon. Jeanneret was also responsible for the fireplace in the main salon which he designed as his own version of a classical base, column and 'entablature' topped with ceramic tiles (also of his own design) which open in a composition celebrating nature with leaves, flowers and birds.

According to Roland Bhend and Pierre-Alaine Luginbuhl,[1] the Villa Jeanneret-Perret excited a good deal of unfavourable comment from the local inhabitants when first built. It was felt that the large windows of the main salon were impractical in such a cold winter climate and that a pergola was more appropriate to the Balkans than to an altitude of 1,000 metres in the Swiss Jura. Apparently the pergola particularly incensed the local poet Jules Baillod. Jeanneret and his parents only lived in the house from 1913 to 1915, during which period his mother gave music lessons in the drawing room. Something of Jeanneret's father's pride in his son's achievement may be understood from a remark attributed to him while standing at the drawing room window looking south; that 'it was as though he had a cathedral behind him'.

1 In an article published in the La Chaux-de-Fonds newspaper *L'Impartial*, 9 September 1963.

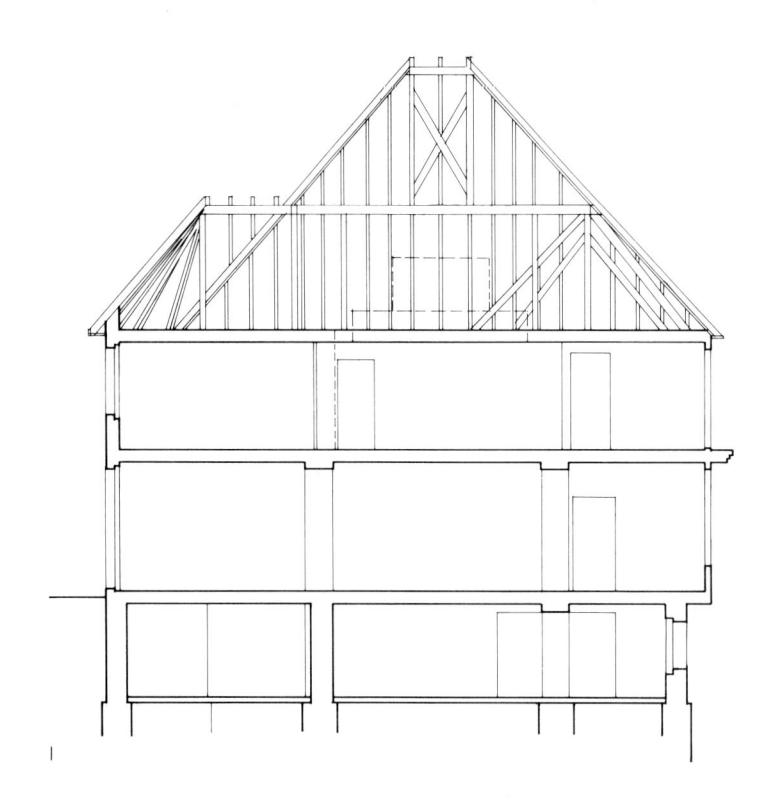

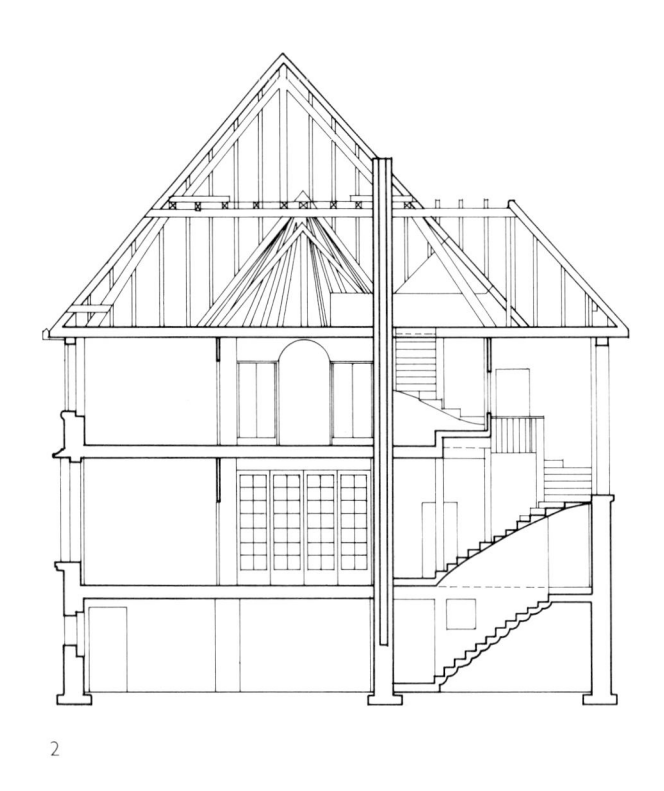

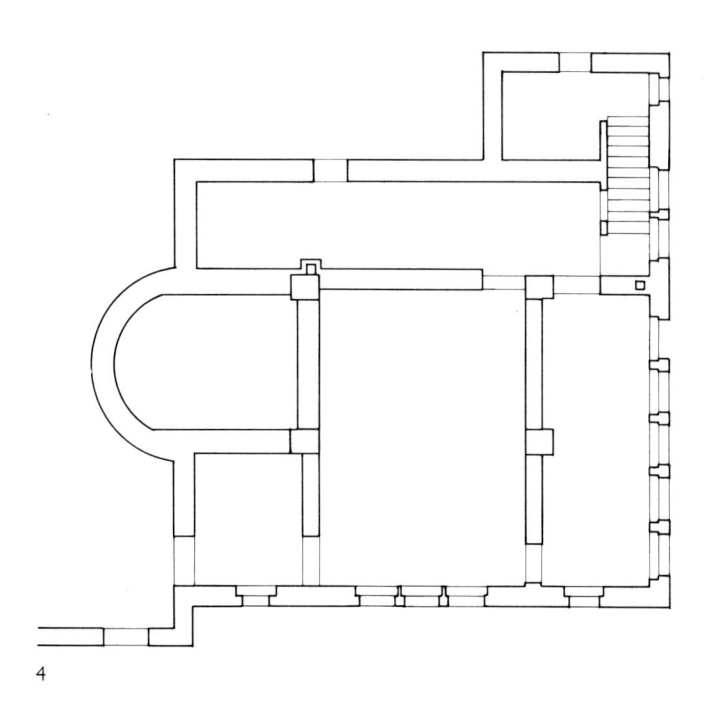

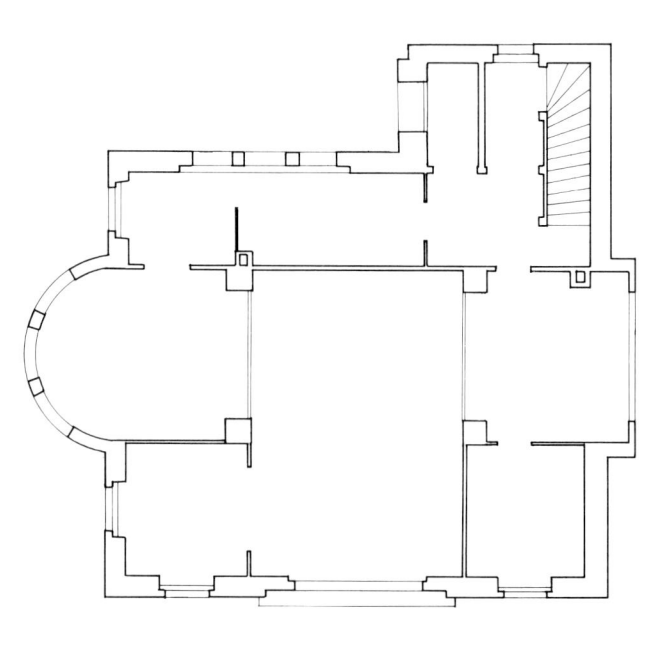

VILLA JEANNERET-PERRET

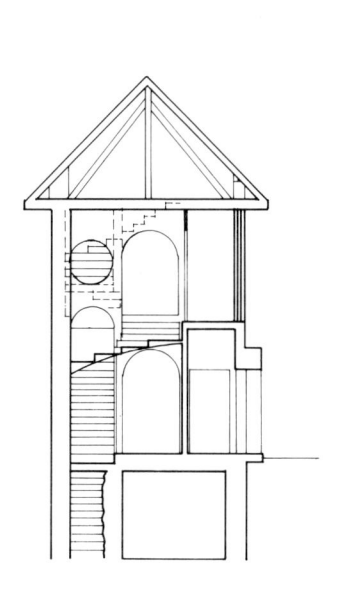

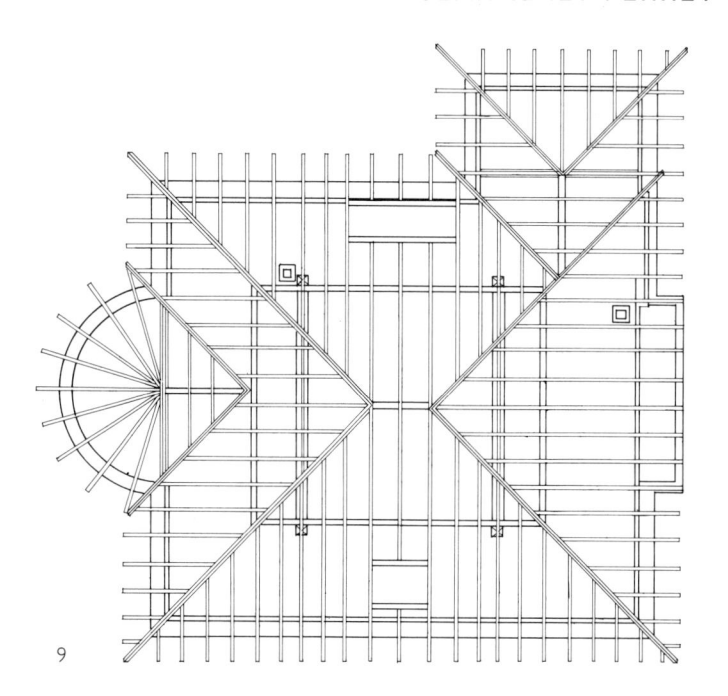

VILLA JEANNERET-PERRET

1 Longitudinal section
2 Cross section with staircase
3 Section through staircase
4 Basement plan
5 Ground floor plan
6 Joist layout at ground floor
7 First floor plan
8 Joist layout at first floor
9 Roof beam structure

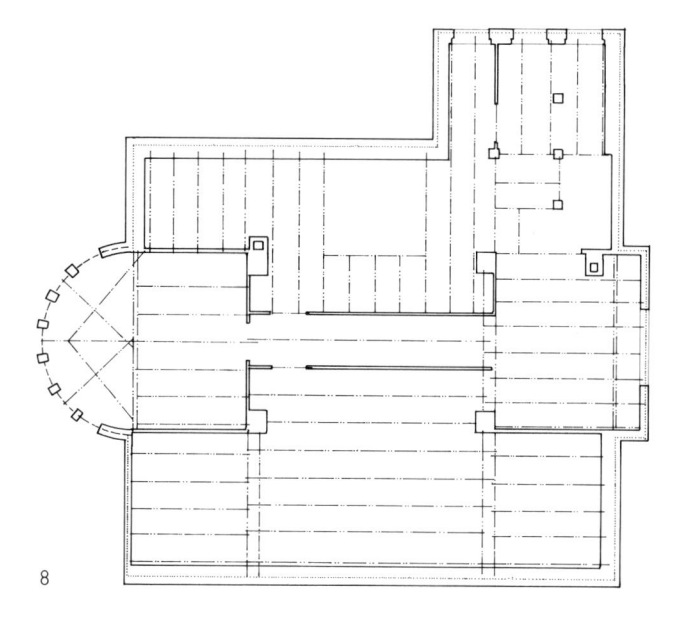

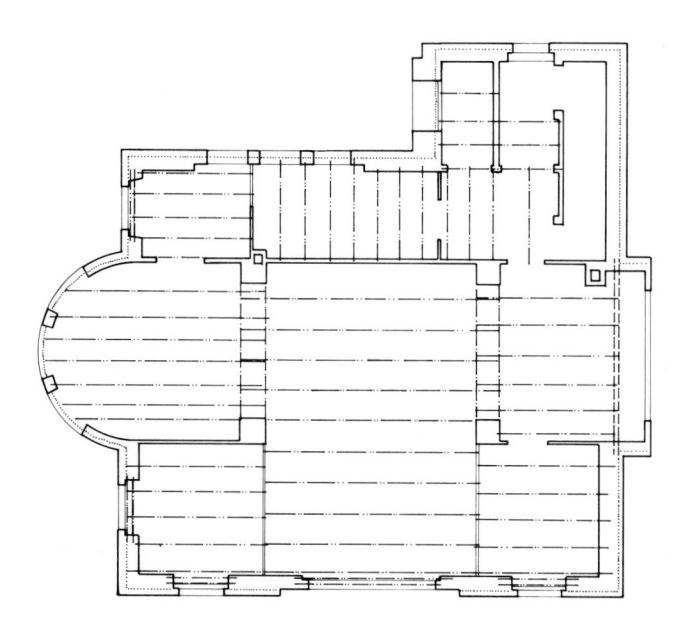

77

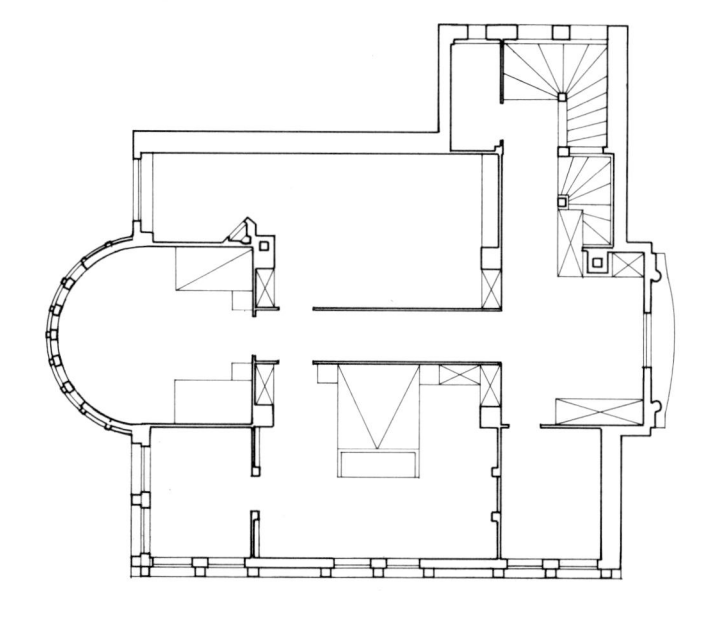

VILLA JEANNERET-PERRET

10 West elevation
11 North elevation
12 South elevation
14 East elevation

VILLA JEANNERET-PERRET

VILLA JEANNERET-PERRET

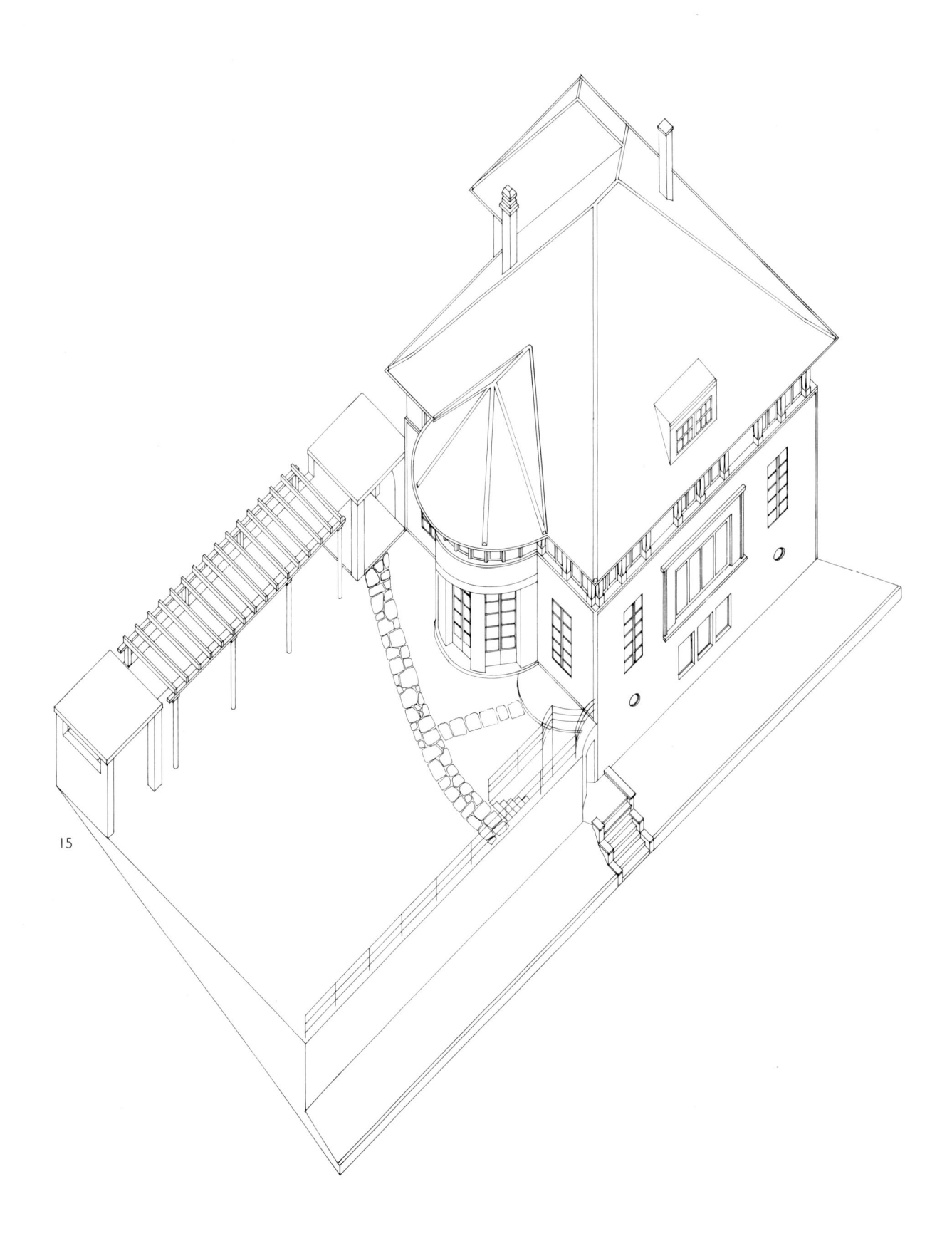

15 Axonometric from the south
16 Cut-away axonometric from the south

VILLA JEANNERET-PERRET

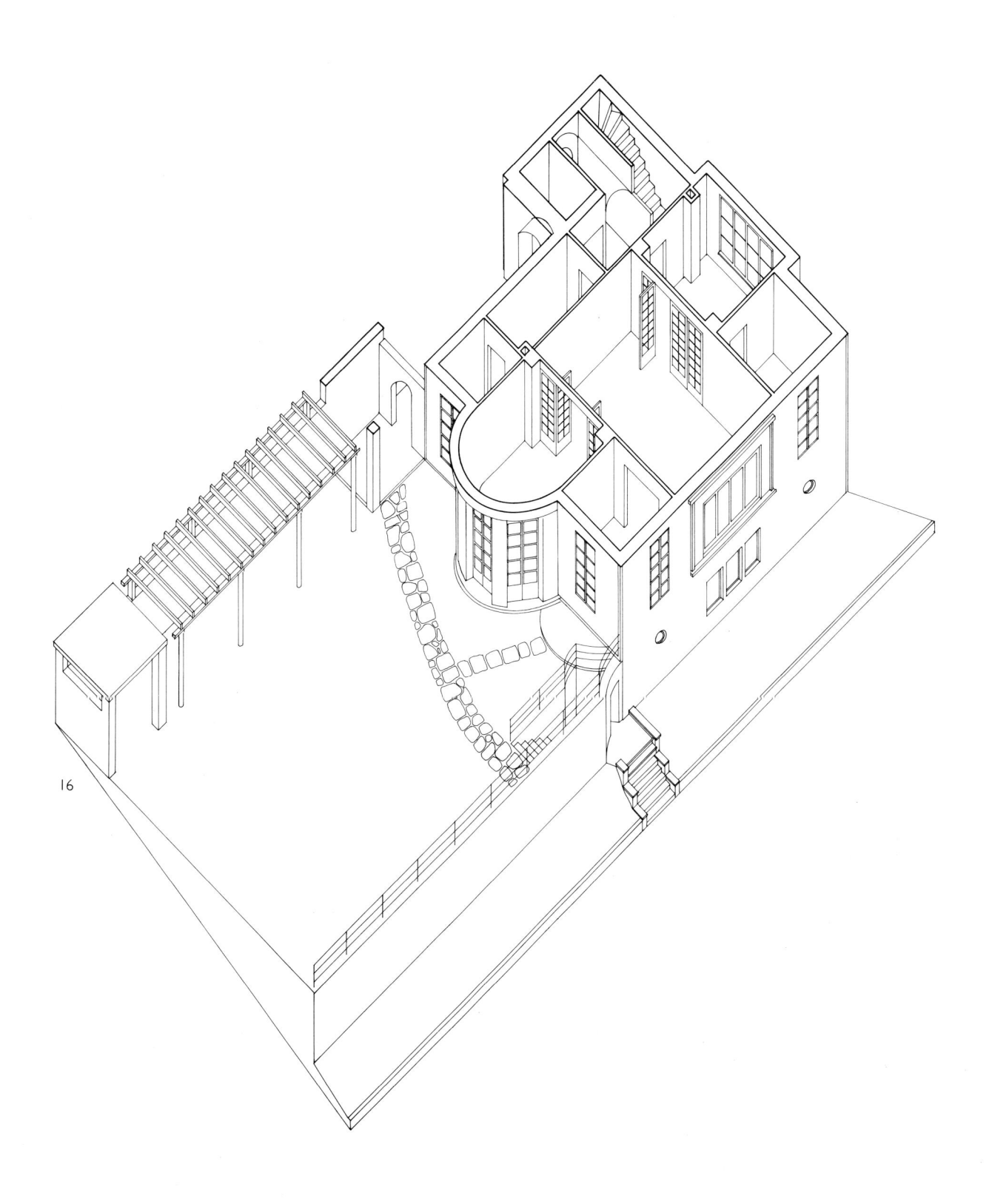

16

VILLA FAVRE-JACOT
1912

VILLA FAVRE-JACOT
Le Locle 1912
Charles-Edouard Jeanneret

This villa was built as a large family residence for the wealthy industrialist and founder of the local Zenith factory, Georges Favre-Jacot. The site consists of a long, narrow piece of land on the side of a hill overlooking Le Locle, the next town along the valley from La Chaux-de-Fonds.

The approach is from the south-east and the rectilinear block comprising the main rooms responds to the linearity of the site by its organisation along the main east-west axis. This becomes the axis of circulation with additions to the main block responding to the entry and to the organisation of terraces and gardens.

The movement progression towards the house is carefully controlled, with an entry zone contained by curved walls which extend forward beyond the main block. A cylindrical vestibule leads to a large central hall which gives access to the salon. The hall and salon each look on to terraces, with the dining area projecting forwards to form a portico with the balcony above. The pediment which surmounts this projection forms part of a series of classical references in which the columns are modified by capitals inspired by nature. The site is laid out with formal gardens, a pergola and a pool, and it was intended that a gazebo should span the road running along the hill immediately below the site.

Perhaps the most interesting feature of the design is the way the circle in front of the house is related to the movement progression. The curved side walls which enclose the space 'embrace' the visitor as they do in a more sophisticated fashion forty years later in the chapel at Ronchamp, and the turning circle involves the motor car in the architecture in a manner which predicts a similar involvement in the Villa Savoye.[1] The 'spokes' of the turning circle help to relate the house to the space in front of it, the radial form fulfilling a similar role to the star-like pattern of the paving in the piazza which links the three buildings of Michelangelo's Campidoglio in Rome.

1   For a detailed analysis of these buildings see G H Baker, *Le Corbusier: An Analysis of Form*, Van Nostrand Reinhold, (Wokingham 1984).

VILLA FAVRE-JACOT

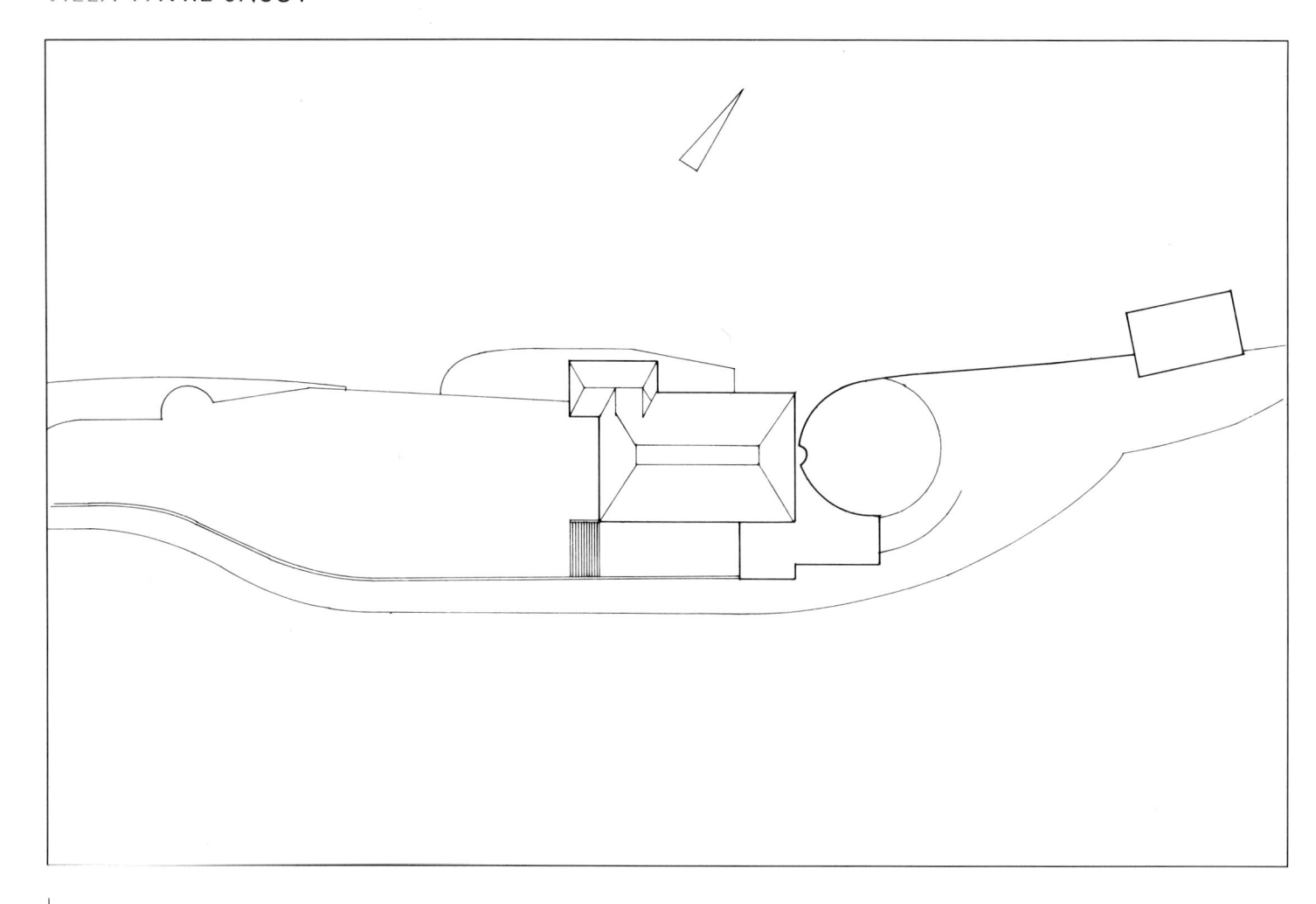

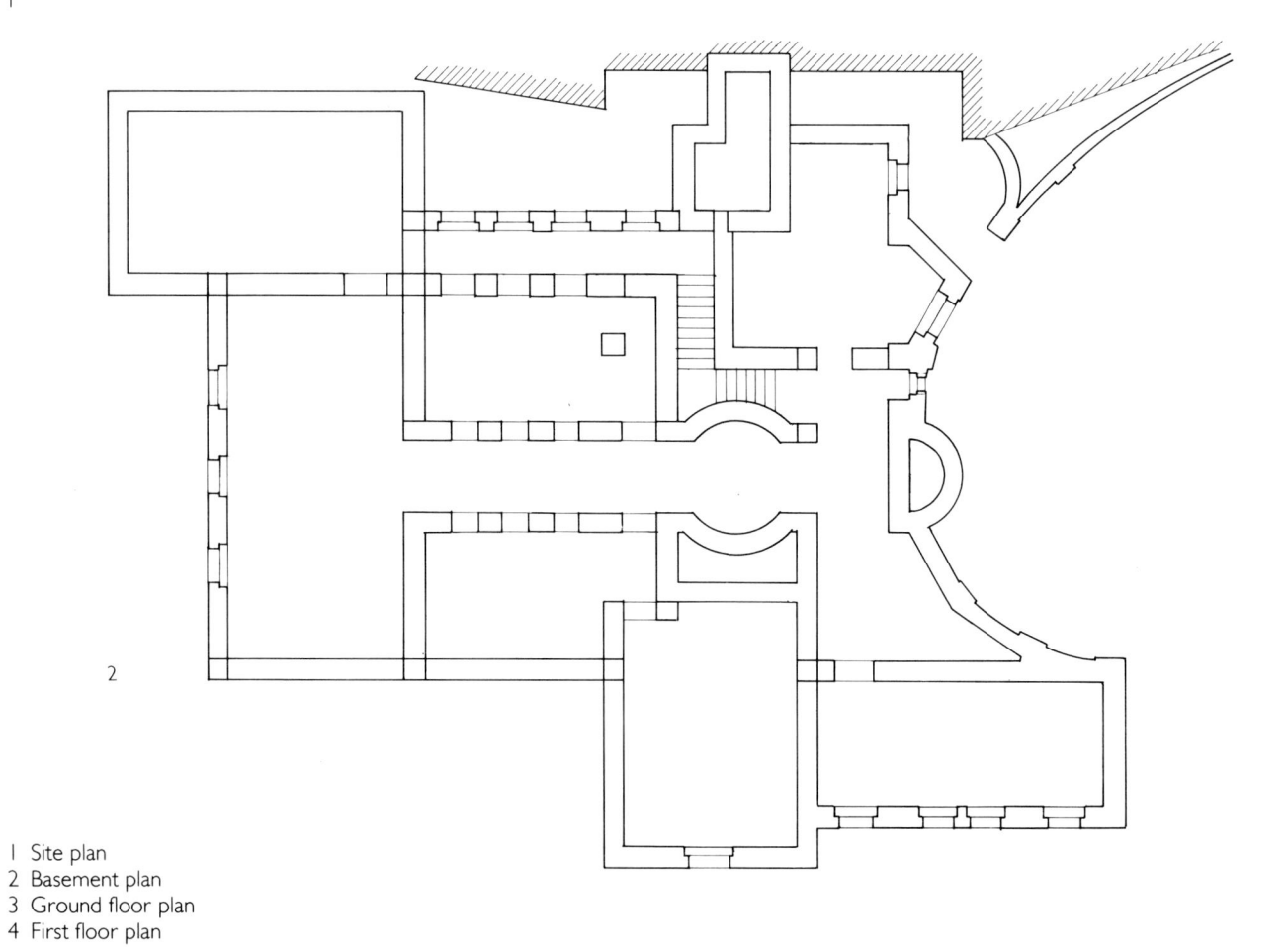

1 Site plan
2 Basement plan
3 Ground floor plan
4 First floor plan

VILLA FAVRE-JACOT

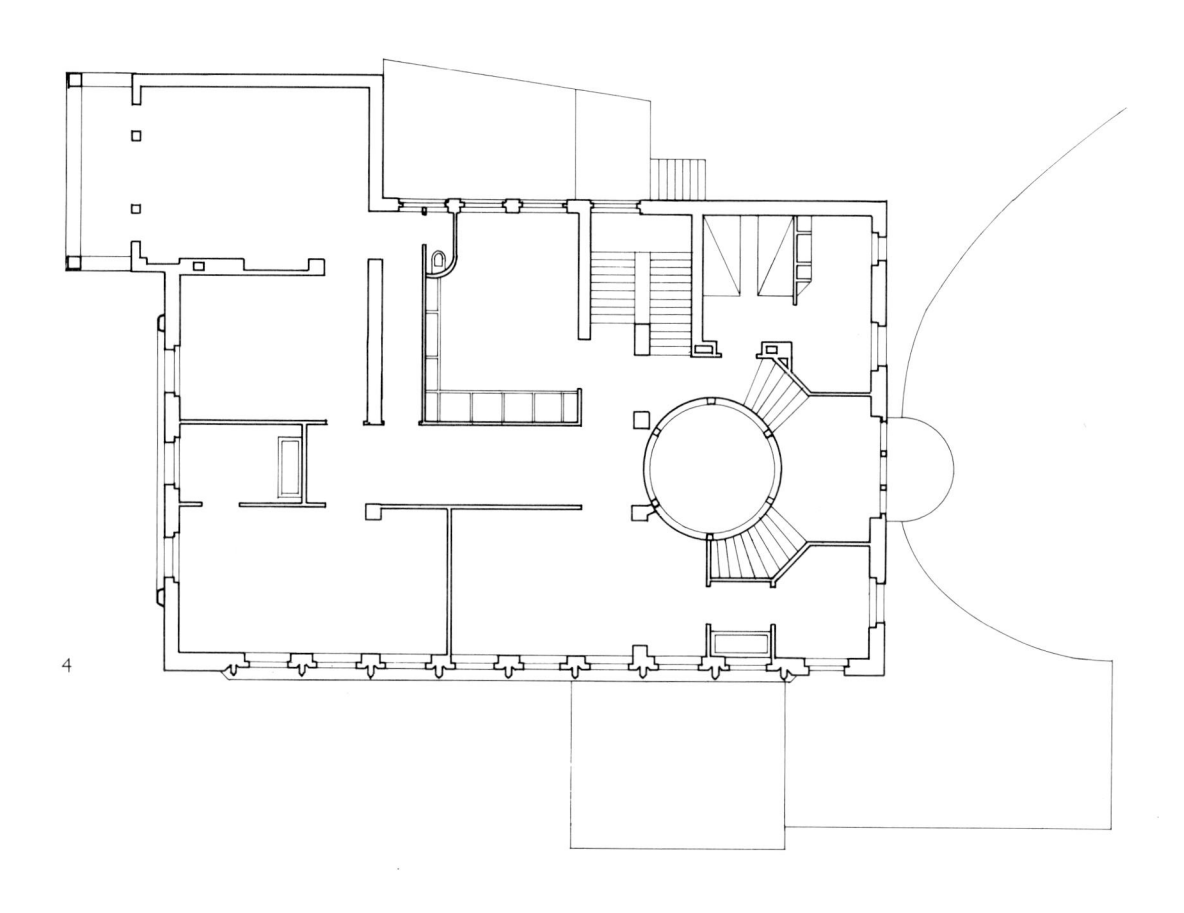

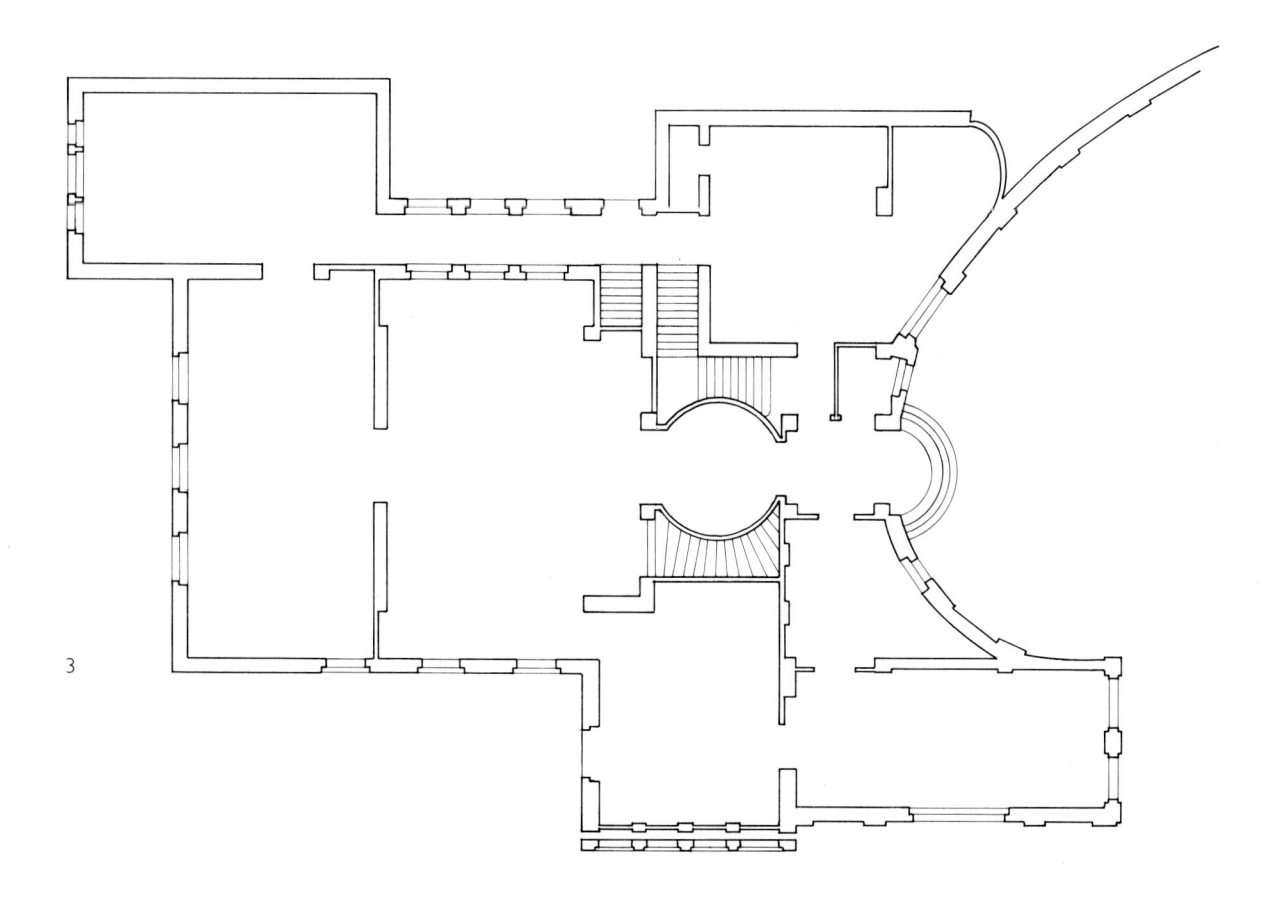

4

3

VILLA FAVRE-JACOT

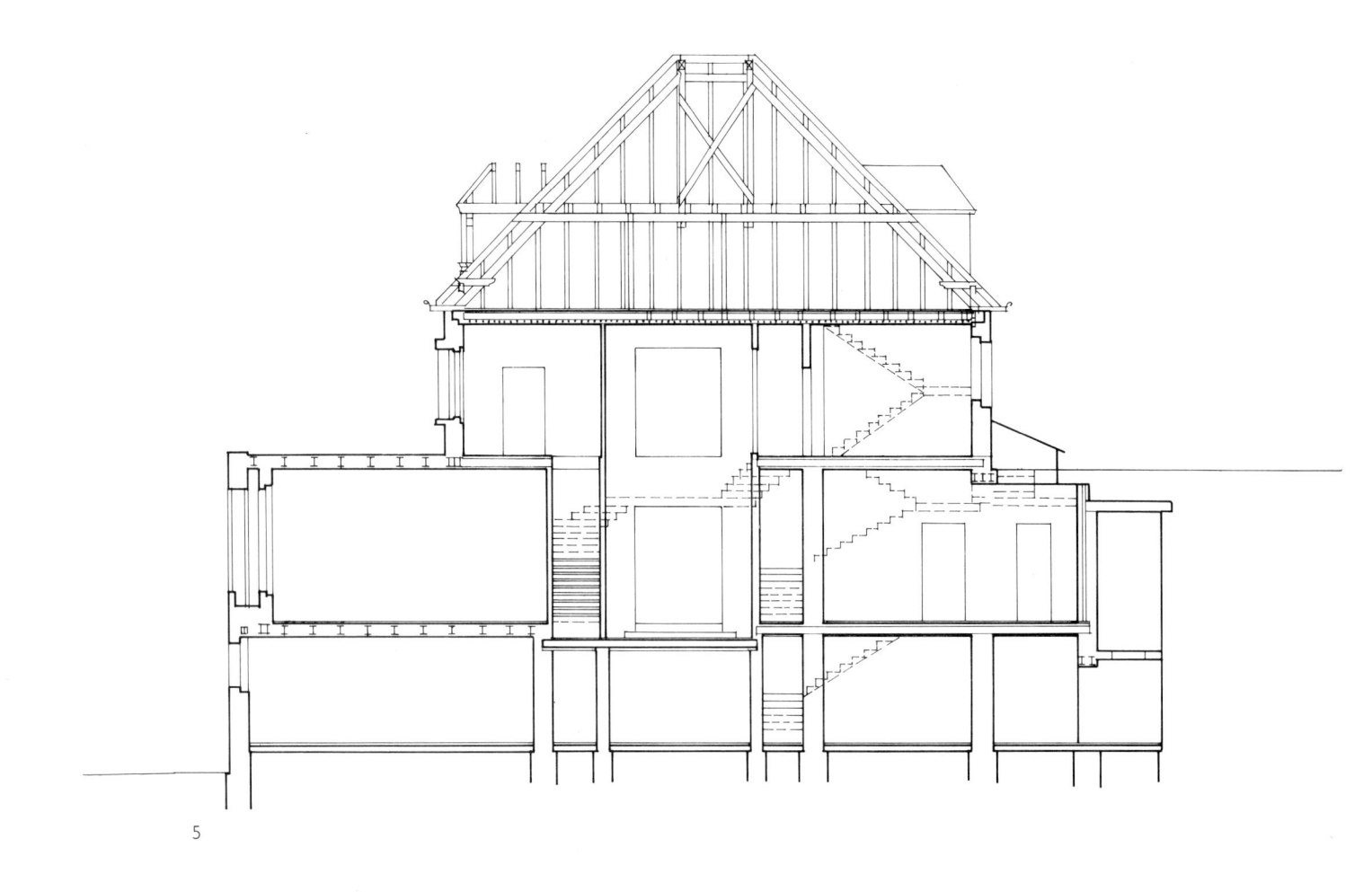

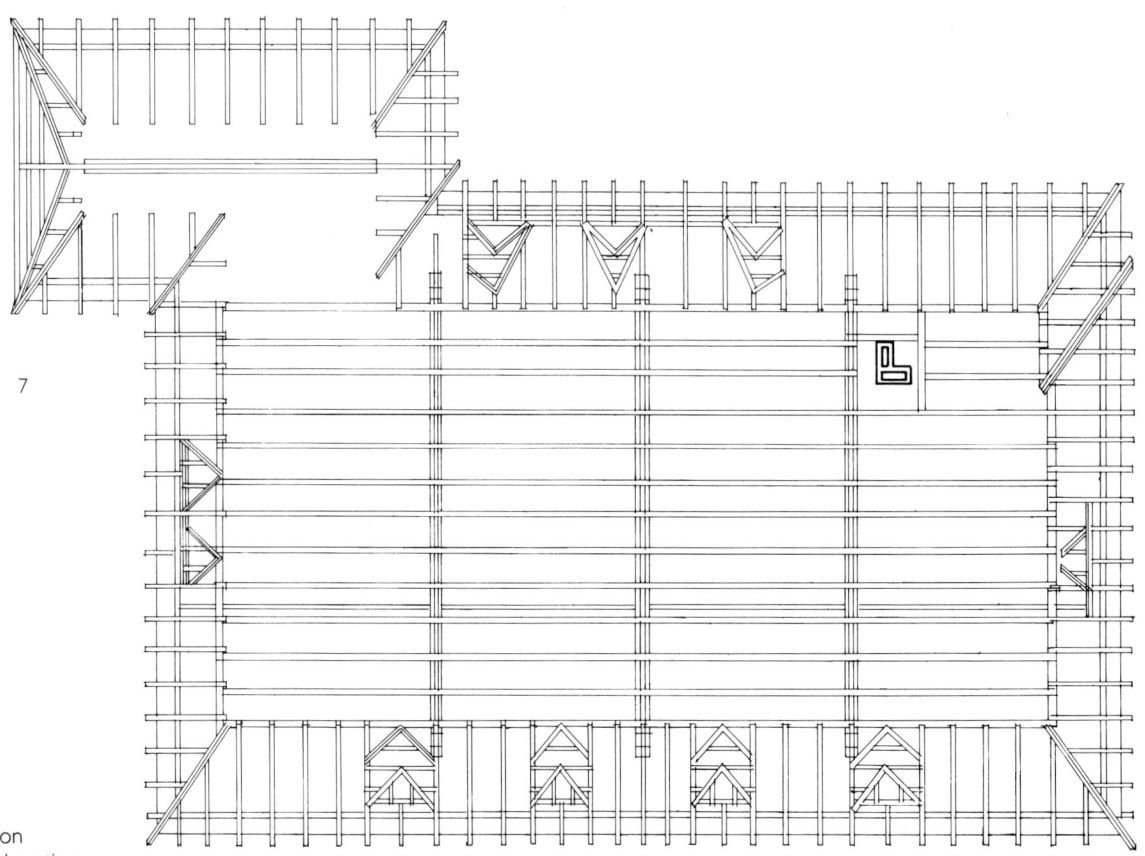

5

7

5 Cross section
6 Longitudinal section
7 Joist plan
8 Roof beam structure

VILLA FAVRE-JACOT

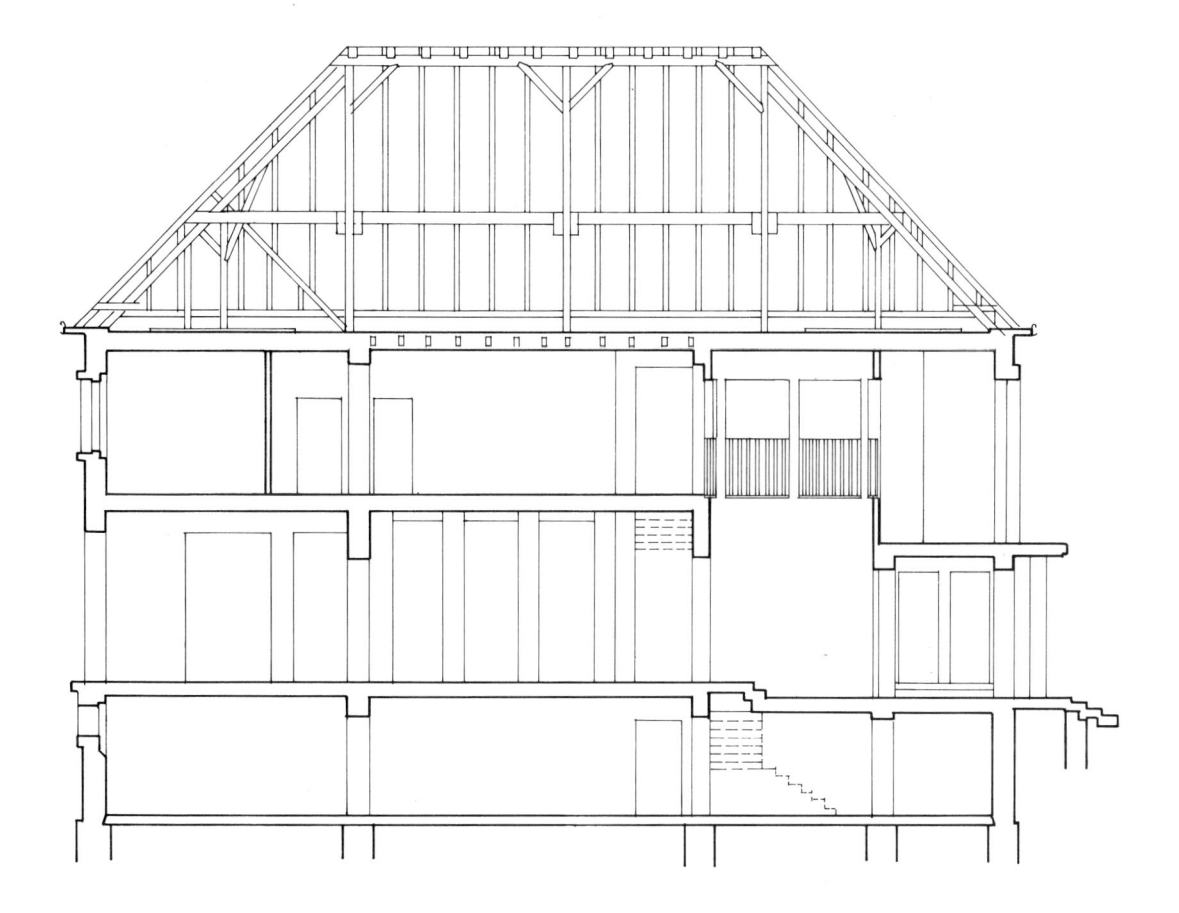

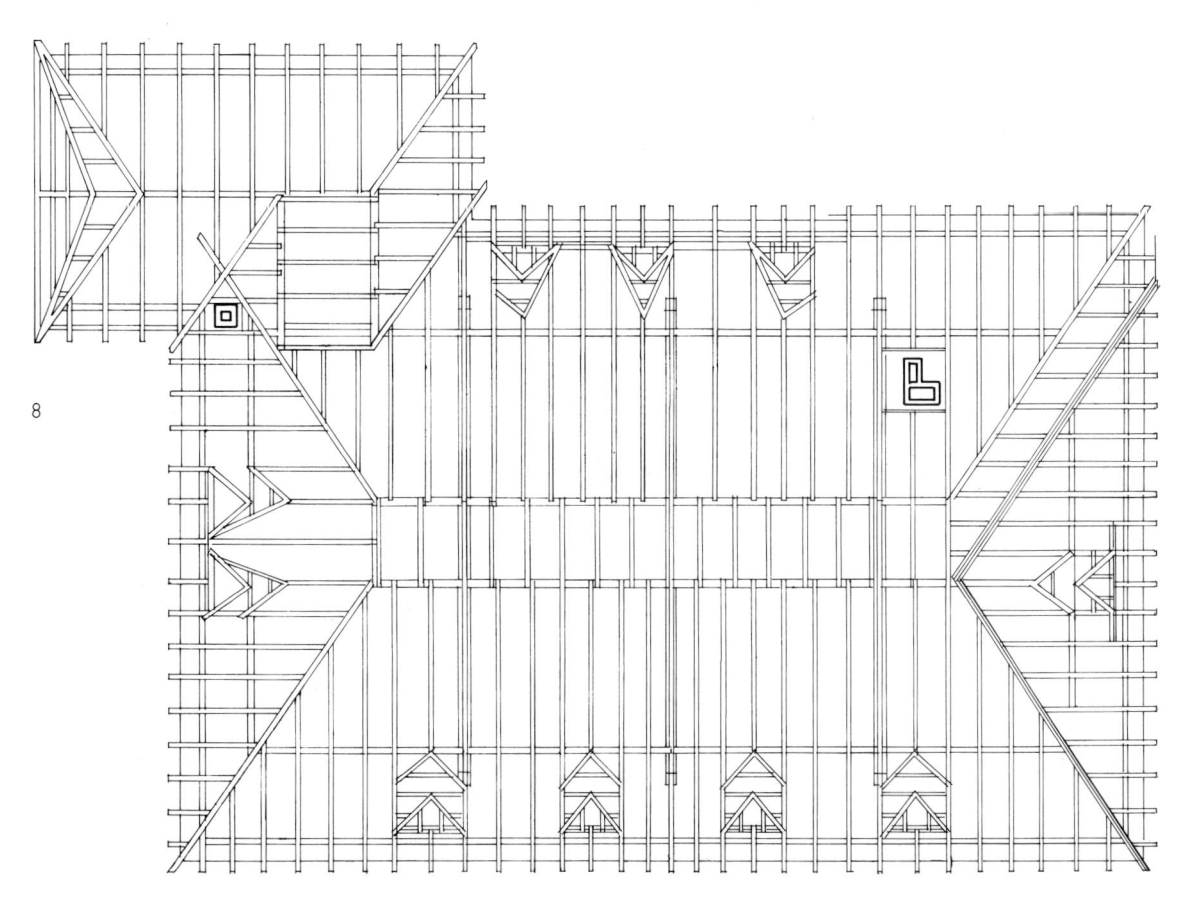

6

8

VILLA FAVRE-JACOT

9

10

9 South elevation
10 North elevation
11 East elevation
12 West elevation

VILLA FAVRE-JACOT

11

12

VILLA FAVRE-JACOT

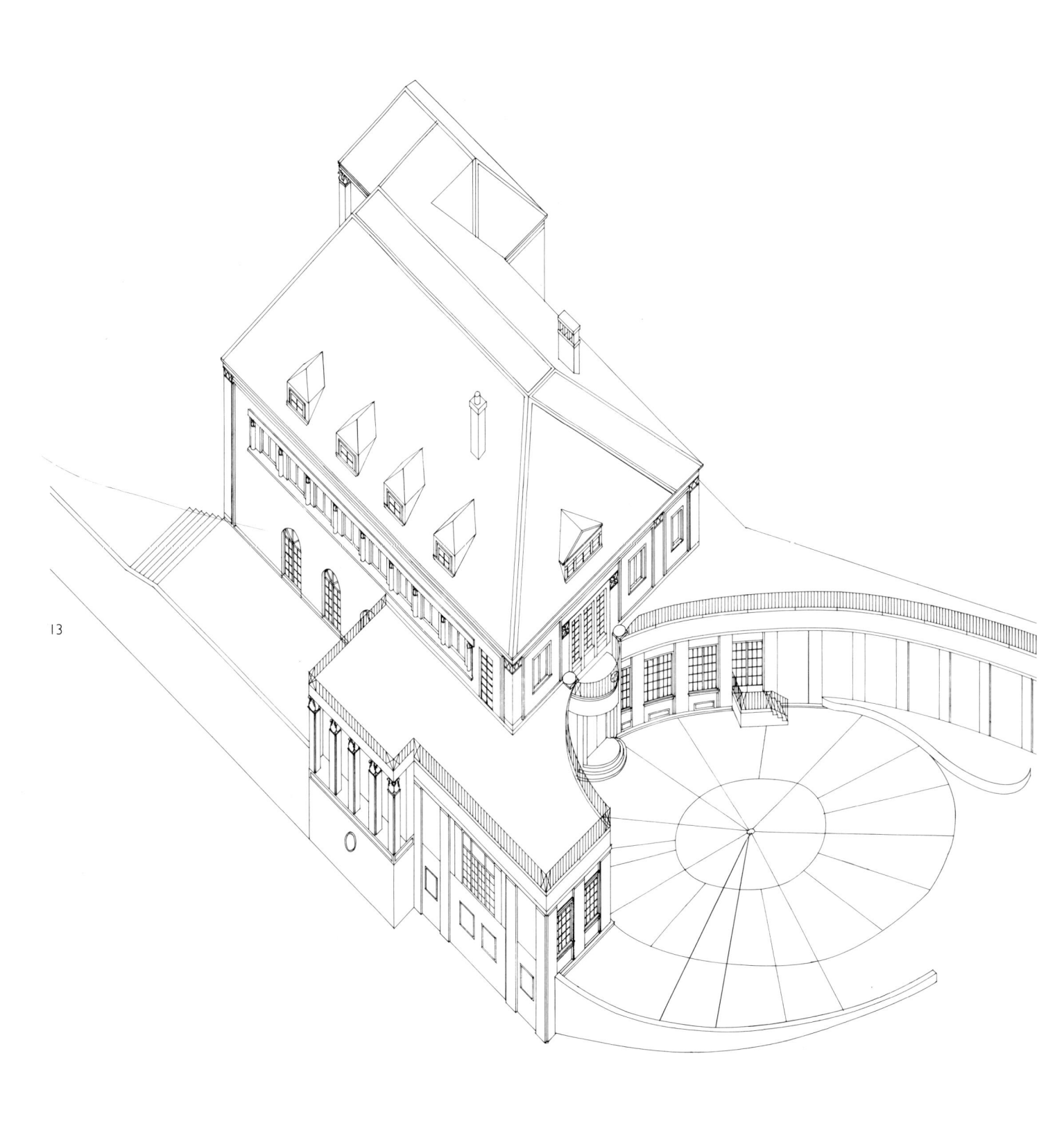

13

13 Axonometric from the east
14 Cut-away axonometric

VILLA FAVRE-JACOT

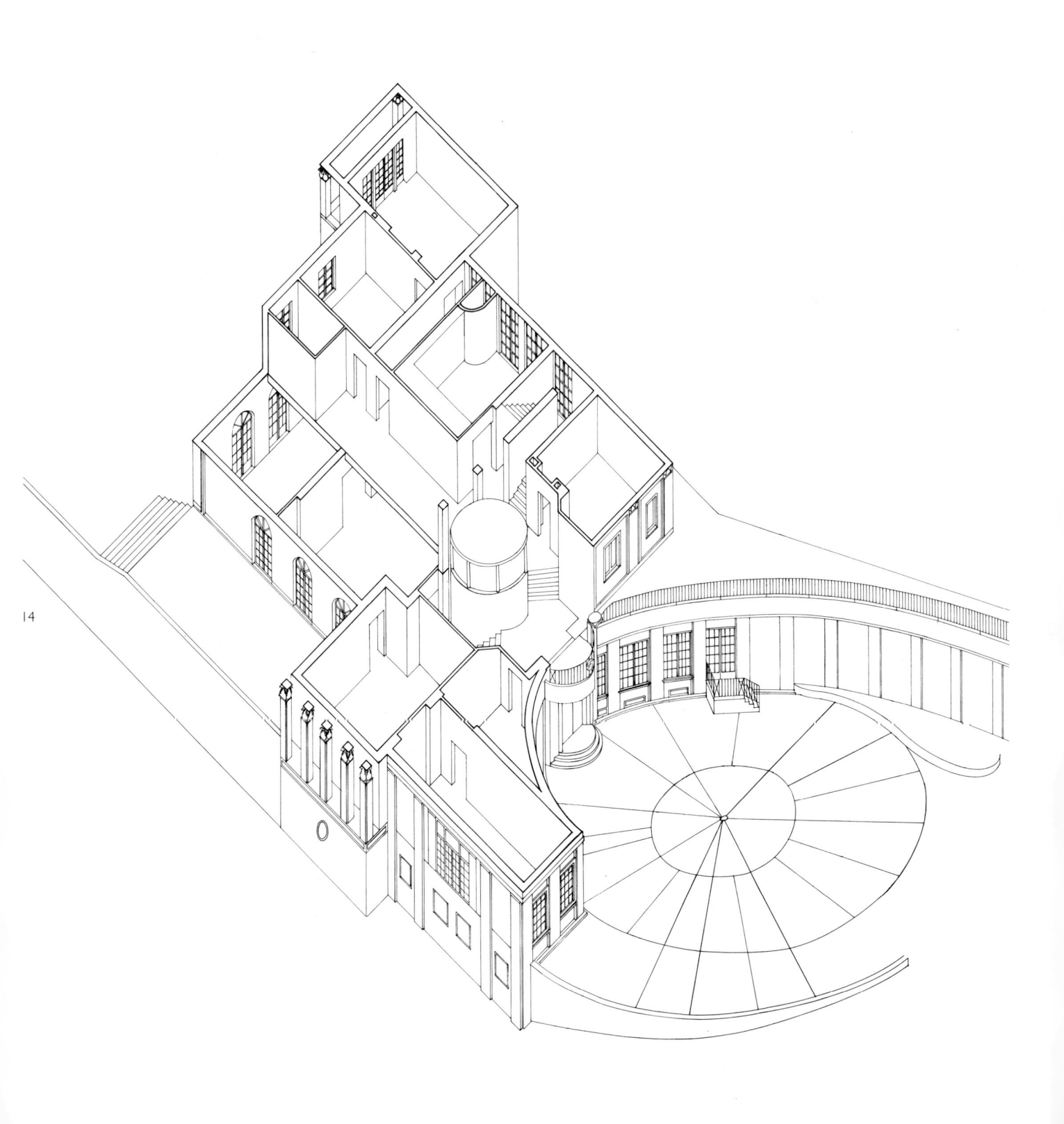

VILLA SCHWOB
1916

VILLA SCHWOB
La Chaux-de-Fonds 1916
Charles-Edouard Jeanneret

This villa was built for Anatole Schwob, a prominent local industrialist, at the corner of the rue du Doubs and the rue de la Fusion on mid-slope in La Chaux-de-Fonds. Because of the alignment of the rue de la Fusion (which runs at an angle down the slope) the site is wedge-shaped at its western end. Access is from the rue du Doubs, which runs along the hillside with the sloping site giving southerly views. The cubic main volume of the villa is located on the southern side, and is separated from the street by an access zone in which the hall and stairs run parallel with the rue du Doubs. This zone is placed immediately behind the flat, largely blank facade which presents the villa to the street. The facade becomes in effect part of the wall which encloses the villa: its symmetrical elevation has two entrances beneath a canopy, the principal entrance to the left leading into a long narrow hall.

The main volume of the house is entered centrally from this hall, and the living area comprises a space which extends vertically on the central lateral axis and longitudinally and horizontally on an axis parallel with the rue du Doubs. Each axis receives emphasis; the lateral by its height, the longitudinal by semicircular bay projections. At ground level, on the south side, the library and study areas extend the horizontal component of the main living space whilst reinforcing the south-facing bias of the plan.

The central space is complex and carefully balanced, with a balcony at first floor level giving access to the main bedrooms. The attic storey is provided with a flat roof, and the southerly bias of the plan is maintained by a roof terrace which runs along the south elevation and extends along each side. This roof terrace is identified by a concrete overhanging edge which acts like a cornice. At ground level, on the west side, the kitchen is placed behind the enclosing wall flanking the rue du Doubs in an extension of the plan which leads to a corner pavilion. A pergola now runs behind the wall on the east side with formal terraced gardens completing the ensemble. The villa is built of reinforced concrete and is faced with a veneer of ochre-coloured bricks arranged in panels.

The villa has central heating concealed in the walls and floors but was criticised initially because of the amount of glass in the main living space and because of the flat roof, both considered impractical for the cold winter climate. Jeanneret became involved in damaging legal proceedings when Anatole Schwob alleged that the villa had cost far more than the architect's estimate. Proceedings began in 1918 and ended in June 1920 with a settlement in which each party admitted some liability. The interior was redesigned by Angelo Mangiarotti of Milan around 1960, although it remains in essence as conceived by Jeanneret.

VILLA SCHWOB

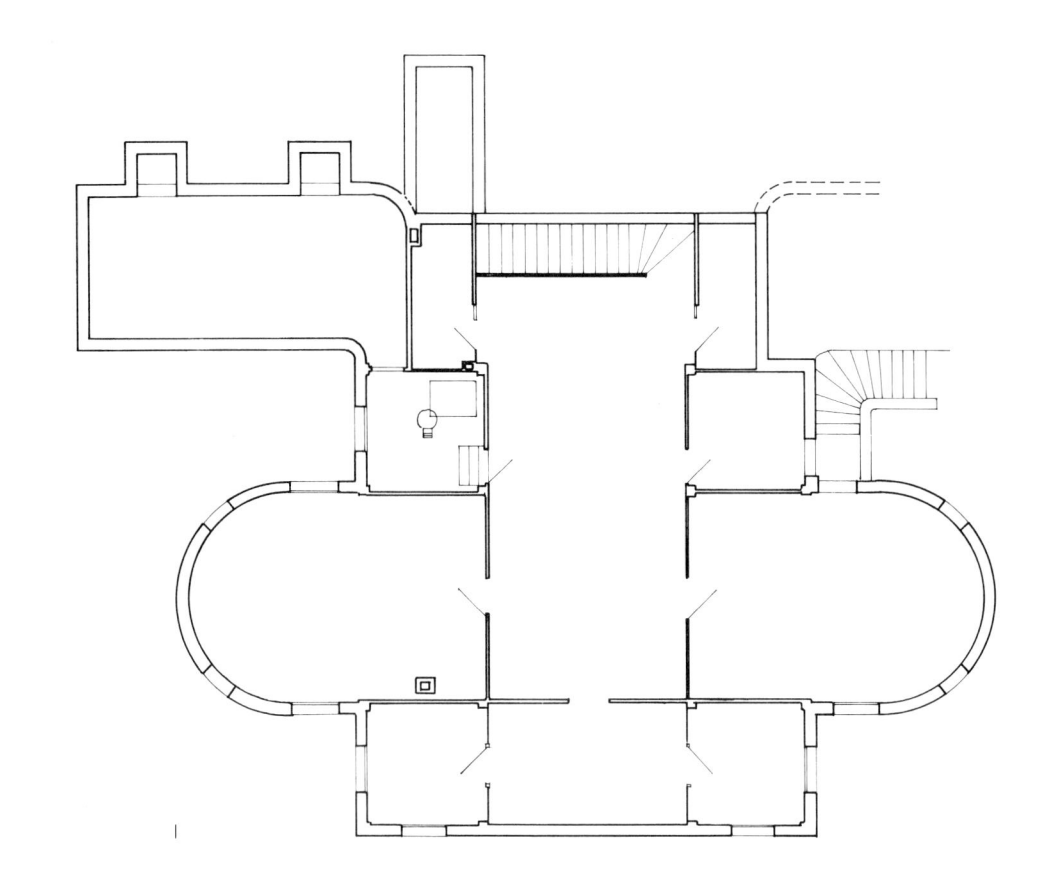

1 Basement plan
2 Ground floor plan
3 First floor plan
4 Second floor plan

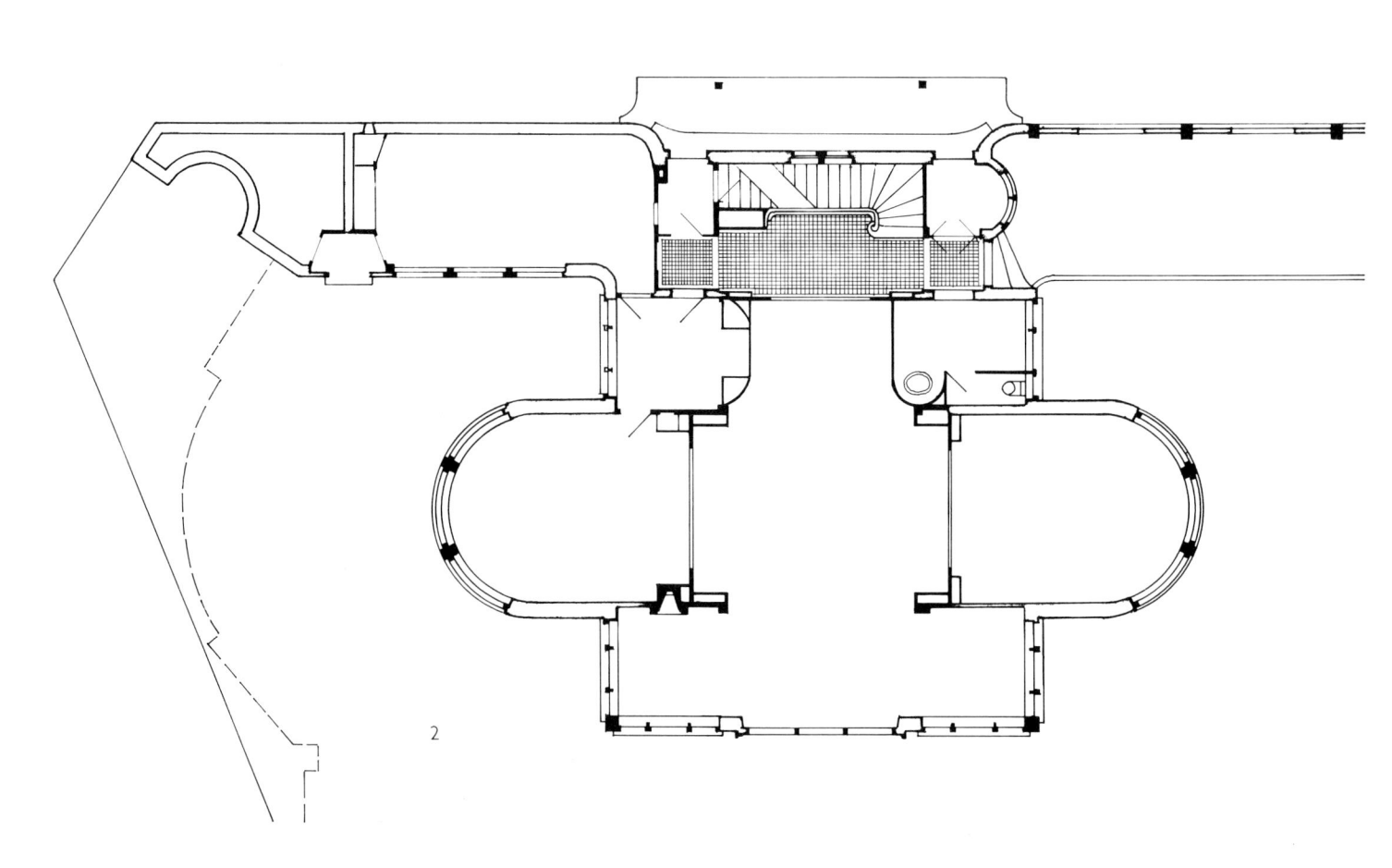

VILLA SCHWOB

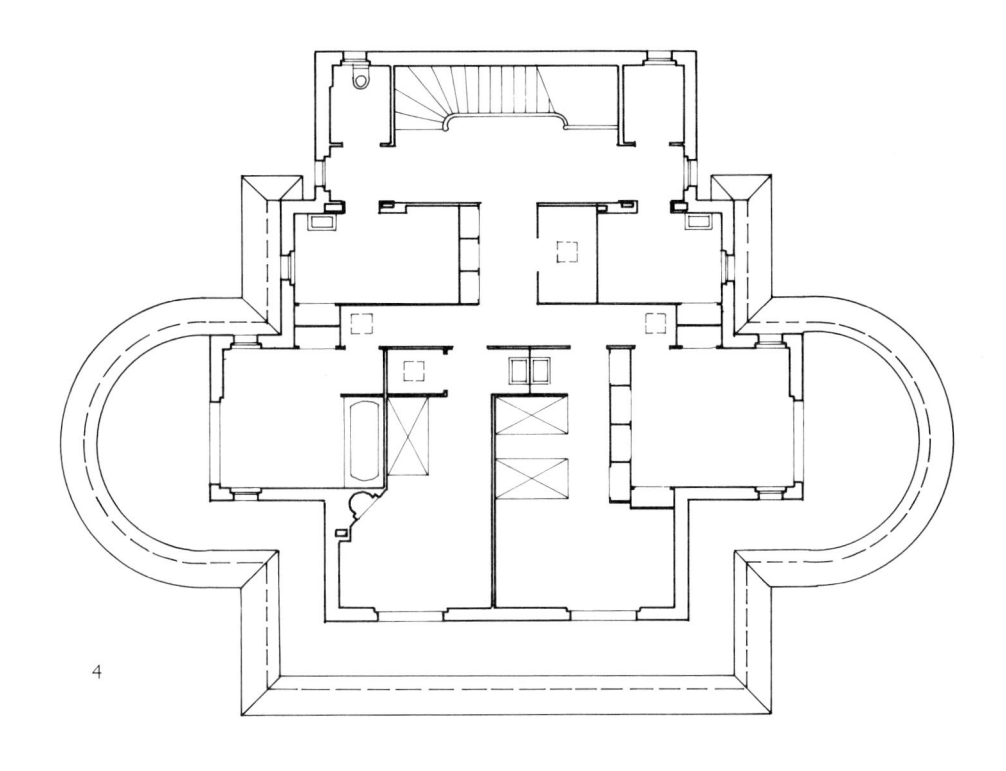

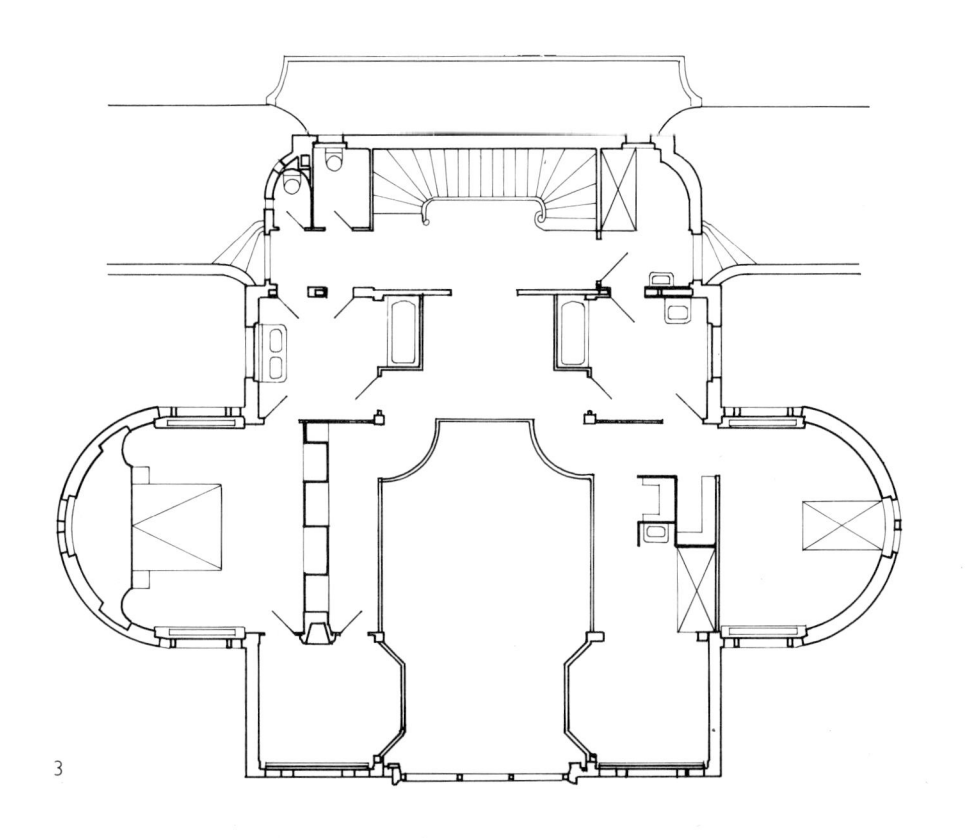

4

3

VILLA SCHWOB

5

6

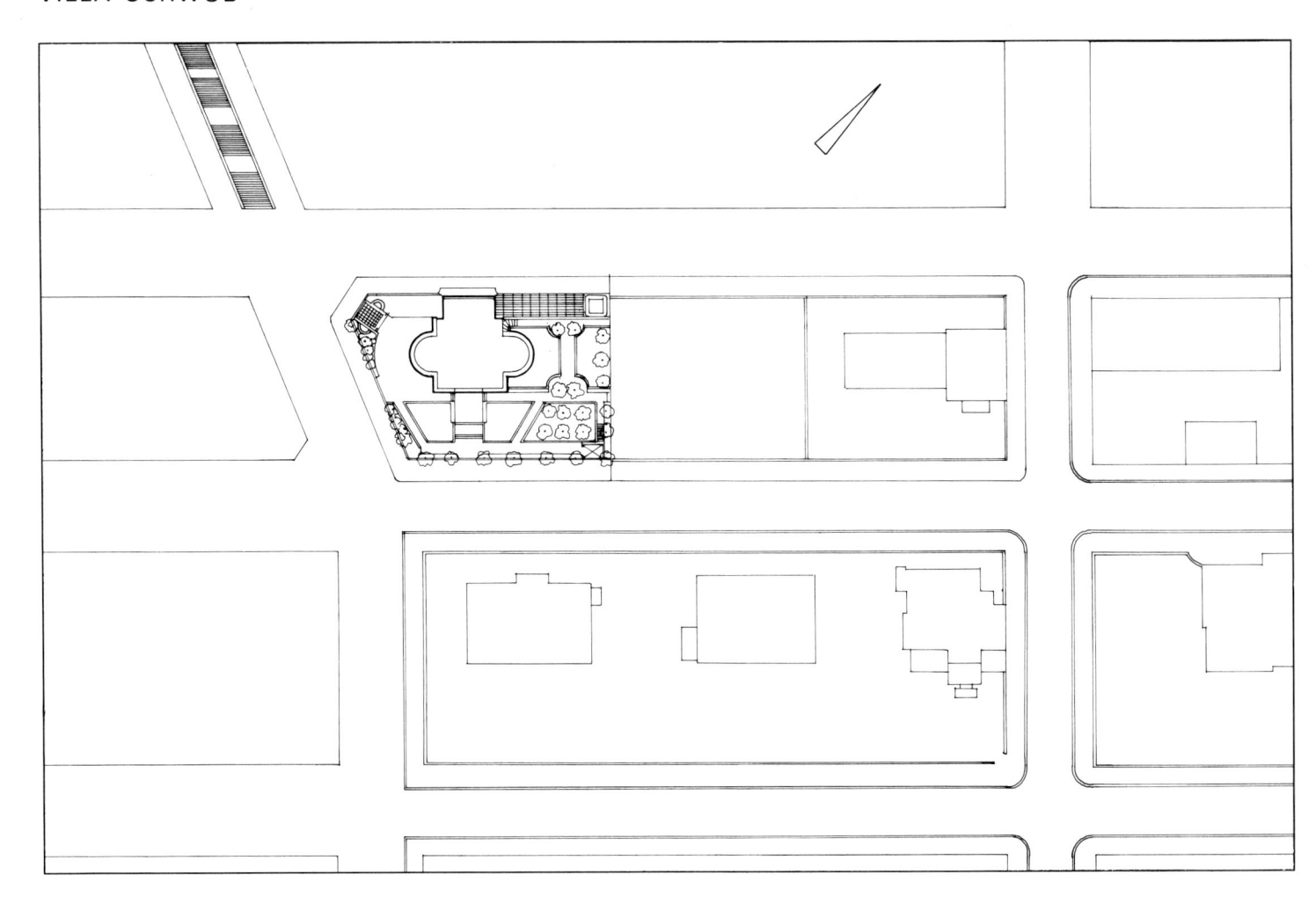

5 Site plan
6 East elevation
7 West elevation
8 Longitudinal section

VILLA SCHWOB

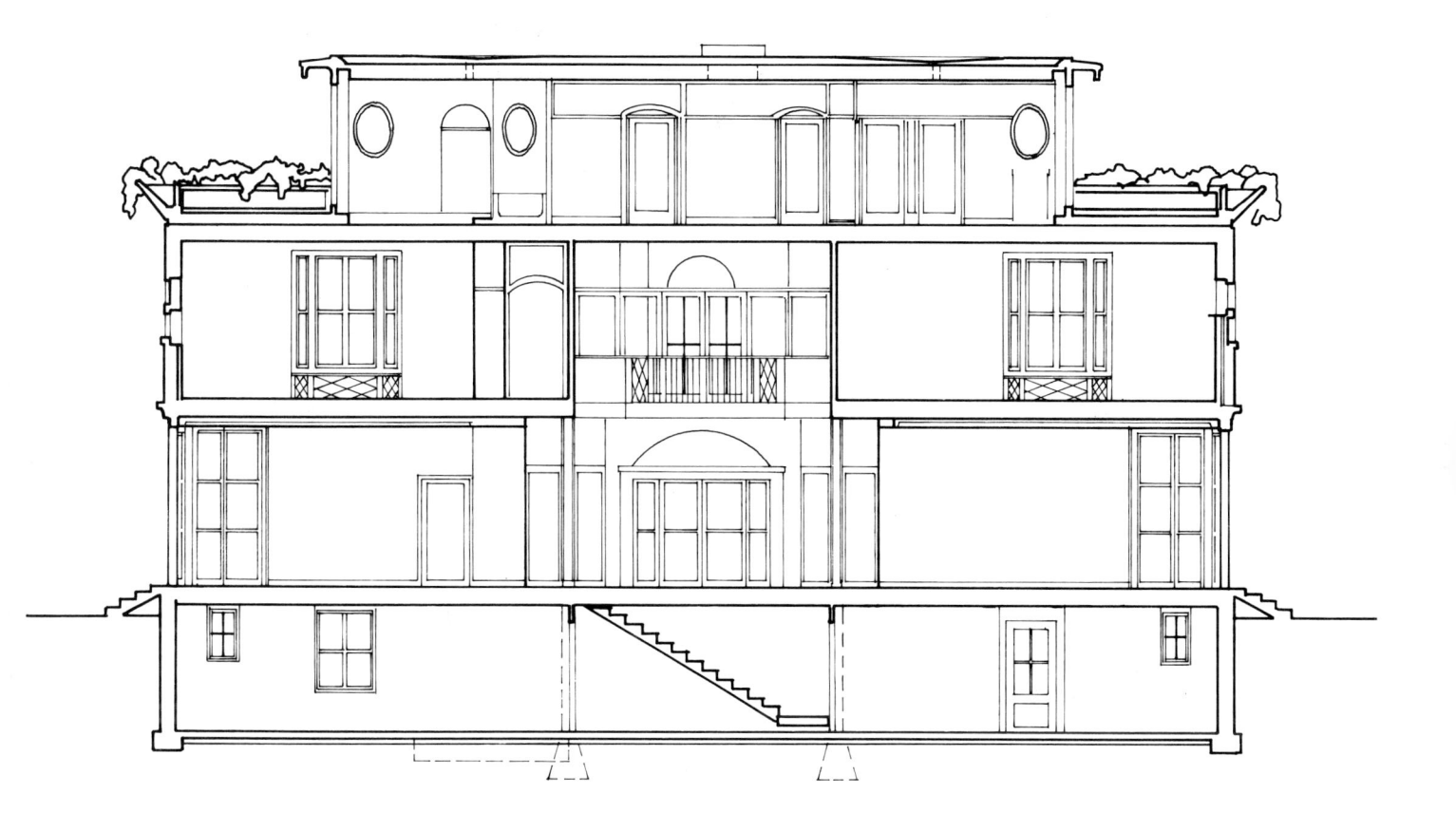

VILLA SCHWOB

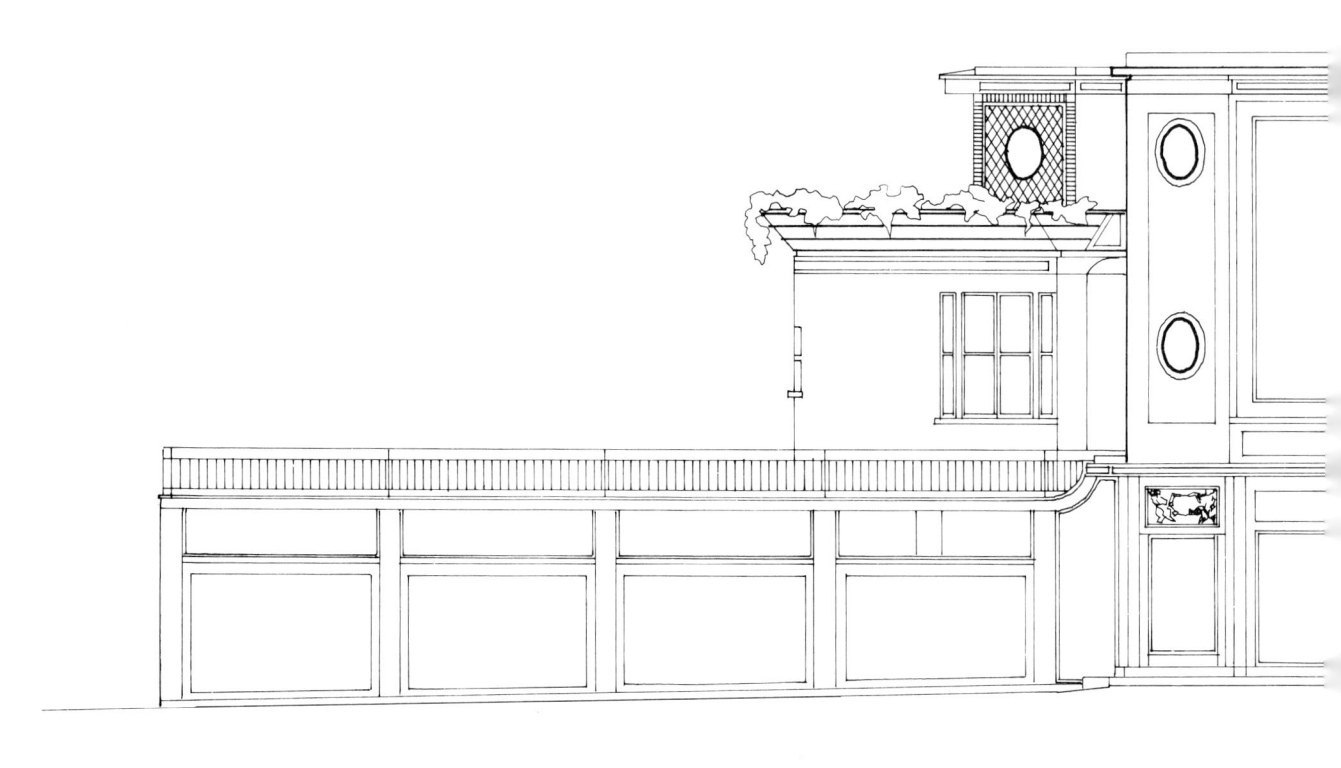

9 South elevation
10 North elevation

VILLA SCHWOB

VILLA SCHWOB

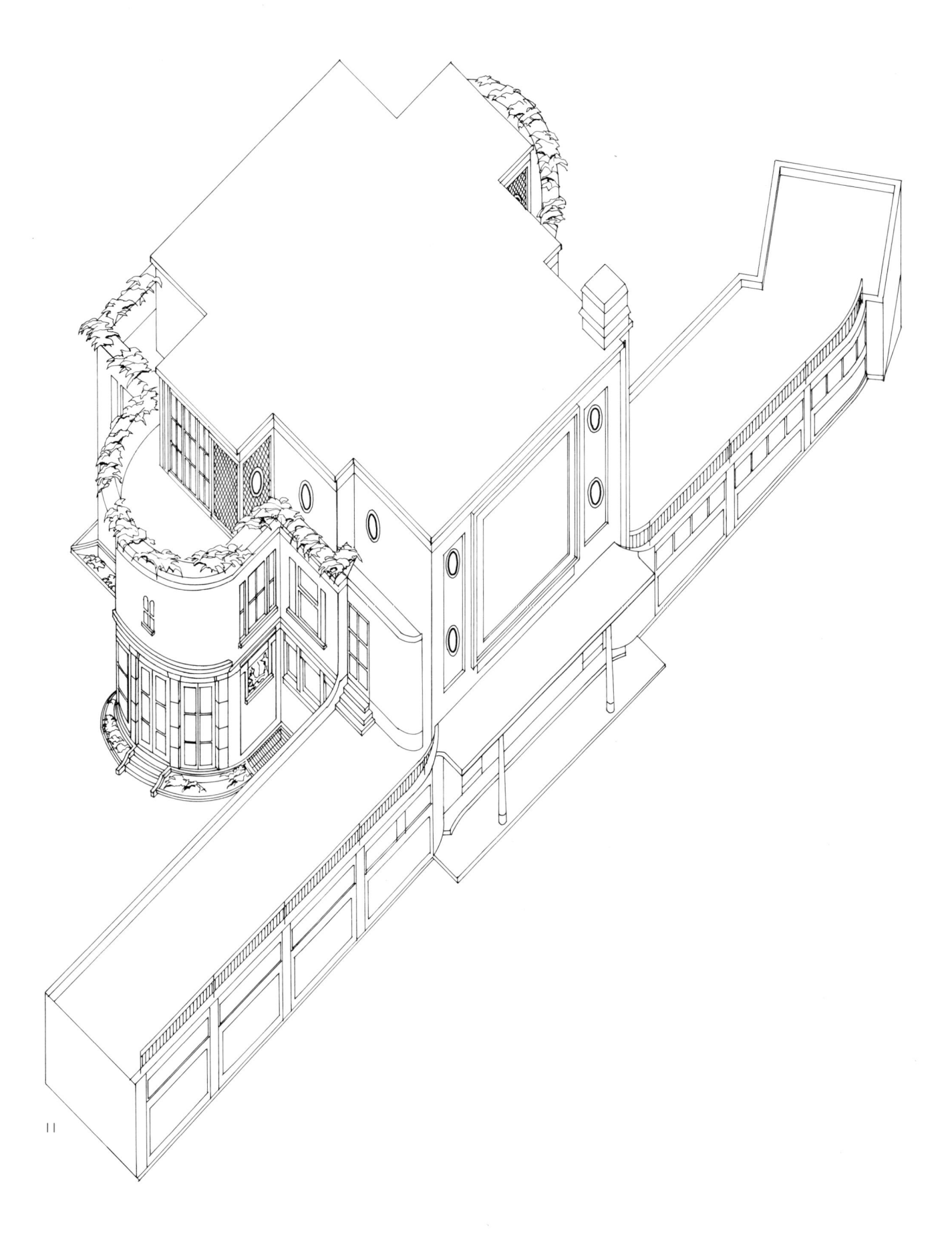

11 Axonometric from the north
12 Cut-away axonometric

VILLA SCHWOB

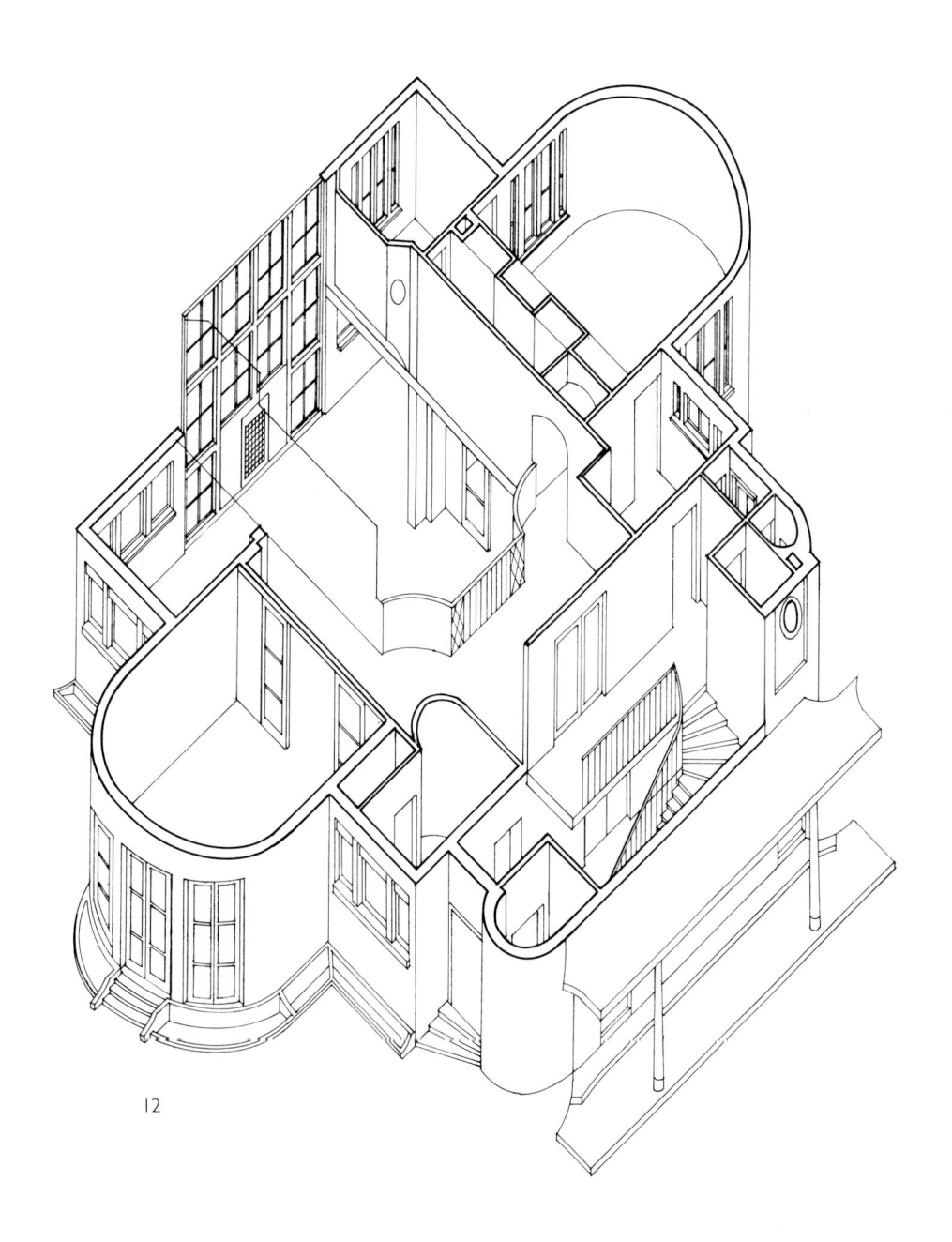

12

LA SCALA CINEMA 1916

LA SCALA CINEMA
La Chaux-de-Fonds 1916
Charles-Edouard Jeanneret

The cinema is located on the lower part of the sloping hillside of La Chaux-de-Fonds between the rue de la Parc and the rue de la Serre: the natural slope is utilised to give a rake to the ground floor seating. The entrance to the cinema is in the rue de la Serre, and the balcony is placed at the opposite end. An escape stair from the balcony runs along the side of the building and leads to the main entrance foyer, whilst further escape is provided by two external staircases flanking the projection booth which juts out into the rue de la Parc. (This booth is a later addition which does not appear in Jeanneret's drawings.)

The cinema is spanned by concrete portal frames with a curved underside from which hangs a barrel-vaulted ceiling, supporting a pitched timber roof. The balcony is of reinforced concrete, providing a clear span with unimpeded views for the downstairs seating.

The arch, which dominates the facade, is flanked on each side by entranceways to the rue de la Serre which are identified by pedimented porches with pilasters above. The north facade is an abstract planar composition in which the external stairs exploit the potency of the oblique – the first appearance of a device which formed an important part of Le Corbusier's architectural language during the 1920s.

According to Marc Emery,[1] the original scheme for the cinema was drawn up by the architect Jean Emery,[2] who collaborated with René Chapallaz to produce a design for the building in June 1916. A competition open to pupils past and present of the Art School was then held for the facade. Jeanneret did not take part in this competition but presented his own design to the client and took over the scheme from Chapallaz (who had been one of the three judges for the competition). Although the elevations of the final design were by Jeanneret, the plan remains as designed by Chapallaz and Jean Emery, and Marc Emery maintains that 'in its functional and structural aspect the cinema is ninety per cent their work'.[3]

1. Marc Emery, *La Chaux-de-Fonds and Jeanneret*, Musée des Beaux-Arts et Musée d'Histoire de La Chaux-de-Fonds, 1983, 'Chapallaz *versus* Jeanneret' p 28.
2. Marc Emery's grandson.
3. *ibid* p 28.

LA SCALA CINEMA

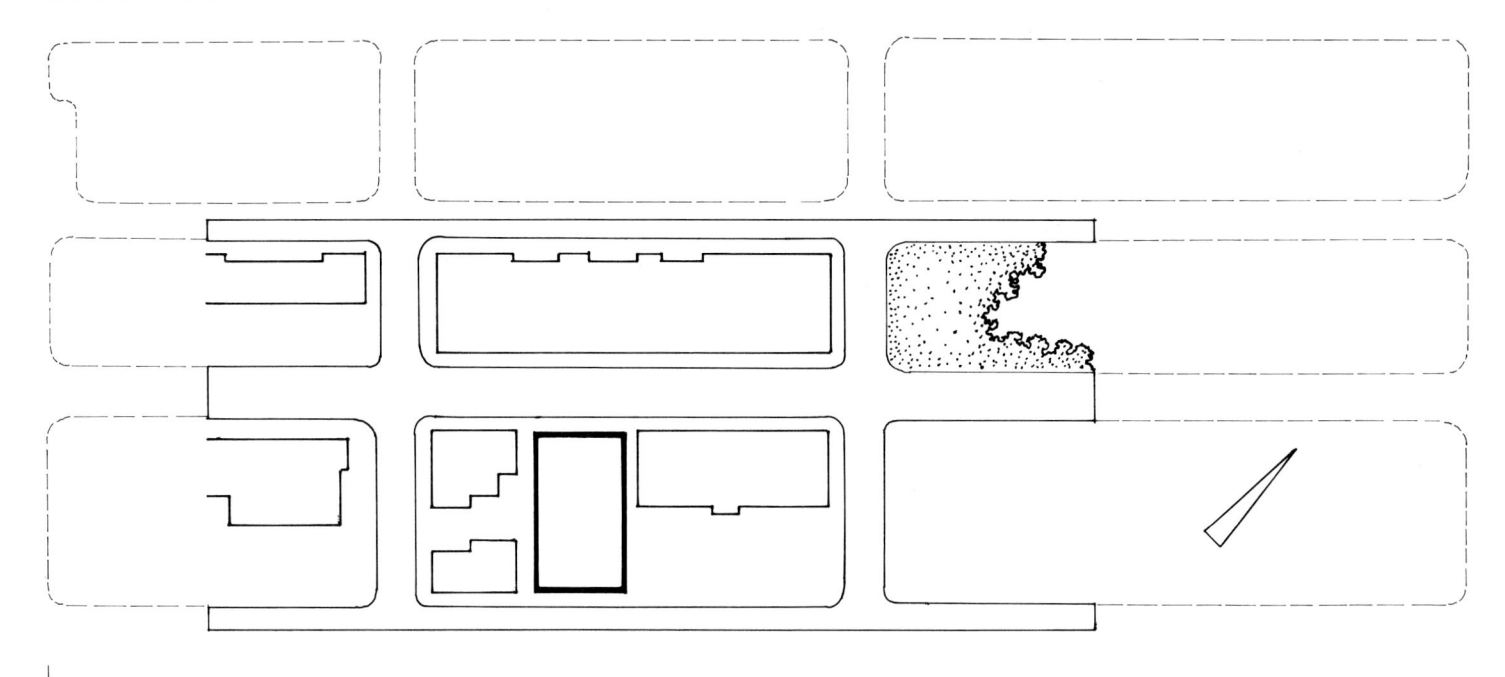

1 Site plan
2 Foundation plan
3 Ground floor plan
4 Plan at gallery level

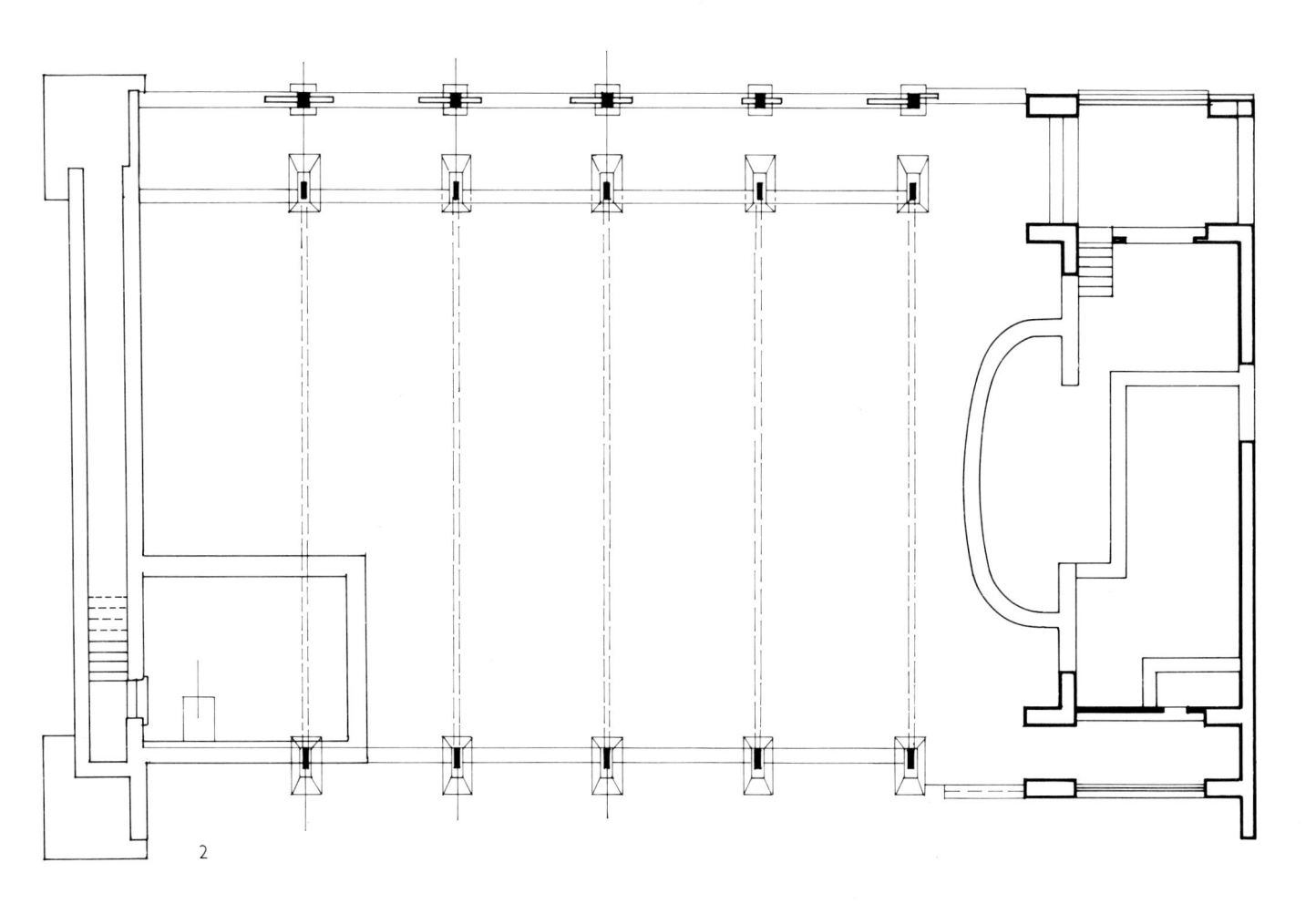

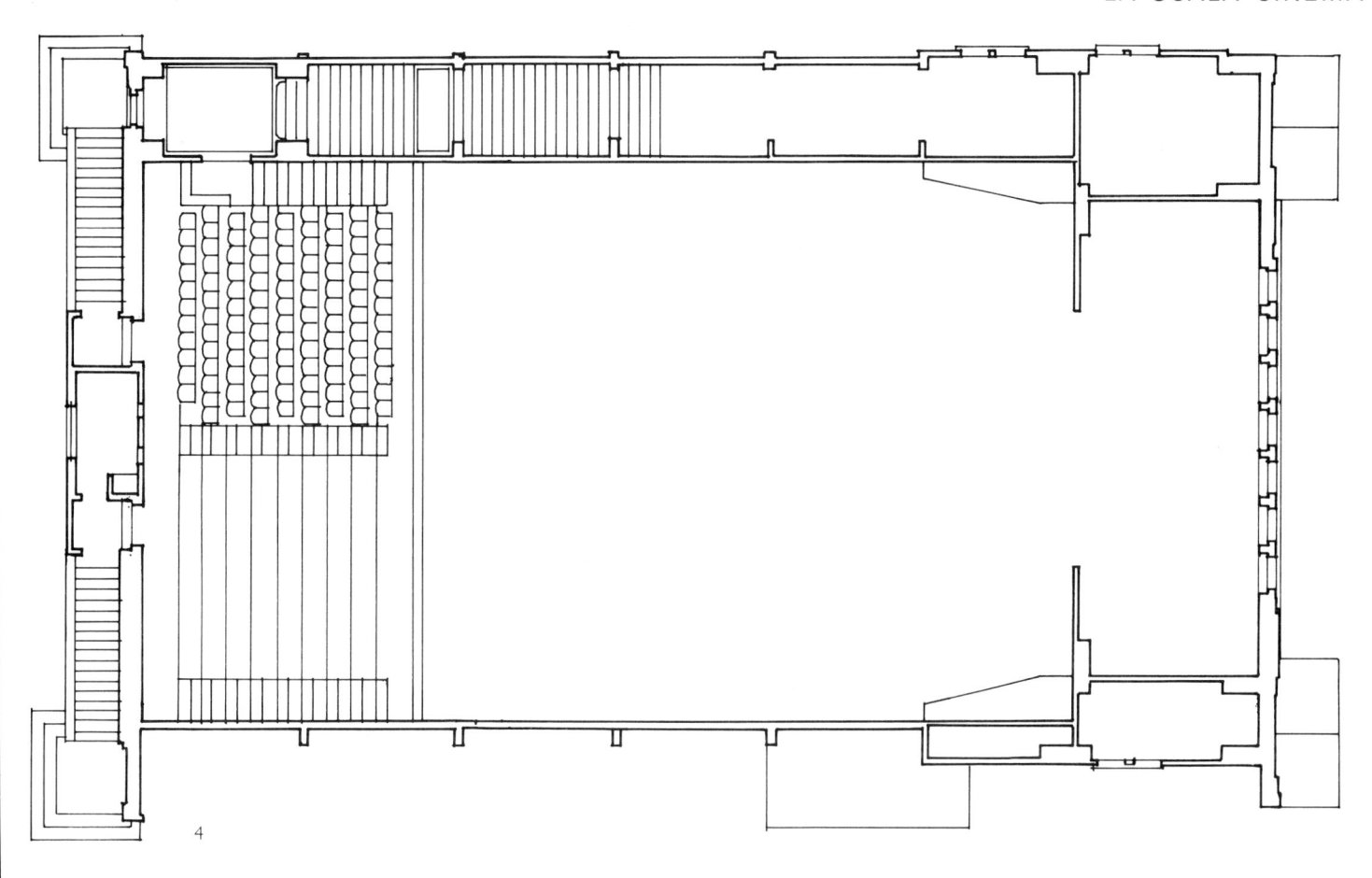

LA SCALA CINEMA

4

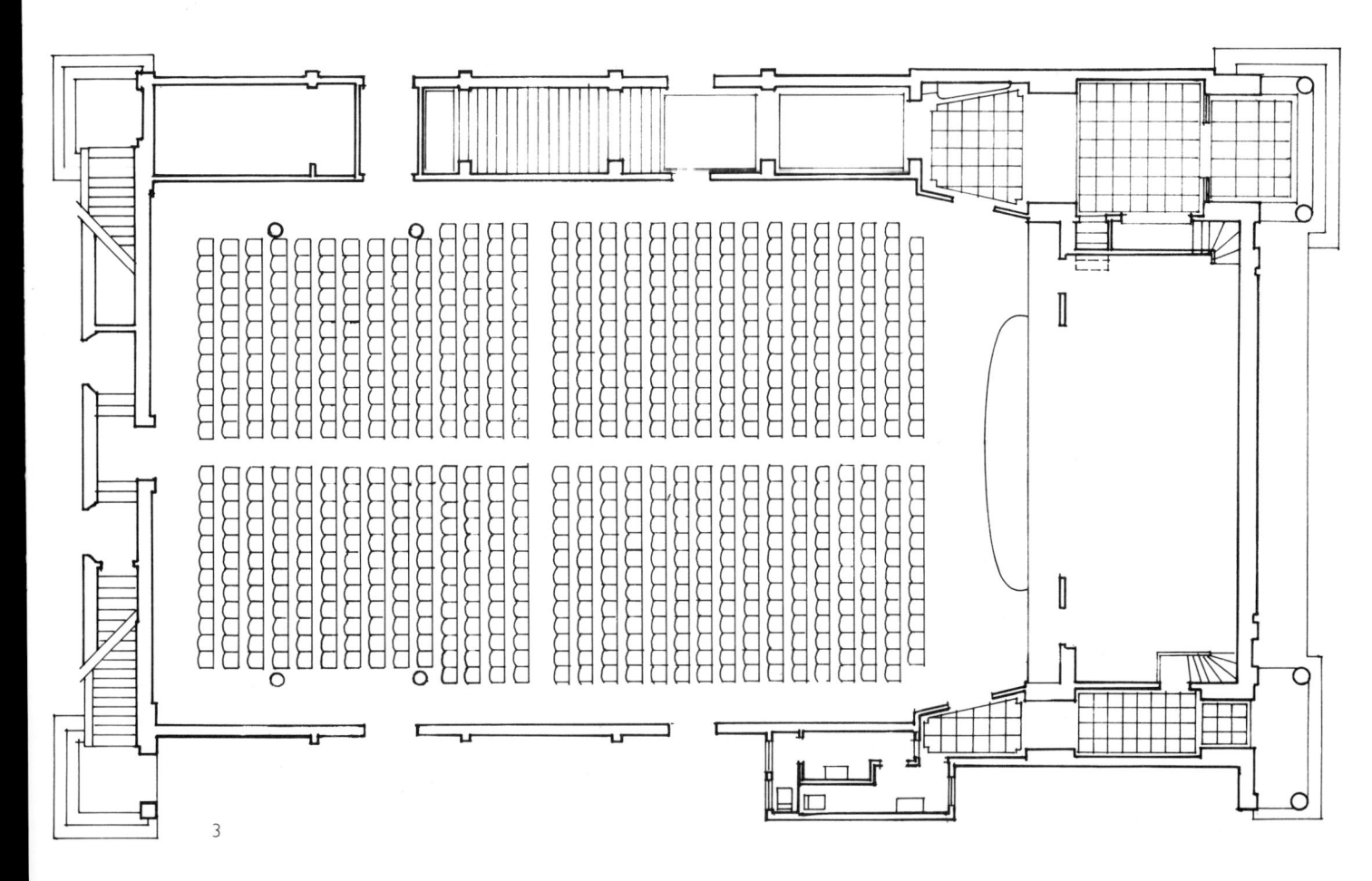

3

LA SCALA CINEMA

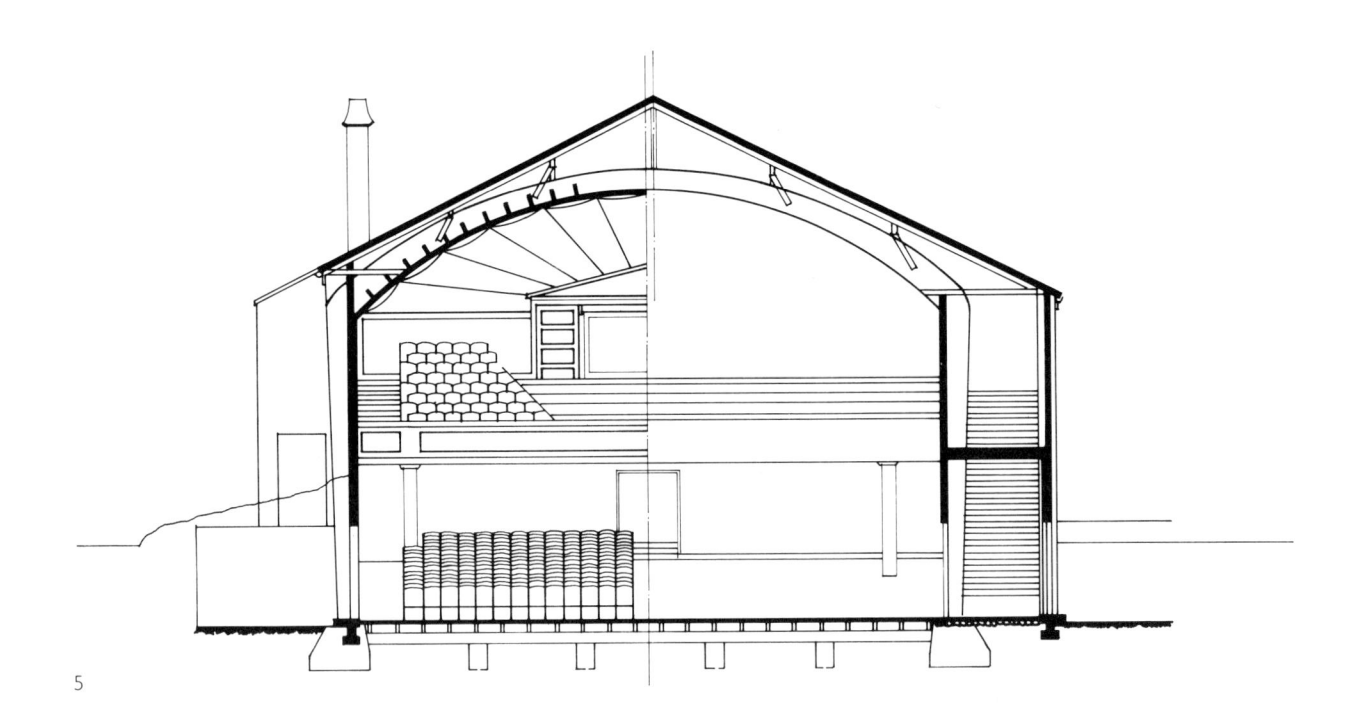

5 Cross section
6 Longitudinal section with interior details
7 Longitudinal section showing foundations and roof structure

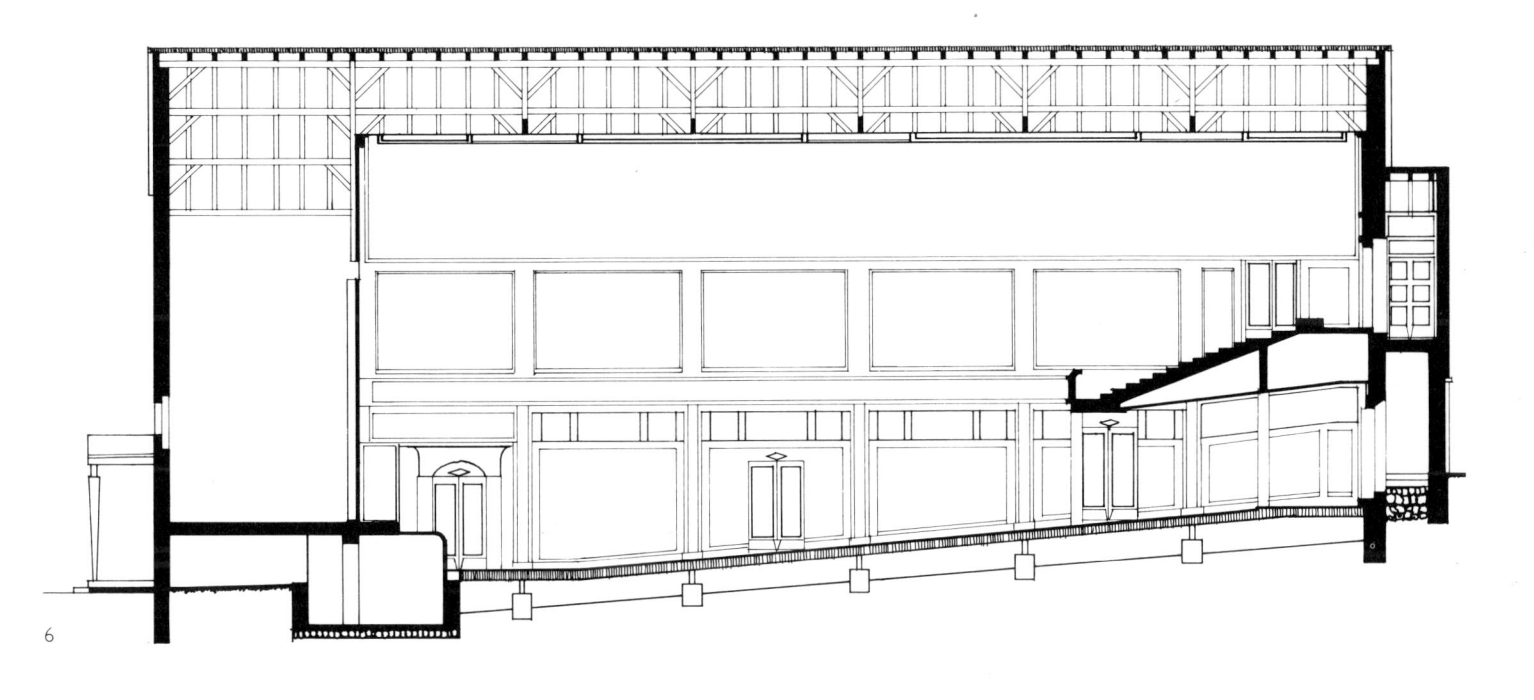

LA SCALA CINEMA

6

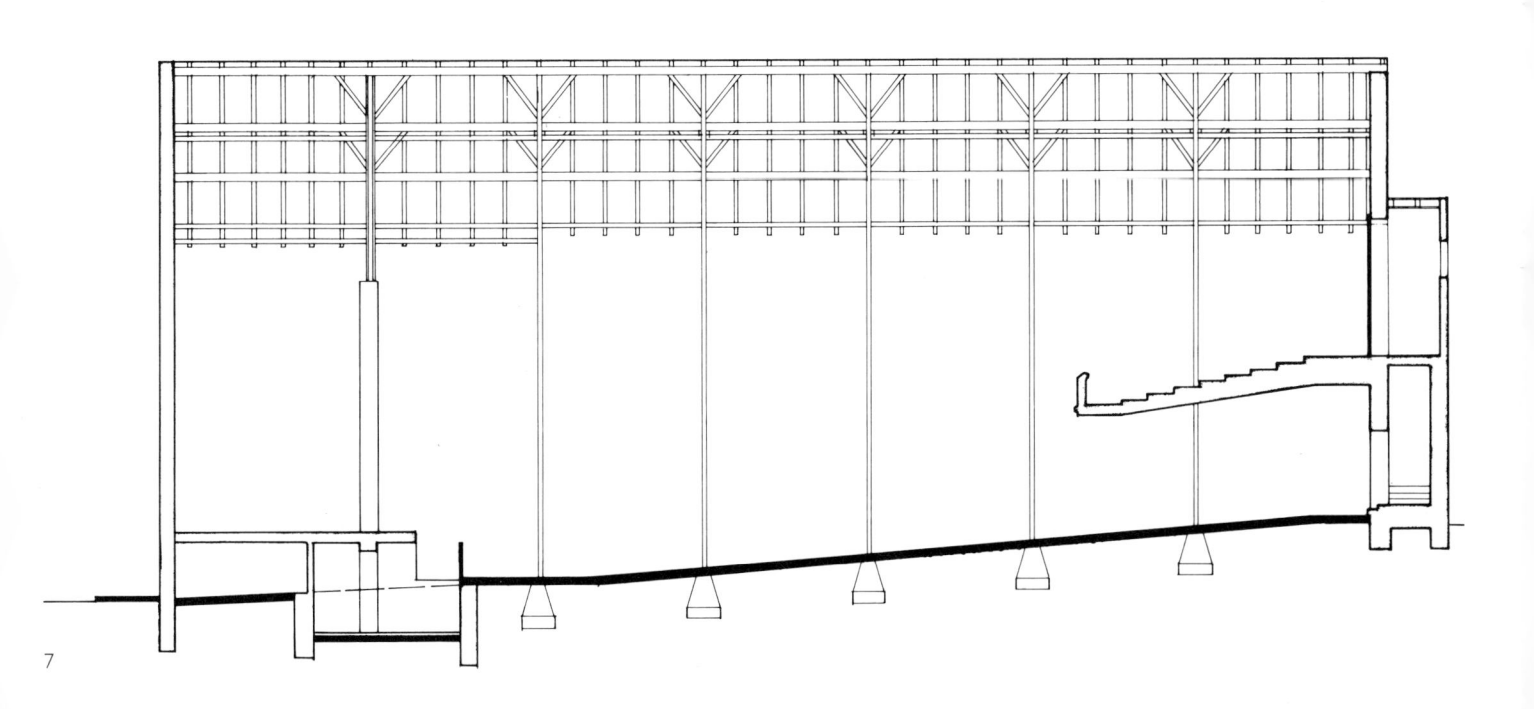

7

LA SCALA CINEMA

8

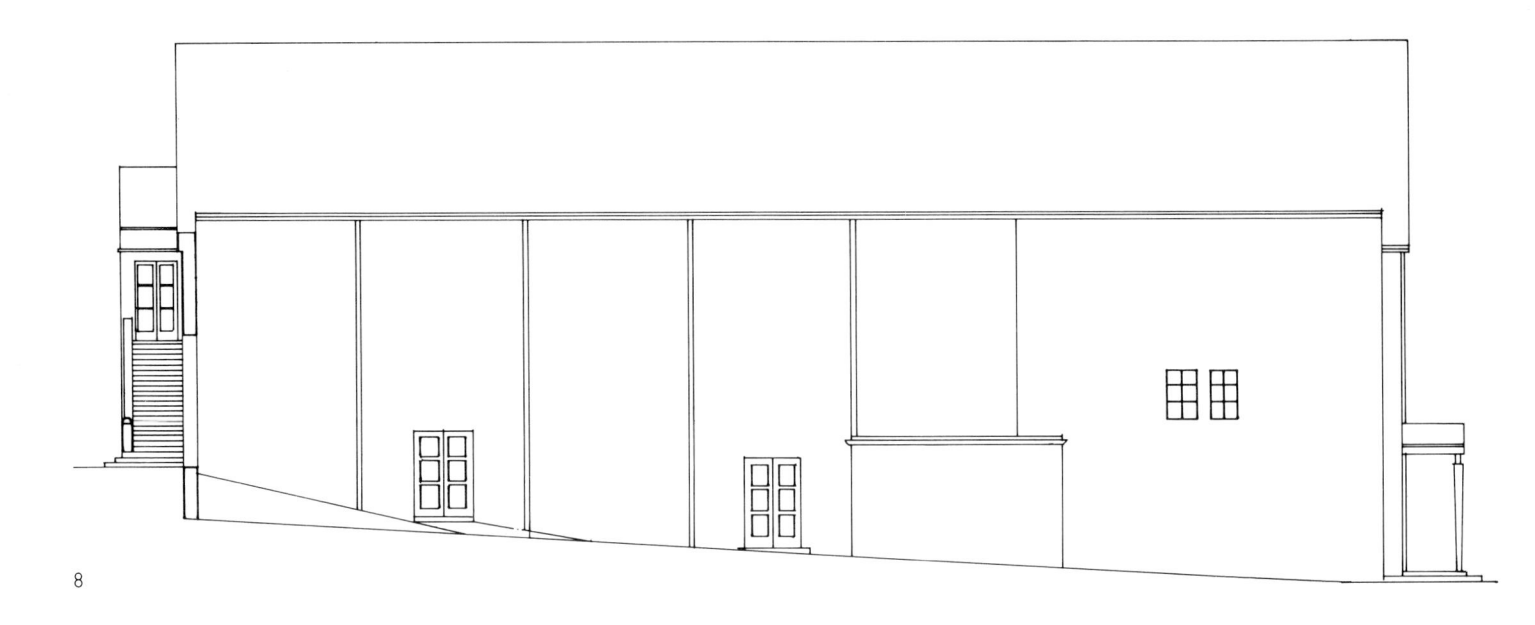

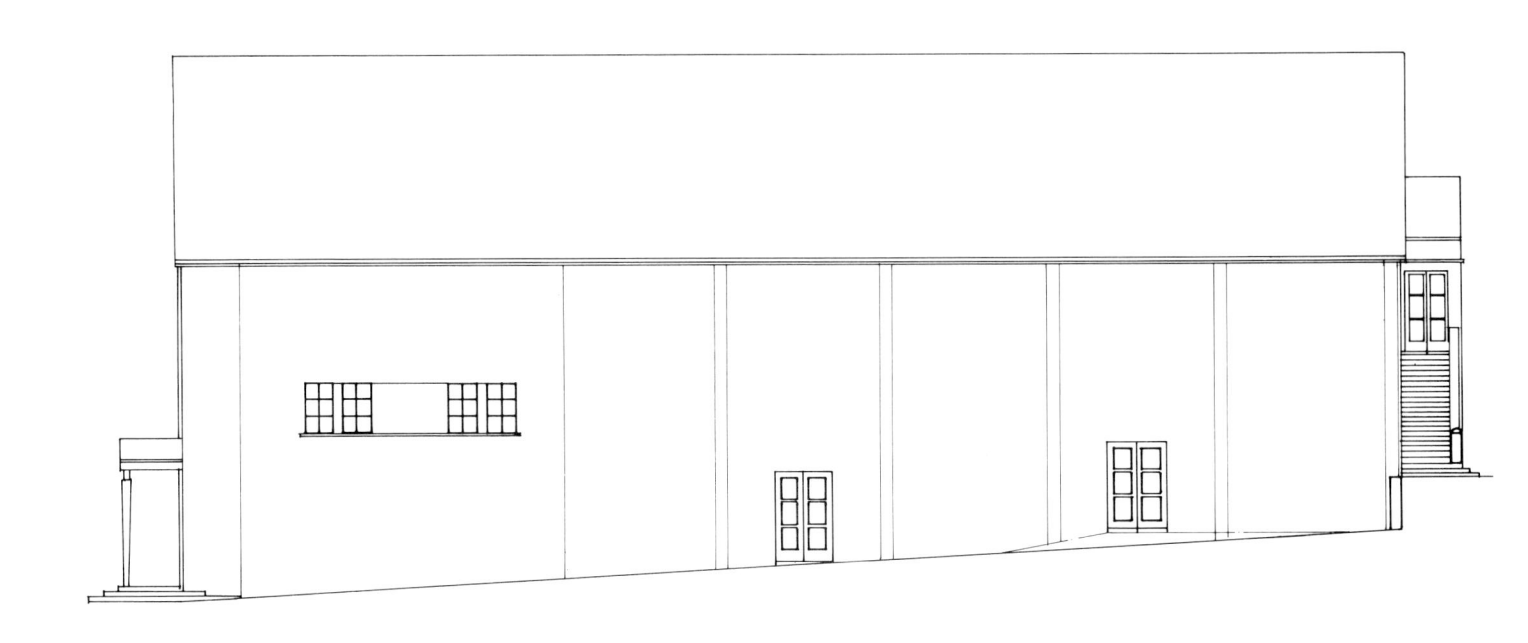

9

8 West elevation
9 East elevation
10 Elevation to rue de la Serre
11 Elevation to rue de la Parc

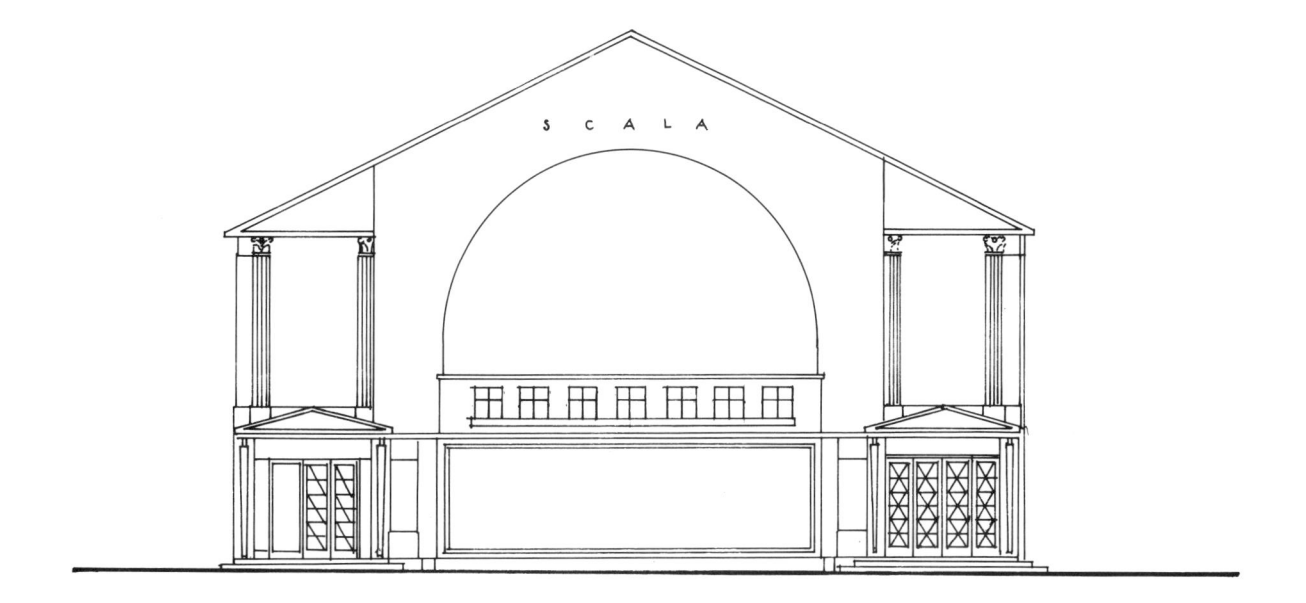

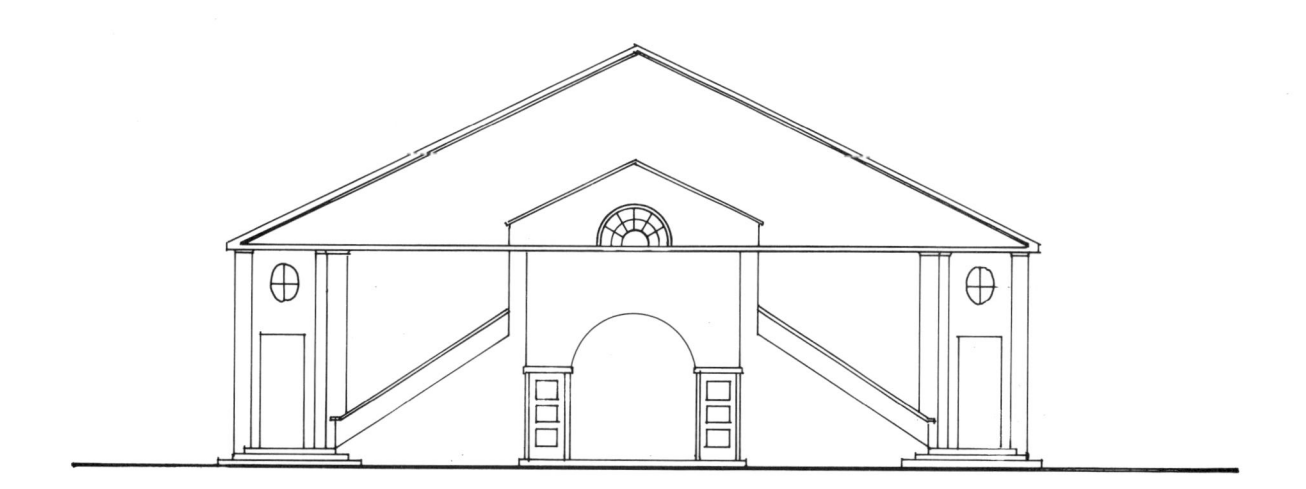

LA SCALA CINEMA

LA SCALA CINEMA

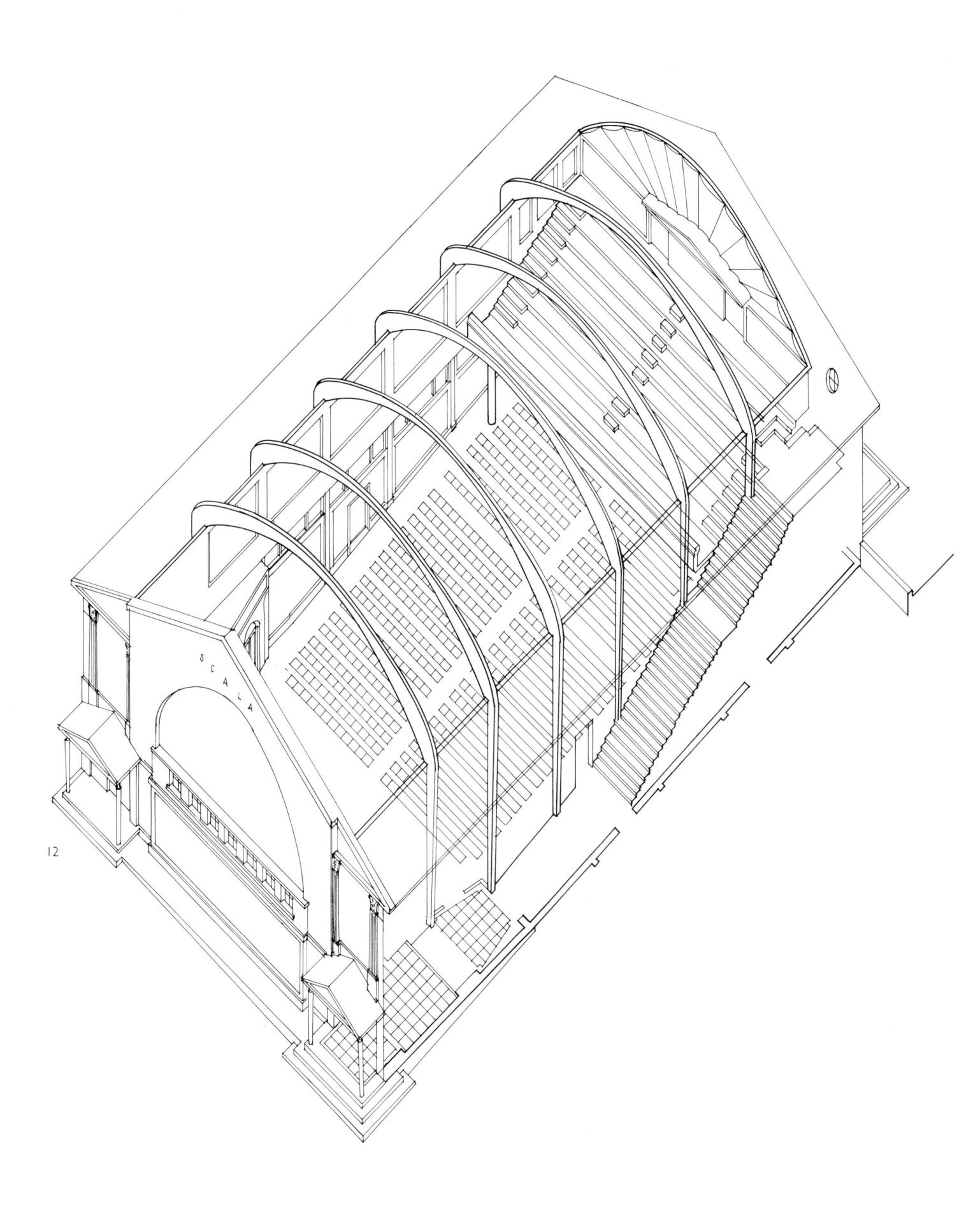

12 Axonometric from the south-west

The Early Projects
1905-1916

112 *From Feeling to Reason:
Jeanneret and Regionalism*
Jacques Gubler

121 *In Time with
the Swiss Watchmakers*
Jacques Gubler

128 The Early Villas
in La Chaux-de-Fonds

130 Selected Bibliography

131 Résumés in French, German,
Spanish and Italian

FROM FEELING TO REASON

From Feeling to Reason: Jeanneret and Regionalism

Jacques Gubler

For Le Corbusier, the issue of *regionalism* entailed an investigation into the 'popular arts'. His ambition, at the time he entered architecture, was to inaugurate a *new local tradition*. The search for himself and the search for the origins of architecture were combined into one. And by scrutinising the organic structure of the cow – the antithesis of the machine – he brought about a near-impossible reconciliation between the philosophies of Voltaire and Rousseau.

The Urban Place

In all of Switzerland, La Chaux-de-Fonds was the only industrial town – apart perhaps from Saint-Gall – where Art Nouveau was ever an issue of public debate. This was probably largely due to the pervasiveness of the watchmaking industry. Before the outbreak of the First World War, the town's industrialists controlled over half the watch production of Switzerland, which in turn accounted for as much as ninety per cent of total world production. Although the population statistics indicate a relatively small town – 17,000 inhabitants in 1860; 36,000 in 1900; 40,000 in 1917 – La Chaux-de-Fonds was, at the turn of the century, the watch capital of the world.[1] It is important to bear this economic pre-eminence in mind, not only because it created a demand for architects, but also because it meant that local cultural traditions – republicanism, economic liberalism, labour and religious movements – were tied to industry.

Throughout the nineteenth century, the physical growth of La Chaux-de-Fonds proceeded in line with the rational planning regulations dictated by the local authorities, the Police du Feu et des Constructions.[2] A fire in 1794 took on the value of a *foundation* in the town's history and *collective memory*. With the rebuilding came rationalisation. A typological formula was prescribed, that of the *massif* – the block or clearly defined terrace row.

The result was a broadly Ponts-et-Chaussées style urbanism. The town's topographical position on both sides of the slope at the bottom of a valley naturally spawned both an orthogonal street pattern *and* longitudinally parallel thoroughfares. But it was the entrepreneurs who codified the architectural typology of La Chaux-de-Fonds. They ensured a remarkable homogeneity in the official policy governing the extension of the 'manufacturing town'. Speculation revolved less around the land, which was in the hands of a few wealthy cattle-owners, than around the capacity of the buildings to accommodate flats or workshops with equal ease. The resulting buildings had, from a formal point of view, a distinctly Neo-Classical flavour, being volumetric blocks whose gables could be read as pediments. The predominant type was that of the apartment house on a slope with road, stair, WC and kitchen stationed uphill: bedrooms, garden and outside extensions (workshop, terrace, garage, storeroom) downhill. Usually, there were two dwelling units facing one another off a shared landing, each with a central corridor servicing the individual, independent rooms. This plan, remarkable for its social utility, went back to the eighteenth-century patrician houses of Neuchâtel.

1 Watch manufacturing in La Chaux-de-Fonds in 1900
2 Aerial view of La Chaux-de-Fonds in the evening, c 1920

FROM FEELING TO REASON

The homogeneous nature of entrepreneurial production at La Chaux-de-Fonds – the emphasis on raw materials (asphalt, metal castings, girders, stone of varied origin and, from 1901, Hennebique reinforced concrete) – made the architecture produced there from the 1890s onwards somewhat trivial and at times delightfully vulgar. And this was precisely what L'Eplattenier and his students were reacting against when they left town and took refuge in the forest of Pouillerel.

In 1900 Pouillerel was a primitive mountain pasture overlooking La Chaux-de-Fonds. It provided a relatively exotic destination for family walks on Sundays with, on a clear day, views of 'the blue line of the Vosges'. Living on the fringe of Pouillerel at that time required stamina, as the only way to get there was by a long trek on foot. Nevertheless, L'Eplattenier set the exodus from La Chaux-de-Fonds in motion in 1901 when he began construction of his house and workshop at Pouillerel.

Like van de Velde or Behrens, Charles L'Eplattenier (1874-1946) was originally a painter who came to architecture via the arts and crafts. He studied at Prague and Paris, and knew of Charles Blanc, Ruskin, Galle and Grasset. On meeting Clement Heaton, he also became familiar with the English Arts and Crafts tradition. Appointed professor at the School of Art in La Chaux-de-Fonds in 1897,[3] he was not yet thirty when Charles-Edouard Jeanneret (1887-1965) became his pupil, around 1902.[4] First, L'Eplattenier taught drawing, which he saw as an essential object lesson and route to knowledge. To observe, with pencil in hand, plant, mineral and animal in order to transcribe their geometric order according to the rationalist method outlined by Viollet-le-Duc in *Histoire d'un dessinateur* (1879) and later developed by Grasset and Provensal;[5] to discover the underlying 'true' form so as to be able to pour into it the plastic identity of the craftsman's product, be it comb, fan, candlestick or watchcase – these were the goals of the drawing exercise. Whether the end product was a knick-knack or a 'useful object' was of no great importance. If need be, an umbrella stand and a small clock could merge in an identical casing. However, the 'supreme stage' of the form lay in the work of architecture; a collective synthesis of the 'major' and 'minor' arts (a *Gesamtkunstwerk*). L'Eplattenier organised his students in a series of studios devoted to different craft techniques.

3 Postcard showing 'The Summit of Pouillerel', c 1906
4 Villa Fallet, detail of the western facade. The white limestone corbelling, a metaphor of the 'rock', evokes and interprets the mineral in a similar manner to Jeanneret's watchcase (see p 123)

The Place of Nature

The Villa Fallet should be understood as the *collective manifesto* of the Art School. It was intended to prove that L'Eplattenier and his students had achieved a maturity in their work although, admittedly, they needed the practical experience of Chapallaz, whom L'Eplattenier had met during construction of his own house, to master the project, obtain planning permission and supervise the site.

Chapallaz (1881-1976) received his architectural training during a five-year apprenticeship with the important Zurich practice of Otto Pfleghard and Max Haefeli, who were then working on the Schatzalp sanatorium in Davos and the Zur Trülle commercial block in the Bahnhofstrasse in Zurich. At the same time, he attended classes at the Zurich School of Applied Arts. In 1902, he was hired by an entrepreneur in La Chaux-de-Fonds and, in 1906, he opened his own practice in the neighbouring town of Tavannes, where he married the daughter of the director of the Tavannes Watch Company. With L'Eplattenier and his followers, Chapallaz played the role of master builder. Jeanneret's task was to assist him – the stage-manager of the Villa Fallet.

The brief for the Villa Fallet was for a well-appointed family house. The client, Louis Fallet (1879-1956), was a small industrialist specialising in the 'artistic decoration' of watchcases who trusted L'Eplattenier implicitly. The plans, drawn up by Chapallaz, were approved in 1906, and the house was moved into in August 1907. The Villa Fallet conforms initially to the typological norms for a sloping site – excavated uphill, overflowing downhill, with a basement containing storerooms, laundry room and central heating system. However, the living space is spread over two levels: the salon, kitchen and workshop are on the ground floor; the bedrooms are above. At the very top is a large attic, a high room where the 'spirit' of the house resides. This vertical stratification of day-and-nighttime spaces – derived from nineteenth-century English domestic architecture' – is also found in other large houses built in La Chaux-de-Fonds between 1900 and 1910.[6] The split-level stairwell, which occupies the whole of the northern gable, is an unusual feature which it is tempting, in retrospect, to attribute to Jeanneret, as is the rational clarity of the project as a whole – the grouping of utility rooms in one zone and the division between night and day.

However, what makes the Villa Fallet so unusual is its ornamentation. L'Eplattenier's students saw this house as their 'œuvre de jeunesse'; an opportunity to flaunt their virtuosity. Their aim was to compound a decorative catalogue found *in situ*; to neutralise, or rather, *naturalise* the internationalism of Art Nouveau. The picturesque is here made manifest in all its variations: complex symmetries, contrasting textures and stones, polychromy and elaborate crossing and interpenetration of gables. This grammar of form was undoubtedly indebted to the century-old tradition of the *picturesque* in Britain. There are also similarities with the Villa Majorelle by Sauvage (1898-1900) at Nancy[7] but, at Pouillerel, the *genius loci* must have suggested the ornamental theme of the pine tree and inspired the geometrical combination of the cone and fir in the articulation of the main facades. Certain details emphasise the Jurassic identity of the building: the window on the axis of the western gable is fashioned to look like a miniature gable; and the white limestone corbels, which are anchored in yellow limestone and support blood-red girders, symbolically evoke the rocky mineral. The Villa Fallet is altogether as finely worked as a watchcase; its splendour seems to vindicate Viollet-le-Duc's belief that the workshop was the only place to learn architecture.

The Villa Fallet had a snowball effect, bringing commissions for two more houses to be built nearby. The clients, Albert Stotzer (1872-1939) and Ulysse Jules Jaquemet (1873-1942), were both involved in watchmaking: Stotzer taught mechanics at the watch-making school and Jaquemet was a watchcase finisher. The architectural brief for the two houses was identical: each comprised two separate apartments suitable for rental, one placed on top of the other, with ample service areas in the basement and the attic: a good architectural investment! Chapallaz was the supervising architect. The plans, which he drew up in consultation with Jeanneret, are signed by both men and dated 'January 1908' (in the case of the Villa Stotzer) and '16 April 1908' (for the Villa Jaquemet). Jeanneret was in Vienna at that time, which for him was synonymous with the Wiener Werkstätte.

The Villas Stotzer and Jaquemet show how Chapallaz and Jeanneret were together extending their search for a *regional* style while at the same time rationalising and crystallising their methods. The dominant formal effect in these houses, largely in response to the construction techniques, is that of the 'block'. The floors are reinforced concrete slabs (made by the Hennebique system) anchored in the masonry of the outer walls. The lateral projection of the bow windows can be read as a homage to Muthesius's *Das Englische Haus*[8] or, alternatively, as the beginnings of the 'apsidal' theme developed more fully in Jeanneret's later projects. The local identity is expressed not only by the ochre-yellow limestone, but also by the way the side walls project out beyond the front gable in an arrangement typical of farms in the Jura – a salute to the domain of the cowherds.

It was not long, however, before Jeanneret stood his distance. Vienna's appeal having slightly worn off, he had visited Tuscany and, by the autumn of 1908, was in Paris discovering how the Perret brothers worked.[9] He became disenchanted with the Villas Fallet, Stotzer and Jaquemet. In a letter to L'Eplattenier dated the 22nd and 25th of November, 1908, he explained that Chapallaz had nothing more to teach him, that he was suspicious of the smugness of his fellow students, and that he could no longer accept an architecture based primarily on 'the love of the plastic effect' and the 'eurythmics of forms'[10] – two terms which he undoubtedly related to the aesthetic of the picturesque. What did he propose in its place? Curious as it may seem to readers of Le Corbusier, Jeanneret at that time saw form as opposed to logic, to calculation, and to the death of dreams. The courses, travel and visits to museums and schools – all the efforts he had made to educate himself between 1907 and 1911 – had been undertaken with one aim: to prepare himself to practise architecture in La Chaux-de-Fonds.

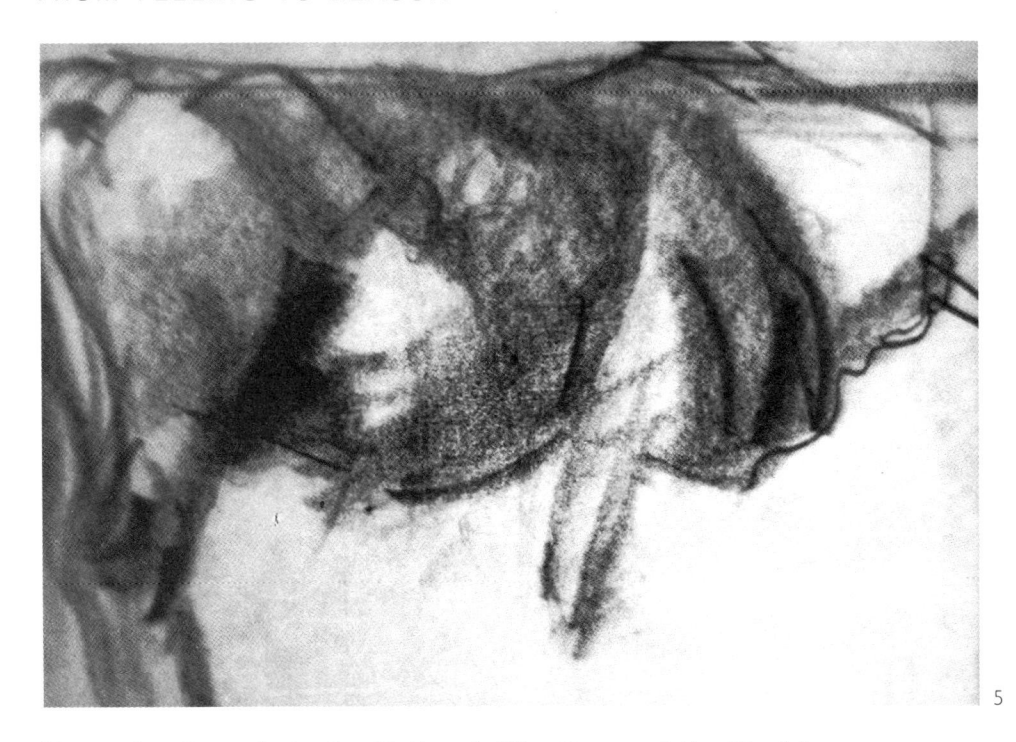

FROM FEELING TO REASON

From the Organic to the Rational: The Cow and the Machine

That the ideas of regionalism could overlap with the advent of Art Nouveau is well demonstrated by Sauvage's early work.[11] Sauvage was part of the rationalist tradition of Viollet-le-Duc, which believed that domestic architecture could learn some valuable lessons from rural architecture, among them economy of materials, adaptation to the climate and respect for the local way of life. Viollet-le-Duc undertook a true ethnography of the house.

Art Nouveau presented a number of contradictions. The most obvious was the conflict between elitism and 'popularity' within production and amongst the clientele. There was a further opposition between encouraging the international spread of ideas and asserting a distinct national identity. This was particulary evident in Catalan Modernism[12] but also felt more or less fervently in Glasgow, Moscow and Prague. However, there was no trace of a secessionist 'Jurassianism' in the 'art movement' of La Chaux-de-Fonds – except perhaps a fleeting reference to the secular antagonism between the 'Upper' and 'Lower' parts of the Neuchâtel canton. Upper Neuchâtel is the republican, anarchist, socialist part of the Jura (containing Le Locle and La Chaux-de-Fonds) where, ever since the eighteenth century, the cow and the watch have represented the two poles of the economy. Lower Neuchâtel contains the capital and is patrician, based around its lakes, more royalist than republican, a producer of excellent wines, chocolates and fish.

So what did L'Eplattenier and his students hope to achieve with their grand scheme of reconciling their town with its 'true nature'? And why did La Chaux-de-Fonds' 'Special School for Arts Applied to Industry' go off to the country to think about botany? Why was Pouillerel seized on as a 'Monte Verità'? Why did they look to nature for an object lesson and for social harmony? Was it not from Rousseau that L'Eplattenier's method of teaching and mythology were derived? Were not L'Eplattenier and his students seeking to regain a 'country whose integral character was still intact'?[13] And can't we hear *Emile* speak when Jeanneret says in 1911, 'Having educated my eyes to the spectacle of things, I shall try to tell you, in sincere words, the beauty that I've encountered'?[14] Did not both L'Eplattenier and Jeanneret communicate in botanical metaphors, dreaming of an art movement which would transcribe 'the logic of the life which develops from the embryo through the roots, the stem and the leaves to become the flower'?[15] And even though Jeanneret dismissed the picturesque quality and formalism of 'his' first three houses in 1908, he continued to hold dear the conviction that architecture proceeded from a sense of mission, from a personal search for truth, which resided in the permanence of 'nature'; in the animal (woman

5 Sketch of a cow by Charles-Edouard Jeanneret, c 1910
6 Theo van Doesburg, 'Aesthetic Transfiguration of an Object', 1925

FROM FEELING TO REASON

remaining for him 'a creature of nature'), geography, the popular arts and geometry. Having absorbed the centres of the architectural world (Tuscany, Venice, Istanbul, Athens, Campanie, Rome) and stayed awhile in the art capitals (Vienna, Paris, Berlin), Jeanneret took back to La Chaux-de-Fonds a quite personal historiography.

Le Corbusier's historiography revolved not around the idea of progress but rather the belief that the present is a crisis to be resolved by architecture. He believed that 'machinism' had upset the natural and organic harmony of the world (do not forget that for Le Corbusier, 'machinism' always began 'a hundred years ago'). The architect, however, had penetrated the secret of both nature and the machine. He had equipped himself with the theoretical means to annul the crisis. The architectural machine could establish the new order, which was in fact a return to the original organic harmony. The cow and the machine, which coexisted only at La Chaux-de-Fonds, provided the two energy-giving and symbolic poles of his solitary effort 'towards an architecture'.

The finest architectural apology for the cow is to be found in Frank Lloyd Wright's autobiography. 'Cow! What a word!... Why is any cow, red, black or white, always just in the right place for a picture in any landscape? Like a cypress tree in Italy, she is never wrongly placed ... Has anyone sung the song of the patient, calf-bearing, milk-flowing, cud-chewing, tail-switching cow? Slow-moving, with fragrant breath and beautiful eyes, the well-behaved, necessary cow, who always seems to occupy the choicest ground anywhere around?'[17]

Wright's physiocratic (Jefferson + Virgil) cow undoubtedly illustrates the tradition of Usonia (the contraction of 'US' and 'Union' proposed by Samuel Butler) in which 'organic architecture' was implanted. Le Corbusier also drew many rough sketches of animals, making his notebooks resemble a full natural history. From La Chaux-de-Fonds to Chandigarh, the cow was depicted as a guardian of nature and its seasons, like a peaceful clock.

On a more general level, it might be said that the avant-gardes in painting and music from 1907 to the outbreak of the First World War set in motion a rhetorical pendulum between the primitive and the mechanical, the sacred and the profane, anonymity and initiation. For does not *Le Sacre du Printemps*, (1912-13), show polychromatic folklore and black and white mechanical modernity as inextricably linked in a contrapuntal relationship? A drawing by Jean Cocteau dated 1913 and entitled *Stravinsky Playing Le Sacre du Printemps* shows the composer thumping away at the keyboard of a piano. The dancer emits electric wires and the spectators are transformed into squares.[18]

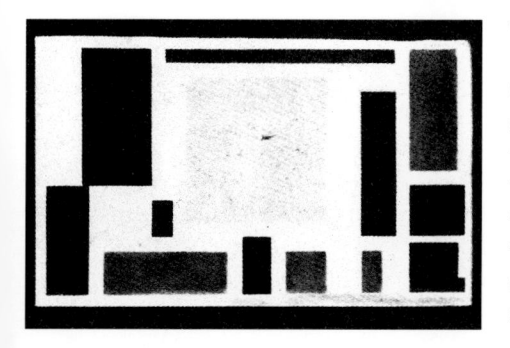

Van Doesburg illustrated, in four stages, the aesthetic transformation of a picturesque object into a plastic configuration.[19] Van Doesburg thought of this as a strictly one-way process, yet, before the First World War, 'popular arts' and modernity were seen to interact. For Jeanneret in 1911, both iron bridges and Danube villages seemed to emerge from the same Breughelian landscape: 'This old Pieter Breughel who sings with all his soul in *Seasons* and *Kermesses* his joie de vivre and his admiration and love for this good earth in which he has his place, which gives him strength and joy because it is full of beauty and health.'[20]

In his *Etude sur le mouvement d'art décoratif en Allemagne* (1912), Jeanneret cast himself as an innovator working towards a 'Renewal'. The first chapter, 'General Considerations', opens with an exposition based on a thesis by Paul Mebes, whose influential work, *Um 1800*, had appeared in 1908.[21] For Mebes, modern architecture had to be based on a platform established 'around 1800'; a platform of Neo-Classicism which Giedion called 'romantic Classicism' in 1922, and Emile Kaufmann called 'autonomous architecture' in 1933. Jeanneret explained: 'Up until the (French) Revolution, the Arts – the faithful expression of the economic and political life and the psychological state of the people – had risen slowly and without eclipse...'[22] Art was thus seen as *eclipsed* by the Revolution. But the reconquest of this Golden Age of Reason was thought by some to still perhaps be possible. If Mebes had known the anonymous, popular and conciliatory architecture of the entrepreneurs of La Chaux-de-Fonds in the nineteenth century, perhaps he would have dedicated a third photographic album to it.

117

FROM FEELING TO REASON

Was Jeanneret, in 1912 on his return from the Orient, when he opened an independent architectural practice at La Chaux-de-Fonds, attempting to rediscover the key to the *last, true* local tradition? Was the northern gable of the La Scala Cinema (1916) a salute to the vernacular pediment of the Jura? Certainly, up until the war, Jeanneret clung onto the thought of reconciling his architecture with his native town: 'I think that it is necessary to be patient, that it is necessary to desire to do what is honest and beautiful, and that in order to marry one's work with what already exists in the region, it is necessary to know how to wait.'[23]

This theme of waiting recalls that of the initial moment. On several different occasions, most notably in 1940-41, Jeanneret thought the time was ripe and, as Le Corbusier, was to go on to promote the radical, yet calm and rational, restoration of the ancestral heritage.

First published in Archithese *3/81. Translated from the French by Pamela Johnston*

NOTES

1. Pierre du Bois, *Les mythologies de la Belle-Epoque, La Chaux-de-Fonds, André Evard et l'Art Nouveau* (Grandson 1975). See also Jacques Gubler, 'In Time with the Swiss Watchmakers', pp 120-7.
2. Marc Emery, 'Réhabilitation urbaine et interdisciplinarité, cas de La Chaux-de-Fonds', thesis paper submitted to EPF-Lausanne, 1979.
3. Paul Seylaz, *Charles L'Eplattenier* (La Chaux-de-Fonds 1974).
4. Allen Brooks, who is working on a monograph of Jeanneret's youth, has noted that Charles-Edouard did not – contrary to what Le Corbusier said – escape compulsory schooling until the age of fifteen. He would thus have entered the Art School in 1902.
5. Paul V Turner, 'La prima formazione di Le Corbusier, 1902-07', postscript to Brian Brace Taylor's *Le Corbusier e Pessac* (Rome 1973), pp 97-108.
6. See Emery, *op cit*.
7. *Henri Sauvage*, catalogue of an exhibition at the SADG Archives d'Architecture Moderne (Brussels 1976), pp 230-3.

7 La Scala cinema, main facade and entrance portico, as built in 1916
8 Villa Schwob under construction, 1917, showing the reinforced concrete skeleton with brick infill

8   Hermann Muthesius, *Das Englische Haus* (Berlin 1904, 2nd edition 1908).
9   Stanislaus von Moos, *Le Corbusier: Elements of a Synthesis* (Cambridge, Mass 1979).
10 Letter to L'Eplattenier dated the 22nd and 25th of November, edited by Frank Jotterand, *Gazette de Lausanne*, 4-5 September 1965.
11 François Loyer, 'Sauvage ou le renoncement', in *Henri Sauvage, op cit*, p 36.
12 Oriol Bohigas, *Arquitectura modernista* (Barcelona 1968); André Barey, *Barcelona: de la ciudad preindustrial al fenomen modernista* (Barcelona 1981).
13 Le Corbusier, *Le Voyage d'Orient*, 'Completed in Naples on the 10th of October 1911 by Charles-Edouard Jeanneret. Re-read on the 17th of July 1965 at 24 Nungesser et Coli by Le Corbusier' (Paris 1966), p 19.
14 *ibid*, p 37.
15 Charles-Edouard Jeanneret, in a letter to L'Eplattenier dated the 26th of February 1908. Quoted from Eleanor Gregh, 'The Dom-Ino Idea', *Oppositions* No 15/16 (Winter 1979-80), p 84.
16 Charles Jencks, *Le Corbusier and the Tragic View of Architecture* (London 1973), pp 99-110.
17 Frank Lloyd Wright, *My Autobiography*, p 26.
18 Jean Cocteau, *Dessins* (2nd edition, Paris 1924), p 119.
19 Theo van Doesburg, *Grundbegriffe der neuen gestaltenden Kunst* (Frankfurt 1925/Mayence 1966), p 18 and plates 5-8.
20 Le Corbusier, *Le Voyage d'Orient, op cit*, p 28.
21 Paul Mebes, *Architektur und Handwerk im letzten Jahrhundert ihrer traditionellen Entwicklung* (Munich 1908), two vols.
22 Charles-Edouard Jeanneret, *Etude sur le mouvement d'art décoratif en Allemagne* (La Chaux-de-Fonds 1912/New York 1968), p 9
23 Charles-Edouard Jeanneret, 'Le renouveau dans l'architecture', *L'Œuvre* I (1914), No 2, p 37.

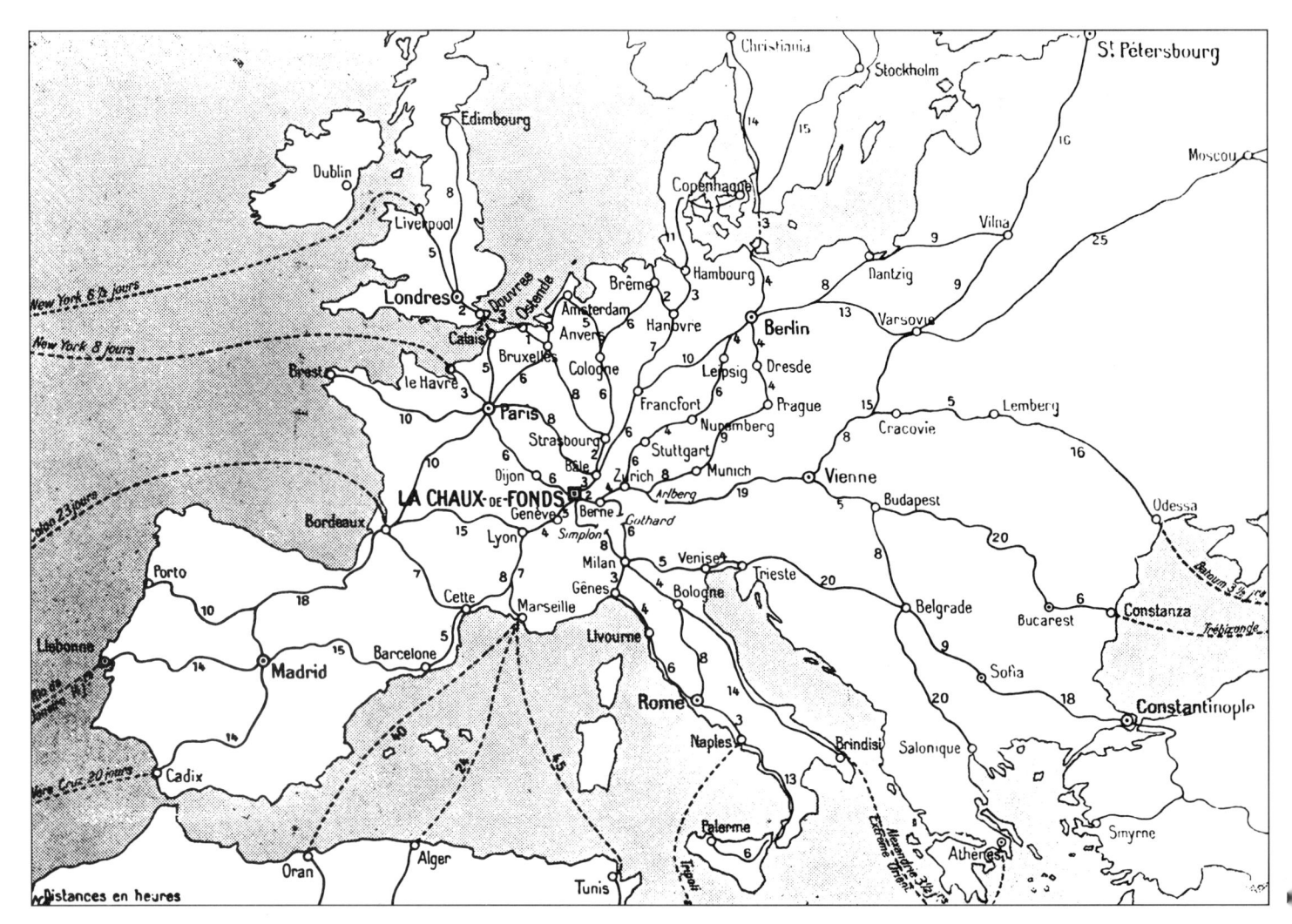

THE SWISS WATCHMAKERS

In Time with the Swiss Watchmakers

Jacques Gubler

The importance of Le Corbusier's first identity – as Charles-Edouard Jeanneret – was revealed only after his death.[1] Born in La Chaux-de-Fonds in 1887, Jeanneret was apprenticed in the Art Nouveau style and partly 'self-taught' in architecture, making initiatory tours which he related to his experience of his native town,[2] where he produced seven built works (six houses and a cinema). His autobiographical *Œuvres complètes* would have us believe that, upon breaking ties with La Chaux-de-Fonds at the age of thirty, Jeanneret became Le Corbusier in the same way that Athena sprang fully armed from the head of Zeus. Once he had chosen Paris as his 'battlefield',[3] the architect divulged his origins only in a few, carefully worded philosophical statements. In the 'Confession', for instance, which formed the afterword to *L'Art décoratif d'aujourd'hui*,[4] he attempted to settle his debt to La Chaux-de-Fonds by acknowledging how much he owed to the 'Master' (Charles L'Eplattenier). Nevertheless, the student kept his distance, less out of respect for his teacher (whose name remained taboo) than out of a desire to dissociate himself from his work, tied up as it was with another century and a province lost in the mountains.

Le Corbusier was grateful to his mentor for having been attuned at the turn of the century to the 'heroic-conquering' Art Nouveau movement, as well as for the fact that he had taught drawing as a cognitive discipline, presented architecture as the synthesis of the major and minor arts and, defining the school as a *workshop*, employed the methods of the craftsman to express form. This was a relatively peaceful 'first chapter', during which Jeanneret devoted himself to searching for a 'regional style' – a search ultimately refuted by the 'brutality of the big cities'.[5] As a butterfly, Le Corbusier wanted to forget his previous life as a caterpillar.

La Chaux-de-Fonds in 1900: World Capital of Watchmaking

At the beginning of the century, the thriving Swiss watchmaking industry accounted for ninety per cent of world production.[6] In 1914, the Watchmakers' Collective of La Chaux-de-Fonds – which had won a Grand Prix at the 1900 World's Fair in Paris – admitted that it controlled sixty per cent, in value terms, of all Swiss exports.[7] The town's economic importance was attributable to the adept manner in which its industrialists had pulled together the diverse manufacturing concerns of the region during the last decade of the nineteenth century to develop multinational markets while annually adapting supply and demand, speculating on precious metals and economic fluctuations and dominating the world market by controlling the middlemen. This industrial evolution, which was typical of the turn of the century, implied neither total mechanisation nor the forcible concentration of production into vast units. Rather, it operated on the principles of centralising management, using rail, post and telegraphic services extensively, organising distribution and after-sales services while also ensuring the close collaboration of banking establishments. Swiss watchmaking was the ultimate model for heterogenous manufacturing, and as such was described rather humorously by Marx in *Das Kapital*: La Chaux-de-Fonds itself was mentioned as a town which could 'be considered as forming a single watchmaking manufacturer'.[8]

1 La Chaux-de-Fonds, watch capital of the world in 1900. From a leaflet published in 1914 by the Watchmakers' Collective
2 Favre-Jacot's factory in Le Locle. The panopticon and glasshouse provided the social and architectural models for watch manufacturing at the turn of the century

THE SWISS WATCHMAKERS

The Society of Watch Manufacturers of La Chaux-de-Fonds (founded in 1886) orchestrated Switzerland's monopoly of the world market on the one hand and, on the other, brought its influence to bear on the final stage of the manufacturing process – the casing. Prolonging the tradition of mechanisation, the employers of La Chaux-de-Fonds used machines to increase control over finishing. But they were also, at a time when Swiss watches were still essentially luxury items, the hauts couturiers of watchmaking, having skilfully adapted by 1900 to the introduction of precious metals – pure gold, platinum and silver – into the manufacture of watchcases and settings. The problem of incorporating ornamentation within the 'industrial arts' had in fact been addressed as early as the mid eighteenth century by watch manufacturers in Geneva, who opened a drawing school for craftsmen involved in the industry. La Chaux-de-Fonds also had an art school which maintained close ties with the watch manufacturers.

The Art School

Apart from public primary and secondary education, which expanded steadily from the first third of the nineteenth century onwards, schooling in La Chaux-de-Fonds developed in two sectors particularly useful to industry: technical specialisation and commerce. The Industrial College (1865), School of Watchmaking (1885) and School of Commerce (1890) expected high standards of their instructors and paid them accordingly. These schools did not so much simulate practical experience as control apprenticeship to the professions – that is what they were equipped for. Thus the School of Watchmaking – in its architecture and equipment – was a factory, while the School of Commerce (which in 1890 had eighteen students, five instructors and fourteen auditors) taught foreign languages and in 1894 introduced typewriters. Drawing featured as an autonomous discipline in the syllabus of both primary and professional schools. As in Geneva, where the arts and crafts were directed towards the manufacture of watches, its teaching was regarded as an integral part of the craftsman's training.

La Chaux-de-Fonds is the only town in Switzerland that may be considered a centre of Art Nouveau,[10] with examples of the style appearing around 1902. At this time, Charles l'Eplattenier (1874-1946), a painter and decorative artist trained in Budapest and Paris, built his house in a clearing in the forest at Pouillerel. He based his villa on the vernacular model of the Jurassian farmhouse and chose his site to signify his will to pitch his tent in relatively wild surroundings and thereby gain a new *experience* useful in the teaching of ornamental composition. Le Corbusier would later see in his 'old master' (who was scarcely thirteen years older than he was) a 'true woodsman'.

L'Eplattenier saw the construction of his house as a kind of rite of initiation – a passage to the age of reason. It also helped him to reformulate his teaching and map out a coherent course of study which could be broken down as follows: stage one, observing, by drawing, mineral and plant forms; two, selecting a repertoire of ornament, a textural and geometric caricature of the above; three, realising the design by an almost alchemical process whereby both primary (wood, stone) and precious (pearls, diamonds, metals) materials are manipulated towards the craftsman's ends. Finally, architecture appears as the transcendent synthesis, the outcome of form.

The Art School at La Chaux-de-Fonds – a product of the arts and crafts tradition – put L'Eplattenier in charge of an advanced course. L'Eplattenier had a personal magnetism which fired his students with enthusiasm – this was probably a prerequisite for the success of his method, which was founded on the intuition and admiration of the teacher. He was directly inspired by the School of Nancy, and Gallé's poetic ideas in particular. However, he was also aware of Art Nouveau and had the school subscribe to the Darmstadt magazine, *Deutsche Kunst und Dekoration* (German Art and Decoration). He also sought to win the confidence of a local patron of the arts, the 'Bureau de Contrôle des Ouvrages d'Or et d'Argent', which was, as its name suggests, a body charged with supervising the working and management of precious metals.

The years 1901-04 corresponded exactly to the swan song of the pocket watch before it was dethroned by the wristwatch. Prized by officers strapped tight in their

3 Postcard showing winter sports below L'Eplattenier's house at Pouillerel, c 1905
4 From left to right, Matthey, Jeanneret and Houriet – three of L'Eplattenier's students working on the sgraffito wall of the Villa Fallet, c 1907
5 Decorative research applied to the watchcase: six of one hundred-and-eight items shown by L'Eplattenier and his students at the 1906 Milan International Exposition
6 *Drinking Fly* watchcase produced by Jeanneret at the Art School under L'Eplattenier's supervision, 1905

THE SWISS WATCHMAKERS

dress uniforms (particularly aristocratic members of the Czar's army), the pocket watch was worn attached to the owner's apparel and opened in the manner of a medal. The craftsmanship of its casing became the philosophical keystone of L'Eplattenier's teaching and the La Chaux-de-Fonds based *Revue Internationale de l'Horlogerie*, which published hundreds of illustrations of watches, monitored his progress in this area. The students at the Art School were introduced in their very first year to a new technique of engraving. How this method differed from others can best be explained by the following example.

Georges Favre-Jacot, the director of Zénith watches (who was to finish his days in a villa built by Jeanneret) commissioned Mucha to produce some drawings on the theme of the Four Seasons for a series of 'artistic watches'. The designs, which won a Grand Prix at the 1900 World's Fair, were then re-transcribed in copper-plate engraving and decorated with niello and enamel – a delicate process requiring a great deal of time.

To put jewellery work within the students' reach, L'Eplattenier and his colleagues introduced a technique called *ramolayé* whereby, as in *repoussé* work, the design was raised in relief, having been hammered through from the underside.[11] This technique led to the decorative motif being geometricised, and even repeated. Retouching and finishing was done by chiselling, applying *champlevé* enamels, and setting stones or pearls. The equipment, materials and framing used at the Art School at La Chaux-de-Fonds produced a result which was near professional, especially to those who were not acquainted with the finer points of the craft.

1906 Milan International Exposition

L'Eplattenier scored a great coup at the 1906 International Exposition in Milan which celebrated the opening of the railway line running from Paris to Milan via Switzerland and the Simplon tunnel. On show there, under the title 'Decorative Research Applied to the Pocket Watch', were one hundred and eight examples of his students' work. The Art School was awarded a Diploma of Honour[12] and, although the Swiss watchmaking pavilion received few visitors on account of its poor location and relatively banal architecture, it nonetheless provided the *Revue Internationale de l'Horlogerie* with a whole collection of images from the exhibition. Among them was the object which, in Le Corbusier's autobiography, became both the masterpiece and indiscretion of his earliest youth. It was a beautifully crafted piece to which the *Revue Internationale de l'Horlogerie* devoted the following description, by way of explaining L'Eplattenier's teaching method. 'A student examined a moss-covered stone. His intention was to render this pebble not as it was in reality but rather as he saw it on different planes; he placed the most salient ones in the middle of the pocket watch and made the others disappear as the case got narrower. He then found a conventional procedure for rendering the moss whereby the upper part of the stone is decorated. In the moss is a fly in quest of a dewdrop, and that is well interpreted – the fly in yellow-gold, the moss in red-gold, copper or steel, and the dewdrop in diamond.'[13]

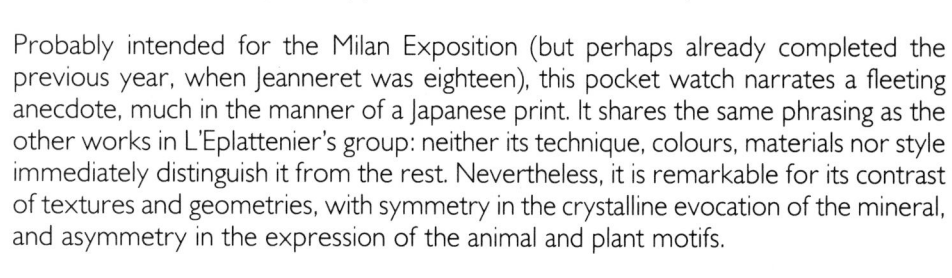

Probably intended for the Milan Exposition (but perhaps already completed the previous year, when Jeanneret was eighteen), this pocket watch narrates a fleeting anecdote, much in the manner of a Japanese print. It shares the same phrasing as the other works in L'Eplattenier's group: neither its technique, colours, materials nor style immediately distinguish it from the rest. Nevertheless, it is remarkable for its contrast of textures and geometries, with symmetry in the crystalline evocation of the mineral, and asymmetry in the expression of the animal and plant motifs.

The Milan Exposition gave L'Eplattenier great credibility with the employers in the watchmaking industry. But in 1906, having grouped his best students in a single workshop, he was already preparing a far more ambitious collective manifesto: a house financed by Louis Fallet, the head of a jewellery firm which specialised in decorating the cases of pocket watches. It is certain that the skills of Fallet's son and successor, a master engraver and chiseller, greatly benefited L'Eplattenier and his students. The Villa Fallet was to be Jeanneret's first architectural experience.

THE SWISS WATCHMAKERS

Jeanneret's Clients

Louis-Edouard Fallet (1879-1956), a sponsor and ardent supporter of the Art School, was not a big industrialist but one of the many small or medium-sized businessmen involved in watch manufacturing. Following the lead of his friend L'Eplattenier, he moved to the forest of Pouillerel.

When L'Eplattenier built his own house he asked a local entrepreneur to design the plans, since he was not recognised as an architect by the 'Police du Feu et des Constructions' – the office which issued all construction permits in the commune. In turn, this entrepreneur put his trust in a young architect, René Chapallaz (1881-1976), who had just set up a practice in the Jura. Chapallaz formed a friendship with L'Eplattenier and it is he who officially functioned as the architecture instructor at the Art School.

Chapallaz's practice was in Tavannes, where he had married the daughter of a prominent businessman, the director of the Tavannes Watch Company. Through his father-in-law, Chapallaz met other influential watchmakers and built villas and factories in both La Chaux-de-Fonds and Le Locle. A self-made man, he benefited greatly from his contact with L'Eplattenier, who left him and Jeanneret to draw up the plans for the Villa Fallet. Jeanneret undoubtedly participated in the discussion of the brief, and it is tempting, in retrospect, to attribute to him the clarity of the basic design and its articulation.

Construction of the Villa Fallet started in 1906 and was completed in 1907, when Jeanneret was twenty years old. The fees paid by the client enabled a few of L'Eplattenier's students, Jeanneret among them, to travel. Already having read extensively, his visual and literary culture was in no way provincial but opened towards France, Germany and Austria (even the *Revue Internationale de l'Horlogerie* published a coffee service by Josef Hoffmann in 1906).[14] Jeanneret discovered Florence in 1907; henceforth used travelling as a permanent source of reflection about architecture. His self-education continued in Vienna in 1908, where he drew close to Josef Hoffmann. While there, Jeanneret maintained contact by letter with a few friends from home, notably L'Eplattenier and Chapallaz.[15]

The success of the Villa Fallet (which was occupied from the month of August 1907 and saw the birth of four children before the father left) brought with it two commissions for the Chapallaz-Jeanneret team. Who were the clients? Ulysse-Jules Jaquemet (1873-1942) was a watchcase polisher who probably also had a hand in the business affairs of Louis Fallet, his brother-in-law. And then there was Albert Stotzer (1872-1939), also married to a Fallet, who taught mechanics at the School of Watchmaking at La Chaux-de-Fonds and contributed columns on industry and electricity to the *Revue Internationale de l'Horlogerie*. Fallet, Jaquemet and Stotzer, all comfortably off in their thirties, belonged to the new bourgeoisie of La Chaux-de-Fonds, which called itself 'progressive' because it believed that industrial progress would overcome economic crises and that work well done would bring prosperity to all – as their own experiences proved.

The Villas Jaquemet and Stotzer were well-sited, rented apartment blocks designed to look like family homes. Their outside form expands on several themes evident in the Villa Fallet: vernacular elements, systematisation of plan, simplification of chromatic and picturesque effects and the crystallisation of form in an articulated block. This volumetric simplification corresponded to the construction technique, in which masonry load-bearing walls supported the wood framework and reinforced concrete floors. These floors were designed in Lausanne under the supervision of the engineer Samuel de Mollins, who held the Swiss licence to Hennebique's patent.

7   1906 advertisement for Louis-Edouard Fallet's firm
8   Sketch for a *secrétaire*, c 1915
9   The garden of the parent's house with the father, mother, two sons and family cat
10 Villa Favre-Jacot, section in perspective showing the ground floor, 1912. Heliographic print in brown

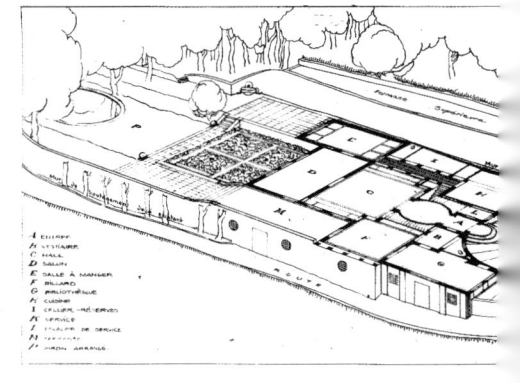

THE SWISS WATCHMAKERS

Reinforced concrete had already become a standard building material in La Chaux-de-Fonds by 1908. Because of the city's altitude of 1,000m the construction season was relatively short – only seven months on average. From 1905 onwards, the most productive entrepreneurs tended to use Hennebique slabs in place of rough masonry flooring, a system which also influenced the structure. Given added impetus by the development of Swiss cemeteries, the use of reinforced concrete spread throughout Switzerland during the years 1893-94.

Although faced with competition from Germany, the Hennebique system predominated in Bâle, the Jura region and all of French-speaking Switzerland. Basing most of his advertising claims on the ability of his product to withstand fire and earthquake, Hennebique was a great advocate of *monolithic* architecture, a penchant reflected in the Villas Jaquemet and Stotzer. However, Jeanneret was rather unsatisfied with these projects. Later, at the Perret brothers' practice, he was to learn two principles which were to be useful in his work of 1912-17, namely, that reinforced concrete induced its own profile, and that it was a general enterprise where the drafting table and job site coexisted.

9

From 1905 to 1908, Jeanneret worked in tandem with Chapallaz on a number of small commissions for craftsmen involved in watchmaking, and in November 1912, Jeanneret's own father, a master enameller, moved into a house built by his son. The Villa 'Jeanneret-Perret' contained a workshop with enough room apparently for the master craftsman and two assistants.

10

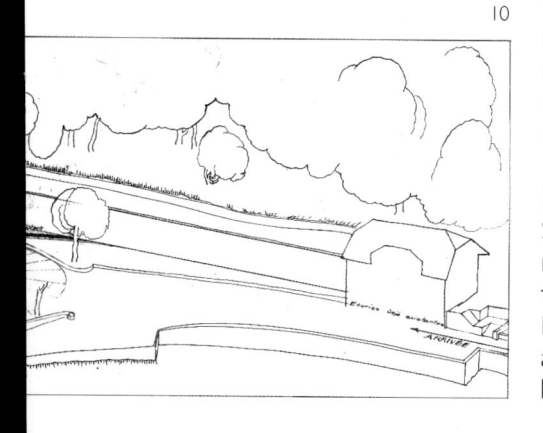

It was only betweeen 1912 and 1917 – after Paris, Berlin, his journey to the East and study of the German decorative arts – that young Jeanneret met the big watchmakers of Neuchâtel and received four commissions: two minor conversions and two large villas. These industrialists were called Favre-Jacot, Ditisheim and Schwob, and operated under the tradenames of Zénith, Vulcain, Cyma and Tavannes Watch.

Known by the tradename Zénith, Georges Favre-Jacot's firm was one of the first in Switzerland to 'make a watch from start to finish', taking American industry as its model. From being a small businessman during the 1870s, Favre-Jacot rose by stages to the rank of a *magnate*. His rise was crowned by a Grand Prix at the 1900 Paris World's Fair where he exhibited the best examples of his work; watches both flat and precise and embellished with designs by Mucha and other contemporary decorative artists. From the 1890s onwards, Georges Favre-Jacot had played a kind of Russian roulette

THE SWISS WATCHMAKERS

and had won both luck and fortune. The choice of trademark – Zénith – connotes well his ambitions and ability to exploit snobbery for commercial purposes.

In 1901, Georges Favre-Jacot had '600 employees producing more than 100,000 watches a year.'[16] As these figures suggest, the Zénith trademark covered both luxury and semi-luxury items. But Favre-Jacot did not work in La Chaux-de-Fonds, his industrial fiefdom being situated in the neighbouring town of Le Locle, where he owned a sizeable amount of land. To enable his firm to fully integrate the manufacture of watches, he developed his own technical services: his mechanical workshop produced most of his machines, while his construction company built his factories. His company was a conglomeration of buildings to which he alone had the key. Omnipresent, not only in his factories but also in the urban and rural landscape, he worked on the technical and tourist infrastructure of the region, opened a quarry and a 'concrete brick' factory and created a complete agricultural model hamlet. He wanted to do it all himself, as in Blaise Cendrars's poem, 'The Creation of the World', where 'God the Father is seated at his roll-top desk'.

Upon reaching retirement age in 1912, Georges Favre-Jacot commissioned Jeanneret to construct a villa which would enable him to overlook his factories and the railway as well as his rural territory. Why this commission? The answer is obvious: he admired Jeanneret for his modern, cosmopolitan culture, his capacity to follow and reinterpret new trends while nevertheless holding to his Jurassian roots in his attempt to formulate a 'new tradition'. Favre-Jacot passed from Grasset to Behrens on an intellectual route already trodden by Jeanneret. His house was classic in its refined concrete profile, yet modern in its access and fittings. As von Moos has pointed out, the oblique unfolding of the villa and its concave entrance echoed the steering wheel of Favre-Jacot's automobile.

Jeanneret's last client, Anatole Schwob, belonged to an authentic industrial dynasty, or rather two of them, namely the Schwob Brothers and Schwob and Company, which used the tradenames Tavannes Watch and Cyma. The Schwobs managed the last phase of the watchmaking process, dressing the watches in accordance with annual fluctuations in demand. Being excellent administrators, they controlled several markets and, after the October Revolution in Russia, where they had substantial interests, the two companies amalgamated.

Anatole Schwob was part of the La Chaux-de-Fonds Jewish community, which had come to the town mainly from Hegenheim in Alsace. After opening a cemetery in 1872, a rabbi was obtained in 1888, and a large and beautiful synagogue was finally built in 1896. Cultivating good relations with prominent members of the city and the official church, the Jewish community played an important role in the development of industry in La Chaux-de-Fonds at a time when the town was restructuring the commercial world of watchmaking to its own advantage.

Even after becoming Le Corbusier, Jeanneret did not disown the Villa Schwob and published it in *Towards a New Architecture*, with the qualifier that it was a first tentative application of 'regulating lines'. In fact, this house – designed in the summer of 1916, occupied in the autumn of 1917 and known locally by the nickname of the 'Villa Turque' – was a remarkable achievement.

Although the subject of litigation between client and architect because it seriously exceeded its budget, this house remains one of Le Corbusier's major works. Its masterful execution and resolution are difficult to equal. Moreover, it has retained over the decades its initial function as residence to a great watchmaking industrialist.

In his perennial search for industrial products to promote his architecture, Le Corbusier could hardly forget that Jeanneret had become an architect by responding to the offers and expectations of the Jurassian watchmakers.

11 1905 poster advertising Zénith, Favre-Jacot's tradename
12 Villa Schwob after completion in 1917. The outer walls are coated with yellow brick, and the bays framed with cream limestone

First published in French in the Revue neuchâteloise, No XXIII, 1981. This text was prepared with the help of Gilles Barbey, Allen Brooks and Stanislaus von Moos

THE SWISS WATCHMAKERS

NOTES

1. The first critical assessment of Le Corbusier's 'origins' was made by Stanislaus von Moos in *Le Corbusier: Elements of a Synthesis* (Cambridge, Mass 1979).
2. For example this phrase dating back to 1911: 'Istanbul is an orchard, La Chaux-de-Fonds a mason.' *Le Voyage d'Orient* (Paris 1966), p 119. The book has the note 'Completed in Naples on the 10th of October, 1911, by Charles-Edouard Jeanneret; re-read in Paris on the 17th of July, 1965, 24 rue Nungesser-et-Coli, by Le Corbusier.'
3. Charles-Edouard Jeanneret, *Etude sur le mouvement d'art décoratif en Allemagne* (La Chaux-de-Fonds 1912), p 11.
4. Le Corbusier, *L'Art décoratif d'aujourd'hui* (Paris 1925), p 198.
5. *ibid*, p 201.
6. Henri Rieben, Madeleine Urech, Charles Iffland, *L'Horlogerie et l'Europe* (Lausanne 1959), pp 163-98.
7. 'La Chaux-de-Fonds, première place du commerce horloger du monde', in *Collectivité des Fabricants d'Horlogerie de La Chaux-de-Fonds*, a brochure produced on the occasion of the National Exposition in Berne (La Chaux-de-Fonds 1914), p 9.
8. Karl Marx, *Das Kapital*, 1867, vol IV, p 12, §3, note 32, 'Chaux-de-Fonds, das man als eine einzige Uhrenmanufaktur betrachten kann...'
9. Jacques Gubler, 'Le cas de la "Fabrique" genevoise', in *Nationalisme et internationalisme dans l'architecture moderne de la Suisse* (Lausanne 1975), pp 37-9.
10. Jacques Gubler, 'Switzerland', in *Art Nouveau Architecture*, edited by Frank Russell, (London 1979).
11. 'Les concours annuels de l'Ecole d'Art de La Chaux-de-Fonds', *Revue Internationale de l'Horlogerie*, vol VII (1906), pp 920-1.
12. *Revue Internationale de l'Horlogerie*, vol VII (1906), p 803-04.
13. *Revue Internationale de l'Horlogerie*, vol VII (1906), p 808.
14. *Revue Internationale de l'Horlogerie*, vol VII (1906), p 863.
15. Françoise Very, 'Construire une petite maison, reconstruire le monde', in *Architecture Mouvement Continuité*, No 49 (September 1979), pp 5-8.
16. *Revue Internationale de l'Horlogerie*, vol III (1902), p 310.

PROJECTS

Le Corbusier
The Early Projects 1905-1917

Villa Fallet

Villa Fallet, No 1, chemin de Pouillerel, La Chaux-de-Fonds

Designed in 1905 and built in 1906-07 by Charles-Edouard Jeanneret, in collaboration with René Chapallaz, architect for Louis Fallet. The plans submitted to the planning authorities were drawn by Chapallaz. The house is the collective manifesto of the 'Ateliers d'art réunis', the group of workshops directed by L'Eplattenier. Besides Jeanneret, André Evard and Léon Perrin (who later became known as a painter and a sculptor respectively) also worked on the project. The aim was to achieve a synthesis of Art Nouveau and the typical regional style of the Jura. A variety of materials and colours were used. The execution is of a cottage-industry type, with occasional traces of dilettantism in the decorative detail. The solid construction uses iron girders in the basement and kitchen with wooden beams and floors elsewhere, while the treatment of the residential programme is sound and traditional 'domestic architecture'. The laundry room, heating system, storage cellar and garage are all in the basement. There is a strong division in the plan of the ground floor between the service area (kitchen, ironing room, small storeroom) to the north, which houses the split-level staircase and is defined on the exterior by the northern gable with its large window; and the living space to the south, which comprises a large and small room, as well as a veranda/conservatory. The living room is extended on the outside by a terrace which forms a covered way. The terrace was later enlarged at the south-west corner. There are three bedrooms on the upper floor. With the exception of the kitchen, all the floors are covered in linoleum. The garden is excavated and planted with trees.

Villa Stotzer

Villa Stotzer, No 6, chemin de Pouillerel, La Chaux-de-Fonds

Apartment house designed and constructed for Albert Stotzer-Fallet in 1908 by Charles-Edouard Jeanneret in collaboration with René Chapallaz, architect, and W Hollinger, entrepreneur. The plans submitted to the authorities are co-signed 'Tavannes, Vienna, Jan 1908'. The house comprises two superimposed apartments with one large and three small rooms, a kitchen, and a bathroom/WC in each. The basement is designed as a service area. There are Hennebique reinforced concrete slabs on the ground and upper floors. Samuel de Mollins of Lausanne were the engineers. This house was intended to define an identifiable massive structure in the Jura tradition: the side walls of the southern gable are extended forwards to form corner-pilasters and the resulting picturesque profile recalls the organic nature of the 'Prairie School'.

Villa Jaquemet

Villa Jaquemet, No 8, chemin de Pouillerel, La Chaux-de-Fonds

Apartment house designed and built in 1908 by Charles-Edouard Jeanneret in collaboration with René Chapallaz, architect for Jules Jaquemet-Fallet. The plans submitted to the planning authorities bear both their signatures and two place names – Tavannes and Vienna. The Villa Jaquemet can be seen as the alter-ego of the Villa Stotzer. They have identical programmes – two superimposed apartments – and identical solutions, although all the gables vary. The sloping roofs to the east and west accommodate balconies whose lines evoke contemplation of the landscape rather than observation of the hunt. There are Hennebique reinforced concrete slabs on the ground and upper floors which are anchored directly to the stonework of the supporting walls. The engineers were Samuel de Mollins of Lausanne.

Villa Jeanneret-Perret

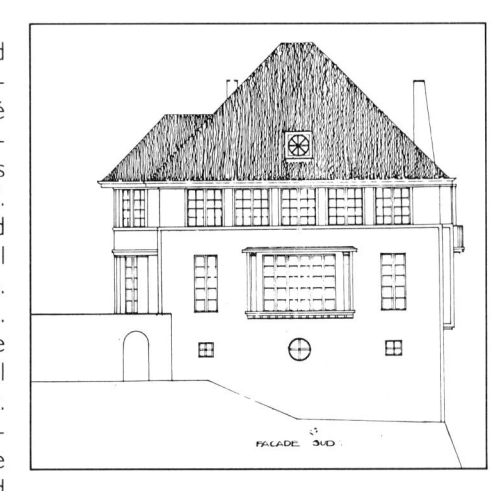

Villa Jeanneret-Perret, No 12, chemin de Pouillerel, La Chaux-de-Fonds

Villa designed in 1912 by Charles-Edouard Jeanneret, architect for his father, Georges-Edouard Jeanneret-Perret, and known locally as the 'White House'. The house as built does not correspond exactly to the plans delivered to the authorities in March-April 1912, for it has an additional watchmaker's workroom in the basement. The plan is cross-axial. The service area to the north, comprising the pantry, kitchen, vestibule and staircase, is very clearly defined. The east-west axis orders a dining room and east apse, a large living room and an anteroom: the effect of transparency was obtained by the use of movable sliding partitions, made largely of glass. The north-south axis orders the large living room with a fireplace and views out over the countryside. The living area on the ground floor extends out into the garden. There are bedrooms on the upper floor, a 'long window' on the south side, and a studio-bedroom with a mansard roof that the young architect reserved for himself. In construction relatively complex and mixed, it uses both iron girders and wood beams. The supporting walls incorporate concrete parts moulded on site. Construction was by Albert Bourquin and Charles Nuding Co.

Villa Favre-Jacot

Villa Favre-Jacot, No 6, côte des Billodes, Le Locle

Villa designed in 1912 by Charles-Edouard Jeanneret, architect for Georges Favre-Jacot, a wealthy industrialist and founder of the local Zénith factory. A rectilinear block comprises the main rooms, responding to the linearity of the site. A cylindrical vestibule leads to a large central hall which gives access to the salon – the hall and salon both overlook terraces. The dining area projects forward to form a portico, its pediment being part of a series of classical references in which the columns are modified by capitals inspired by nature. Curved walls extend forward beyond the main block to create an entry zone, embracing the visitor and linking the movement progression to the architecture – an idea that was developed in a more sophisticated fashion in the Ronchamp Chapel and Villa Savoye. The site is laid out with formal gardens, a pergola and pool, and it was intended that a gazebo should span the road along the hill immediately below the site.

Ditisheim Conversion

Conversion of the second floor in a house for Jules Ditisheim, No 11, rue de la Paix, La Chaux-de-Fonds

This residential building dating from 1856-69 contains three living levels and conforms to the 'anonymous' formula of a vernacular block with a two-cornered gable. In 1913 the second floor was converted into a single apartment. Charles-Edouard Jeanneret was the architect for Jules Ditisheim: he planned the installation of central heating, the creation of a smoking room, and the removal of one WC.

La Scala Cinema

La Scala cinema, No 52, rue de la Serre, La Chaux-de-Fonds

La Scala cinema designed in 1916 by Charles-Edouard Jeanneret, architect for Edmond Meyer. 1,000-seat auditorium with entrance and screen to the south side. Mixed structure: reinforced concrete foundations supporting timber frames built to the specifications of the Hetzer company of Zurich. The technical drawings were also completed in Zurich. In 1930, due to the introduction of the 'talkies', the projection room was rebuilt on axis with the north face; in 1937 an iron framework was introduced; and in 1971 the cinema was completely renovated after a fire so that now only the northern gable gives some indication of the original state. The architect wished to assert a greater presence in the urban landscape through aspiring to (self-)sufficient proportions. The grammar of the building was clearly inspired by French Neo-Classicism, although it evokes Behrens more than Perret. The facade is reduced to a gable form in keeping with the vernacular tradition of the Jura farmhouse.

Spillmann Conversion

Conversion of a second floor flat for C R Spillmann, No 51, rue du Nord, La Chaux-de-Fonds

Residential building and workshop built c 1890 for C R Spillmann. The ground floor originally housed a workshop and the upper floor a single apartment. The building has a block effect with an axial pediment on the southern face. Trees are planted to the south. The metal canopy was added around 1904 and in 1916 Charles-Edouard Jeanneret converted the upper floor into an office.

Schwob Library

Library at Raphaël Schwob's house, No 1221, rue du Temple-Allemand, La Chaux-de-Fonds

Villa designed in 1913 by Léon Boillot, architect for Raphaël Schwob. A major project, the ground floor consists of a large central hall, a suite comprising a library, living room, and billiards room (which later became a music room), as well as a dining room, pantry and kitchen; the upper floor comprises four bedrooms, two dressing rooms and two bathrooms, while a games room, four bedrooms and bathrooms take up the attic space. As a whole, the villa is evocative of the French 'hôtel particulier'. The furniture, wooden panels and decoration in the library are by Charles-Edouard Jeanneret and date from 1917.

Villa Schwob

Villa Schwob, No 167, rue du Doubs, La Chaux-de-Fonds

Villa designed between September and December 1916 and built in 1917 by Charles-Edouard Jeanneret, architect for Anatole Schwob, a watch manufacturer. The house is a block articulated as two lateral 'apses'. On the ground floor this device joins a games room and a dining room to the large living room: effects of transparency result. On the upper floor, the apses accommodate two bedrooms. The attic contains a solarium on the western side. Access is beneath the northern portico while the eastern entrance leads to a sheltering vestibule. To the west, the service entrance is grafted onto the kitchen. A wall conceals the kitchen and a conservatory whose plan reflects in miniature that of the house. Privacy is further ensured by blocking out the view of the residential building to the north. The composition has a subtle asymmetry. The Neo-Grecian cornices, the ochre-yellow baked clay brick flooring and the design of the attic have earned this building its local nickname of the 'Turkish House'. A remarkable conversion of the interior was made around 1960 by A Mangiarotti, architect, of Milan.

Selected Bibliography

WORKS ON LE CORBUSIER'S FORMATIVE YEARS

Books

Pierre du Bois, *Les mythologies de la Belle-Epoque, La Chaux-de-Fonds, André Evard et l'Art Nouveau* (Grandson 1975).
William J R Curtis, *Le Corbusier: Ideas and Forms* (Oxford 1986). See especially 'The Formative Years of Charles-Edouard Jeanneret', pp 16-37.
Giuliano Gresleri and Italo Zannier, *Viaggio in Orienti, Gli Inediti di Charles-Edouard Jeanneret, Fotografe e Scrittore* (Venice and Paris 1984).
Charles-Edouard Jeanneret, *Le Voyage d'Orient*, (Ms 1911, published Paris 1966).
Charles-Edouard Jeanneret, *Etude sur le mouvement d'art décoratif en Allemagne* (La Chaux-de-Fonds 1912/New York 1968).
Charles Jencks, *Le Corbusier and the Tragic View of Architecture* (London 1973), pp 99-110.
Stanislaus von Moos, *Le Corbusier: L'architecte et son mythe* (Paris 1971).
Stanislaus von Moos, *Le Corbusier: Elements of a Synthesis* (Cambridge, Mass 1979). Originally published as *Le Corbusier: Elemente einer Synthese* (Stuttgart 1968).
M P M Sekler, *The Early Drawings of Charles-Edouard Jeanneret* (New York and London 1977).
Paul Seylaz, *Charles L'Eplattenier* (La Chaux-de-Fonds 1974).
Paul V Turner, *The Education of Le Corbusier: A Study of the Development of Le Corbusier's Thought 1900-1920* (New York 1977).

Periodicals and articles

archithese 2-83, special issue devoted to 'La Chaux-de-Fonds und Jeanneret'.
Le Corbusier, 'Le renouveau dans l'architecture', in *L'Œuvre* I (1914), No 2, p 37.
Jacques Gubler, 'The Temperate Presence of Art Nouveau', in Frank Russell (ed), *Art Nouveau Architecture* (London 1979), pp 159-70.
Paul V Turner, 'La prima formazione di Le Corbusier, 1902-07', postscript to Brian Brace Taylor's *Le Corbusier e Pessac* (Rome 1973), pp 97-108.

Exhibition catalogue

Martin Steinmann and I Noseda (eds), *La Chaux-de-Fonds et Jeanneret (Avant Le Corbusier)* (Niederteufen 1983).

Résumé en français

Le centième anniversaire de la naissance de Le Corbusier (1887) est l'occasion pour nous de procéder à une récapitulation de son oeuvre. En tant qu'architecte le plus influent de la première moitié du vingtième siècle, il est principalement connu dans les années 20 pour avoir été à la tête du Mouvement Moderne et dans les années 50 pour cette série de bâtiments impressionnants et sculpturaux que sont l'Unité d'habitation à Marseilles, la chapelle de Ronchamp, le couvent à La Tourette, Chandigarh et les maisons Jaoul. Inévitablement, après trois décennies, la déification inconditionnelle des maîtres de l'architecture Moderne et de leurs icônes est passée de mode. Après une si courte période il semble également inévitable que les maîtres, y compris Le Corbusier, aient à faire l'objet de critiques, même si les critiques sont au mieux mal informés ou au pire malveillants.

Il est clair qu'il faudra plus de temps avant qu'une position objective et dénuée de toute passion puisse être prise concernant le role de Le Corbusier dans l'architecture au vingtième siècle. Quoiqu'il en soit, l'avis actuel est faussé par d'importants lacunes dans la connaissance de beaucoup de gens ce qui empêche ainsi une compréhension complète de ses objectifs et de ses buts. Il est rarement tenu compte de la manière dont les créations de Le Corbusier ont été affectées par les influences de sa formation et par les idées prédominantes d'une époque durant laquelle des changements importants intervenaient pratiquement toutes les décennies. Par exemple, on ne sait pas d'une manière générale jusqu'à quel point les circonstances de sa formation à La Chaux-de-Fonds l'ont mis sur la voie de ses réalisations futures.

En ce sens, il est regrettable que maintenant avec le temps, la période la moins connue de sa vie semble être probablement la plus importante. Jusqu'il y a peu, les premières années à La Chaux-de-Fonds ont été si négligées que encore maintenant beaucoup ignorent l'existence de ses textes, ses cahiers de dessins et ses constructions créés entre 1914 et 1916, sous son véritable nom de Charles-Edouard Jeanneret. Cette Monographie remédie à ce problème en s'attardant à ses premières maisons construites à et près de La Chaux-de-Fonds. Véritables exemples sur pièces, ces maisons crystallisent la position philosophique de Jeanneret et montrent l'origine du développement de sa technique de conception. Mieux que toutes autres formes d'expression, la partie construite de son oeuvre exprime clairement les intentions de l'architecte et ces premières maisons expliquent les changements provoqués d'abord par l'étude et ensuite par les voyages dans sa perception de l'architecture.

Vu la méconnaissance de ces oeuvres, cette Monographie a pour tâche de donner un aperçu complet de ses premières maisons, à l'aide de plans et d'illustrations. Geoffrey Baker a été chargé de redessiner plans, sections et élévations existants de ces constructions, et de fournir des axonométries. En plus d'avoir fourni toutes les illustrations des maisons, il a écrit un article dans lequel chaque maison est analysée en relation avec son milieu et en rapport avec l'évolution de la technique de conception de Jeanneret. Baker étudie aussi de quelle manière l'éducation de Jeanneret à La Chaux-de-Fonds et sa formation au cours de divers voyages d'études ont affecté son développement en tant qu'architecte et expose en détail les changements de technique qui sont intervenus dans son passage d'un style local vers un approche plus classique. Il apparaît que ce développement a pris place suite à une prise de conscience du potentiel de la géométrie. Il a exploité ce potentiel dans ses dernières villas en incluant dans le concept géométrique les mouvements vers et dans le bâtiment.

L'étude de Baker se complète par deux essais écrits par Jacques Gubler. Le premier intitulé 'From Feeling to Reason: Jeanneret and Regionalism' est une étude sur les premières réalisations à La Chaux-de-Fonds en les replaçant dans le contexte de l'éducation de Jeanneret. Son ouvrage couvre les deux sujets qui ont préoccupé Le Corbusier toute sa vie: la nature et la machine. Le deuxième ouvrage, 'In Time with the Swiss Watchmakers', révèle comment le début de la carrière de Jeanneret à été influencé par la prédominance de l'industrie horlogère dans sa ville natale et il retrace son évolution d'apprenti graveur de boitiers de montres vers l'architecture en passant par les commandes des fabricants de montres de La Chaux-de-Fonds.

Deutsche Zusammenfassung

Der hundertste Jahrestag der Geburt Le Corbusiers im Jahr 1987 ist willkommener Anlaß für eine grundlegende Neubewertung seines Oeuvres. Dieser, für die erste Hälfte des 20 Jahrhunderts einflußreichste Architekt, wurde berühmt als führender Vertreter des Modernismus während der 20er Jahre und für eine Reihe von wuchtigen und skulpturähnlichen Gebäuden, die er in den 50er Jahren schuf. Hierzu zählen die Unité in Marseilles, die Kapelle von Ronchamp, das Kloster in La Tourette, die Jaoul Häuser und Chandigarh. Wie nicht anders zu erwarten, haben sich nach nun drei Jahrzehnten die vorherrschenden Trends in der Architektur deutlich verändert. Der Abwendung von der unkritischen Kanonisierung der Meister der modernen Architektur und ihrer Leitbilder, folgte die Hinwendung zu einer pluralistischen Kakophonie der Stile und Bildbereiche. Nach so kurzer Zeit scheint es auch unvermeidlich, daß die Meister – und unter ihnen auch Le Corbusier – ins Kreuzfeuer der Kritik geraten sollten, selbst wenn diese Kritik bestenfalls der Unkenntnis und schlimmstenfalls der Mißgunst entspringt.

Es bedarf offensichtlich einer größeren zeitlichen Distanz, um eine objektive und unvoreingenommene Einschätzung der Bedeutung Le Corbusiers für das 20 Jahrhundert vorzunehmen. Momentane Beurteilungen sind beeinträchtigt durch weithin bestehende Wissenslücken, die ein echtes Verständnis seiner Ziele und Prinzipien behindern. Nur selten wird in Betracht gezogen in welchem Ausmaß Le Corbusiers kreatives Schaffen geprägt wurde durch den Zeitgeist einer historischen Epoche, in der fast jedes neue Jahrzehnt fundamentale Veränderungen mit sich brachte. So wird etwa häufig unterschätzt inwieweit die besonderen Umstände seiner Ausbildung in La Chaux-de-Fonds den Ausgangspunkt aller späteren Errungenschaften bilden.

Es ist daher bedauernswert, daß die rückblickend für Le Corbusier wohl wichtigste Schaffensperiode, auch gleichzeitig seine am wenigsten beachtete ist. Bis vor kurzem wurde seinen frühen Jahre in La Chaux-de-Fonds so wenig Aufmerksamkeit geschenkt, daß auch heute noch eine weitgehende Unkenntnis der Schriften, Skizzenbüchern, und Gebäude, die er unter seinem Familiennamen Charles-Edouard Jeanneret zwischen 1904 und 1916 schuf, zu verzeichnen ist. Die vorliegende Monografie beabsichtigt die Schließung dieser Lücke durch eine dokumentarische Erfassung der Häuser aus der frühen Schaffensperiode in und bei La Chaux-de-Fonds. Als ausgeführte Bauwerke sind diese Kristallisationspunkte der philosophischen Position Jeannerets, und Indizien für die Anfänge seiner entwurfstechnischen Entwicklung. Das realisierte Bauwerk bringt die Absicht des Architekten klarer zum Ausdruck als andere ihm zur Verfügung stehende Darstellungsmittel, und diese frühen Häuser von Le Corbusiers illustrieren den Wandel seines Architekturverständnisses, der zunächst durch Studien und später durch Reisen bewirkt wurde.

Da über diese Werke so wenig bekannt ist, beabsichtigt diese Monografie eine umfassende dokumentarische Erfassung der frühen Häuser mit Hilfe von Zeichnungen und Illustrationen. Geoffrey Baker wurde beauftragt, existierende Pläne, Ausschnitte und Aufrisse neu zu zeichnen und axonometrische Darstellungen zu erstellen. Zusätzlich zum Gros der Häuser-Illustrationen hat er einen Abschnitt beigetragen, in dem jedes Haus im Bezug zu seinem Umfeld und im Kontext der sich herausbildenden Entwurfstechnik Le Corbusiers analysiert wird. Baker befaßt sich ebenfalls damit, wie Jeannerets Ausbildung in La Chaux-de-Fonds und im Rahmen einiger Studienreisen seine Entwicklung im Bereich des Entwurfs beeinflußten. Er behandelt im Detail die Veränderungen der Technik, die sich im Zuge seiner Entwicklung von einer dem Lokalkolorit verpflichteten Bauweise hin zu einem klassischeren Ansatz abzeichneten. Es wird aufgezeigt, daß diese Veränderung der Erkenntnis des Potentials der Geometrie entsprang. In die Villen der späten Schaffensperiode wurde diese so inkorporiert, daß die Bewegung zum Gebäude hin und in das Gebäude hinein Teil des geometrischen Konzepts bildete. Bakers Studie wird ergänzt durch zwei Beiträge von Jacques Gubler. In seinem ersten Aufsatz mit dem Titel: 'From Feeling to Reason: Jeanneret and Regionalism' liefert er den Hintergrund für die frühen Projekte in La Chaux-de-Fonds, indem er sie in den Zusammenhang der Ausbildung Le Corbusiers stellt. Seine Erörterungen umfassen das Themenpaar Natur und Maschine, das Le Corbusier zeitlebens beschäftigte. Der zweite Aufsatz: 'In Time with the Swiss Watchmakers' zeigt auf, wie sehr Jeannerets früher Werdegang durch die vorherrschende Stellung der Uhrenindustrie in seinem Geburtsort beeinflußt war. Er verfolgt seine Entwicklung vom Graveur-lehrling für Uhrengehäuse zum Architekten über Auftragsarbeiten für Uhrenfabrikanten in La Chaux-de-Fonds.

Resumen en espagñol

El centenario del nacimiento de Le Corbusier en 1887 nos proporciona la oportunidad de emprender una exhaustiva revaloración de su obra. Como el arquitecto de mayor influencia en la primera mitad del siglo XX, es más conocido como líder del Movimiento Modernista en los años veinte y por su poderosa y escultórica serie de edificios en los años cincuenta que incluye la Unité de Marsellas, la capilla de Ronchamp, el monasterio de La Tourette, las casas de Jaoul, y Chandigarh. Inevitablemente, tres décadas más tarde el péndulo de la moda arquitectónica ha sufrido un giro que va desde una deificación falta de sentido crítico de los grandes maestros de la arquitectura modernista y sus iconos hacia una cacofonía pluralista de imágenes y estilos. Tras tan corto periodo de tiempo parece también inevitable que los grandes maestros, incluyendo a Le Corbusier, sean objeto de ataques, incluso si las críticas son en el mejor de los casos infundadas y en el peor malévolas.

Ciertamente ha de transcurrir más tiempo antes de que se pueda formar una opinión objetiva e imparcial sobre el papel de Le Corbusier en el siglo XX. Sin embargo, el enfoque actual se ve deteriorado por considerables lagunas en el saber de muchas personas, lo que les impide una correcta comprensión de sus propósitos y objetivos. Rara vez se toma en consideración la manera en que la producción creativa de Le Corbusier se vio afectada por las influencias formativas sobre él y por el espíritu de una época en la que se estaban produciendo cambios significativos casi década tras década. Por ejemplo no se suele entender en qué medida las circunstancias que rodearon a su etapa de formación en La Chaux-de-Fonds abrieron el camino para sus posteriores logros.

En este sentido es realmente desafortunado el hecho de que el período menos conocido de su vida sea considerado ahora, retrospectivamente, como probablemente el más importante. Sus primeros años en La Chaux-de-Fonds se han visto hasta muy recientemente tan relegados que incluso en la actualidad muchas personas no están familiarizadas con los escritos, esbozos y edificios creados bajo su verdadero nombre, Charles-Edouard Jeanneret, entre 1904 y 1916. Esta Monografía intenta paliar tal deficiencia documentando sus primeras casas en La Chaux-de-Fonds y sus alrededores. Como trabajos arquitectónicos, estas casas cristalizan la opinión filosófica de Jeanneret y muestran cómo su técnica de diseño comenzaba a desarrollarse. Los trabajos arquitectónicos reflejan las intenciones del arquitecto con más claridad que sus otras formas de expresión, y estas primeras casas explican los cambios en la percepción de la arquitectura de Jeanneret, ocasionados primero por el estudio y segundo por los viajes.

Como se conoce tan poco sobre estos trabajos, esta Monografía va dirigida a elaborar una documentación exhaustiva de sus primeras casas por lo que se refiere a dibujos e ilustraciones. Geoffrey Baker ha sido encargado de reproducir los planos existentes, secciones y alzado de tales edificios, y de proporcionar sus proyecciones axonométricas. Además de facilitar la mayoria de las ilustraciones de las casas, ha escrito un artículo en el que se analiza cada casa en relación con su contexto y se examina en relación con la técnica de diseño de Jeanneret, que estaba en fase de desarrollo. Baker también plantea la manera en que la formación de Jeanneret en La Chaux-de-Fonds y en sus varios viajes de estudio afectaron a su desarrollo como diseñador, y asimismo detalla los cambios en su técnica que tuvieron lugar cuando se alejaba de unas imágenes vernáculas locales hacia un enfoque más clásico. Este desarrollo parece haber tenido lugar como resultado de la toma de conciencia sobre las posibilidades de la geometría que afloró en sus últimos chalets, de manera que el movimiento hacia y adentro del edificio se convirtió en parte del concepto geométrico.

El estudio de Baker se ve complementado por dos ensayos escritos por Jacques Gubler. El primero de ellos, 'From Feeling to Reason: Jeanneret and Regionalism', recoge las bases de sus primeros proyectos en La Chaux-de-Fonds, situándolos en el contexto de la educación de Jeanneret. Su planteamiento abarca los inseparables tópicos de la naturaleza y la máquina, que preocuparon a Le Corbusier a lo largo de toda su vida. El segundo ensayo, 'In Time with the Swiss Watchmakers', revela cómo al comienzo de su carrera Jeanneret se vio influenciado por el predominio de la industria relojera en su ciudad natal, y sigue su evolución desde aprendiz de grabador de cajas de reloj hasta arquitecto a través de los encargos de fabricantes de relojes de La Chaux-de-Fonds.

Sommario in italiano

Il centenario della nascita di Le Corbusier (1887) è un'ottimo spunto per rivalutare a pieno la sua opera. Le Corbusier fu indubbiamente l'architetto più influente della prima metà del novecento, ma la sua fama è sopratutto legata al Movimento Moderno degli anni venti, di cui fu tra i maggiori esponenti e agli imponenti e scultorei edifici degli anni cinquanta, quali l'Unité a Marsiglia, la cappella di Ronchamp, il monastero a La Tourette, le case Jaoul, e Chandigarh. E' inevitabile che a distanza di trent'anni il pendolo della moda architettonica si sia spostato allontanandosi dalla deificazione acritica dei maestri dell'architettura modernista e delle loro icone, verso una cacofonia pluralistica di immagini e stili. Dopo trent'anni, pare inoltre inevitabile che i maestri, Le Corbusier compreso, vengano presi di mira dalla critica, che tuttavia è nel migliore dei casi disomogenea e mal peggiore, malevola.

Naturalmente è necessario che trascorra ancora del tempo prima di poter formulare un giudizio spassionato ed obiettivo dell'opera di Le Corbusier nel ventesimo secolo. Tuttavia la valutazione attuale soffre spesso di notevoli lacune che ostacolano l'esatta comprensione degli scopi e degli obiettivi dell'artista. Raramente si considera quanta influenza ebbero le sue prime esperienze sulla sua attività creativa, e l'importanza dello spirito dell'epoca, un'epoca di profondi e rapidi cambiamenti. Non è chiaro, per esempio, fino a che punto la sua formazione artistica a La Chaux-de-Fonds fu significativa nella evoluzione che lo portò alle ultime opere.

E' un peccato che si sappia cosi poco su quello che ora appare probabilmente il periodo più importante della sua vita. In anni recenti il periodo di La Chaux-de-Fonds è stato talmente trascurato che solo pochi conoscono gli scritti, i disegni e gli edifici creati dall'artista sotto il suo vero nome, Charles-Edouard Jeanneret, tra il 1904 e il 1916. Questa Monografia si propone di remediare a tali lacune attraverso una ricca documentazione delle case di La Chaux-de-Fonds e dei dintorni. Sono case che cristallizzano la visione filosofica di Jeanneret e illustrano l'evoluzione della sua tecnica progettistica. Le opere edilizie esplicano i suoi principi meglio di ogni altra forma espressiva di cui si servi e le sue prime case illustrano chiaramente la sua nuova percezione dell'architettura, derivata prima dallo studio e poi dai viaggi.

Questa Monografia fornisce un'ampia documentazione delle prime case di Le Corbusier, opere poco conosciute e poco studiate, attraverso numerosi disegni e illustrazioni. Geoffrey Baker ne ha ridisegnato le piante, le sezioni e i prospetti e ne ha fornito le assonometrie. Ha inoltre raccolto gran parte delle illustrazioni correlandole con un'analisi dettagliata di ogni casa in relazione al contesto e all'evoluzione della tecnica progettistica dell'artista. Baker discute inoltre il modo in cui la formazione di Jeanneret a La Chaux-de-Fonds e i suoi numerosi viaggi di studio abbiano influenzato la sua evoluzione di architetto, e come egli sia passato da un'arte ricca di suggestioni locali a un'approccio più classico. Questa evoluzione ebbe luogo grazie alla sua scoperta della forza potenziale della geometria, che vide realizzata nelle sue ultime ville, e che sfrutta il movimento verso l'edificio e al suo interno, quale parte del concepto geometrico.

Lo studio di Baker è integrato da due saggi di Jacques Gubler. Il primo, 'From Feeling to Reason: Jeanneret and Regionalism', illustra i primi progetti del periodo di La Chaux-de-Fonds nel contesto della sua formazione artistica. La trattazione abbraccia la duplice tematica della natura e della macchina, tema che fu caro a Le Corbusier tutta la vita. Il secondo, 'In time with the Swiss Watchmakers', rivela quanto i primi anni della carriera di Jeanneret furono influenzati dalla forte presenza dell'industria orologiera nella sua città natia e ne ripercorre le tappe, dagli anni in cui era apprendista incisore di casse di orologi fino ai giorni della sua fama di architetto, attraverso le commissioni degli orologiai di La Chaux-de-Fonds.

ARCHITECTU

ARCHITECTURAL DESIGN is internationally recognised as being foremost among a small number of publications providing up-to-date information on architecture of the present and past. Each issue presents an in-depth analysis of a theme of relevance to architectural practice today, whether it be the work of an important new architect, a currently influential figure or movement, or the emergence of a new style or consensus of opinion. The high standard of writing, editorial selection and presentation has made Architectural Design one of the world's most progressive architectural magazines and essential reading for anyone interested in the art of architecture.

Themes covered recently by Architectural Design include that of **Post-Modernism and Discontinuity**, illustrated by projects by high-profile architects such as James Stirling, Leon Krier, Terry Farrell, Jeremy Dixon and James Gowan; and **Neoclassical Architecture in Copenhagen and Athens**, guest-edited by Lisbet B Jørgensen and Demetri Porphyrios, which reproduces rare material to reveal the fascinating achievements of some eighteenth- and nineteenth-century Danish architects. **A House for Today** looks at the implications of the architectural heritage for modern domestic design, and particularly large-scale housing development. Lucien Steil's **Tradition and Architecture** surveys the use of traditional principles in contemporary projects, ranging from the smallest private house to the grand municipal arts complex, in a wide range of European countries, as well as the United States.

ART & DESIGN is now published bi-monthly and is specially designed to provide a lasting record of some of the most significant current debates, with contributions from well-known experts in their respective fields, and a free graphic by a notable contemporary artist in each issue. The first double issue devotes its pages to the subject of **Twentieth-Century British Art**, whilst **The Post-Modern Object** takes a critical look at the area of product design. A&D 5/6-1987 **Abstract Art**, reassesses abstract art from the pioneering work of artists such as Kandinsky and Malevich through that of post-war Americans such as Jackson Pollock and Marc Rothko, up to its latest expression today.

You may subscribe to either magazine alone – or to both at a special rate. A combined subscription will give you annually six issues of Architectural Design and six issues of Art & Design at a saving of over £35 or US$75 on their value if purchased individually. Please fill in the form opposite and return it NOW to:

Subscriptions Department
ACADEMY GROUP LTD
7/8 Holland Street
London **W8 4NA**
✆ **01-402 2141**

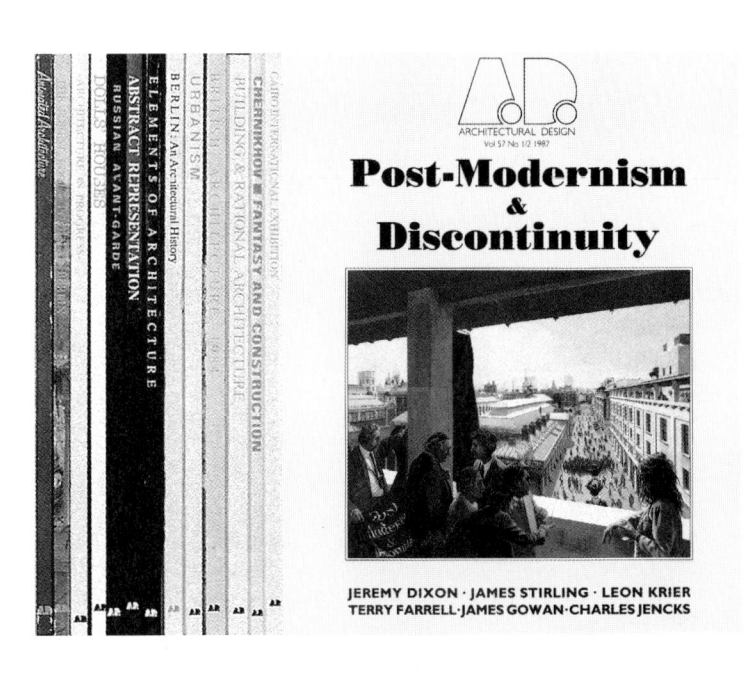

… RAL DESIGN AD ART & DESIGN

✂ - ✂

1987 SUBSCRIPTION RATES FOR ARCHITECTURAL DESIGN & ART AND DESIGN

☐ I wish to subscribe to *Architectural Design* at the full rate
☐ I wish to subscribe to AD at the student rate

☐ I wish to subscribe to *Art & Design* at the full rate
☐ I wish to subscribe to A&D at the student rate

☐ I wish to subscribe to AD and A&D at the full rate
☐ I wish to subscribe to AD and A&D at the student rate

☐ I am a new subscriber. Please send me a free issue of the magazine(s) I am subscribing to

☐ Starting date: Issue No................................Year................................
(Subscriptions may be back dated)

☐ Payment endorsed by Cheque/ Postal Order/ Draft
Value £ / US$ ....

☐ Please charge £................................to my credit card

Expiry date: ....

Account No: ☐☐☐☐☐☐☐☐☐☐☐☐☐

☐ American Express   ☐ Access/ Masterchage/ Eurocard
☐ Diners Club   ☐ Barclaycard/ Visa

ARCHITECTURAL DESIGN	UK	EUROPE	OVERSEAS
Full rate	£45.00	£55.00	US$85.00
Student rate	£39.50	£49.50	US$75.00
ART & DESIGN			
Full rate	£29.50	£34.00	US$49.50
Student rate	£25.00	£29.50	US$45.00
ARCHITECTURAL DESIGN AND ART & DESIGN			
Full combined rate	£59.50	£69.50	US$105.00
Student combined rate	£55.00	£65.00	US$95.00

Signature ....
Name ....
Address ....
....
....

Please send this form with your payment/ credit card authority direct to:

SUBSCRIPTIONS DEPT
ACADEMY GROUP LTD
7/8 HOLLAND ST
LONDON W8 4NA

ARCHITECTURAL Monographs

SUBSCRIPTION RATES

For four issues inc. postage and packing

	UK	Europe	Overseas
Full rate	£45.00	£55.00	US$79.50
Students	£39.50	£39.00	US$69.50

FILL IN THE COUPON AND SEND IT NOW

THE MAGAZINE DEVOTED TO THE WORK OF INDIVIDUAL ARCHITECTS

Architectural Monographs provides up-to-date information on the work of pioneering architects, ranging from the forerunners of the Modern Movement to the best of architects working today. Each issue of Architectural Monographs provides a carefully chosen selection of the architect's work illustrated with drawings and photographs many of which are in colour. Essays by leading architectural writers are fully complemented by extensive chronologies and bibliographies. The express aim of Architectural Monographs is to maintain a high standard of editorial content and reproduction without advertising and at a modest price.

Summaries in French, German, Italian and Spanish

Please add £1.50/US$3.00 per issue for p&p

☐ **2 Hector Guimard**
A catalogue of Guimard's architecture from the early works and the Paris Metro to the full flowering of Art Nouveau in the Castel Béranger and the ingenious apartment buildings of the 1920s.
122 pages including 8 in colour
ISBN 0 85670 363 X
£9.95/US$19.95

☐ **4 Alvar Aalto**
Four leading architectural writers offer their interpretations of Alvar Aalto's enigmatic but profoundly influential work. Many specially commissioned photographs in colour.
126 pages including 16 in colour
ISBN 0 85670 421 0
£12.95/US$24.95

☐ **6 Edwin Lutyens**
Sir Edwin Lutyens dominated the architecture of Britain and its Empire from the turn of the century to the Second World War. Here is a selection of the country houses that provided the mainstay of his career. The second edition contains seven new gatefolds in full colour.
110 pages, 30 in colour (including 7 gatefolds)
ISBN 0 85670 422 9
£12.95/US$24.95*

☐ **7 A & P Smithson**
The Smithsons collaborated on the design and production of this study of 'The Shift' from a functionalist view of architecture to one which asks how buildings can be authentically decorated.
110 pages including 24 in colour
ISBN 0 85670 680 9
£9.95/US$19.95

☐ **8 Sir John Soane**
Three important essays and a pictorial description of the architects own house. Sir John Summerson of the Soane Museum writes on the man and his style, David Watkin describes Soane and his contemporaries, and G. Tilman Mellinghoff discusses the Dulwich Picture Gallery and Mausoleum.
128 pages, 44 in colour (including 6 gatefolds)
ISBN 0 85670 805 4
£12.95/US$24.95*

☐ **9 Terry Farrell**
The theory and practice of one of Britain's leading architects and premier Post-Modernist with critical essays by Colin Amery and Charles Jencks and an assessment by the architect himself of the state of British Post-Modernism.
128 pages, 32 in colour (including 4 gatefolds)
ISBN 0 85670 842 9
£12.95/US$24.95*

☐ **10 Richard Rogers + Architects**
The first in-depth analysis of Rogers' work including the early projects with Norman and Wendy Foster, a comprehensive study of the Pompidou Centre, and his many recent commissions including the Lloyd's Building in London.
160 pages, 476 illustrations, including 79 in colour
ISBN 0 85670 786 4
£12.95/US$24.95*

☐ **11 Mies van der Rohe**
A study of the formative years in Europe examining Mies' preoccupations, methods and the range of his work, which included villas, exhibition pavilions and furniture design. Many specially commissioned photographs.
112 pages, over 200 illustrations
ISBN 0 85670 685 X
£12.95/US$24.95*

☐ Please enter my subscription for four consecutive Architectural Monographs
UK & Eire £45.00   Europe £55.00   Overseas US$79.50   Special student discount £5.50/US$10.00

☐ I wish to start with No ....(subscriptions may be backdated)

☐ I am a new subscriber. Please send me my free gift

☐ I wish to order individual Monographs Nos..

☐ Payment enclosed by cheque/postal order/draft.   Amount £/US$ ....

☐ Please charge my credit card account No: (all major cards accepted)

NO: ☐☐☐☐☐☐☐☐☐☐   Expiry date........................

Signature ....
Name ....
Address ....
....

SPECIAL OFFER

New Subscribers will receive a free copy of either the Hector Guimard or the Smithsons Monograph

ACADEMY GROUP LTD, SUBSCRIPTIONS DEPT 7/8 HOLLAND STREET LONDON W8 4NA